Hospitality Service Quality

HOSPITALITY SERVICE QUALITY

Ranvijay Singh

CENTRUM PRESS
NEW DELHI-110002 (INDIA)

CENTRUM PRESS
H.O.: 4360/4, Ansari Road, Daryaganj,
New Delhi-110002 (India)
Tel: 23278000, 23261597, 23255577, 23286875
B.O.: No. 1015, Ist Main Road, BSK IIIrd Stage,
IIIrd Phase, IIIrd Block, Bengaluru-560085 (INDIA)
Tel: 080-41723429
Email: centrumpress@gmail.com
Visit us at: www.centrumpress.com

Hospitality Service Quality

First Edition, 2013

ISBN 978-93-81460-02-3

PRINTED IN INDIA

Printed at Balaji Offset, Delhi.

Contents

Preface

Delivering quality service will be one of the major challenges facing hospitality managers in the opening years of the next millennium. It will be an essential condition for success in the emerging, keenly competitive, global hospitality markets. While the future importance of delivering quality hospitality service is easy to discern and to agree on, doing so presents some difficult and intriguing management issues. Since the delivery of hospitality service always involves people, these issues centre on the management of people, and in particular on the interactions between guests and staff, interactions that are called service encounters. In the eyes of our guests, our hospitality businesses will succeed or fail depending on the cumulative impact of the service encounters in which they have participated. It is easy to check the importance of managing these service encounters. Think back to the last time you visited a hotel or restaurant. How did you feel about the quality of the experience? Was it one that you would recommend to others? What were the specific interactions that made a difference? If you can't remember, is this something that should matter to the hospitality business concerned? Surely something should have gone especially well? Service encounters are the building blocks of quality hospitality service. How can hospitality businesses manage them more effectively? We suggest a two step process in the evaluation of a service chain.

The starting point for hospitality service encounter analysis is specifying clearly the overall service strategy and what it is designed to achieve. Is the purpose cost or service quality leadership? Is it to provide unique service values, customized or standardized, complex or simple, frequent or occasional? Is it to provide service at any reasonable cost? Is service limited to a luxury package, or does it include budget travellers?

Which staff members are involved in providing the service? What skills do they need? What training has been provided? How committed are they to service goals? Is team cooperation or individual empowerment required? What attitudes are appropriate— friendly, open, helpful, warm service, or efficient, unobtrusive, uninvolving, unthreatening service? What staff members deal with guests? How close are the 'backroom' staff to guests? Are staff presentations and appearances appropriate?

How should the service encounter be conducted, given the enterprise culture? Is the management style, and marketing orientation, appropriate for the tasks? Do service providers have the appropriate attitudes? Is the right emphasis being placed on service quality? When hospitality managers have carried out this two step process they will be in an excellent position to make decisions that will both improve the quality of hospitality services provided and guest perceptions of them. Zeroing in on hospitality service quality in this manner will help hospitality businesses meet the service challenges of the millennium, enhance their market positions, and reap the associated profit rewards.

This book contains advanced information about this subject. This book will be a boost for the learners and an essential subject manual. Designing of the book is such that the students will be benefited as far as the their knowledge and examination is concerned.

—Author

1

Introduction

During the twentieth century it grew into what is widely described as the world's largest industry and, for many destinations, it represents a vital source of income, foreign exchange and employment. More importantly, however, tourism is about people. The annual number of international arrivals reached almost 690 million by the end of the last century this figure has continued to increase into the twenty-first century – by 2006, international arrivals had exceeded 840 million. Moreover, an estimated six times that number participate in domestic tourism each year, figures which represent an enormous, yet temporary, migration of people both across international borders and within their own countries.

Tourism has had a long history. Some commentators place its origins in mediaeval pilgrimages, some in the Grand Tours of the eighteenth and nineteenth century, and others in the railway age world of the spa, mountain and seaside resort. But the real rise of tourism as a major pursuit and as a major industry begins in the post war period. UN World Tourism Organization statistics begin in 1950, when 25 million international travellers were recorded. Then the meteoric rise of the tourism industry began, with average year on year growth rates of 6.5% over the period 1950-2007. The year 2007 saw 903 million international arrivals world wide. UNWTO looks forward to 1.6 billion international arrivals by 2020. And far greater numbers holiday in their own countries: it is much easier however to count international arrivals. After 50 plus years of growth, no one working in the industry today can personally recall the pre-growth era. Growth – in numbers – in geographical impacts – in product terms – is regarded as an ongoing and given norm.

But tourism growth can have serious impacts on the environment and the world's peoples:

- It can have powerful physical impacts on places visited-farm and forest land swept away for airport and road construction, hotels, and golf courses-often in scenic regions. Physical impacts can be complex and far-reaching-ski run development clearing trees can open the way to soil erosion, leading to landslides and potential major disasters. Heavily used areas can suffer erosion from sheer numbers of visitors-mountain erosion in the Alps, and Himalayas are classic examples. Whole ecosystems can be damaged.
- It can have serious cultural impacts. Tourists are wealthy and demanding guests. They can dismiss local customs, turn land values and labour markets upside down, make local languages redundant, and shift the balance of political power in favour of distant multinationals. In some scenarios tourism can bring vice and crime.
- More subtly, tourism can destroy the future it promises by rendering the destination dependent on its dollars, then declaring a spoilt destination unfashionable and redundant. This, the operation of the tourism cycle, can effect both large resorts and rural retreats, rich and poor countries alike. Tourism is a volatile, fashion industry: it needs to be understood and well managed.
- In recent years, the impacts of the transport systems that are fundamental to modern tourism growth have been increasingly recognised. They burn large quantities of fuel in a fuel hungry world; they produce large quantities of emissions in a world beset by climate change issues. Climate Change and Transport Issues are major issues that loom over the world of tourism and sustainable tourism.

Sustainable tourism was designed not to stop tourism but to manage it in the interests of all three parties involved-the host habitats and communities, the tourists and the industry itself. It seeks a balance between development and conservation. It seeks to find the best form of tourism for an area taking into account its ecology and its culture. It may mean limits to growth, or in some cases no growth at all. The precautionary principle is important here. Sustainable tourism seeks not just to plan for tourism, but to integrate tourism into a balanced relationship with broader economic development. That is the way in which sustainable tourism fulfils its requirement to think holistically, and one of its approaches to responsibility in business, the triple bottom line.

In many rural areas the watchword is that tourism should be a tool for rural conservation, service retention and diverse development-not just a business for its own sake. In many urban areas, tourism can also work with heritage conservation by using redundant historic buildings for tourism purposes, by injecting tourism expenditures into areas needing urban regeneration, and by bringing jobs and re-training to areas with unemployment/social problems.

But there is a key caveat. Sustainable development cannot be created by planning alone: it needs to work with the market and it needs to work with businesses great and small.

Progress and Problems

Sustainable tourism began as a purely reactive concept to the above issues, trying to stop negative change. Early outlines simply listed the negative impacts down the left side of the page and then had a wish list of their opposites, presumed to be positive outcomes, down the right side of the page.

To be fair to their authors, there were no research findings or exemplars of successful sustainable tourism to draw on. Only gradually did sustainable tourism become pro-active, trying to create positive change. Many commentators – professional as well as amateur – enjoy criticising tourism. The key to achieving sustainable tourism is, however, to carry out analytical review and criticism, then implement effective management techniques, and then carry on a rolling review, criticism and management process.

Tourism Since World War

In 1945 there was practically no tourism. World War II sort of got in the way.

Most people who travelled did so by train or ship. Air travel was still very early in development. Since 1945 the highways have gotten better. Enter interstates. More people travel by car. Train travel (sadly) has declined in the U.S., though it remains strong in many other countries.

- Air travel has boomed. Ship travel is now largely cruise-oriented.
- Travel is more expensive in some ways, but cheaper in others.
- Many more people have travelled in 2006 than had travelled—other than through military service—in 1945.

According to the World Tourism Organization (WTO) international tourist arrivals grew from 93 million in 1963 to 284 million in 1981 *(WTO 1997)*. By 1990 arrivals had reached 456 million and are expected to double by 2010 *(WTO 1997)*. However, after the recent international terrorist events these expectations are not likely to be met. It appears that the stage is set for the continued growth of tourism in the developed world in the quaternary sector of the economy. Many developing nations are also moving towards a more service-based economy as governments begin to comprehend the potential economic magnitude of the industry. In recent years the most rapid growth of the tourism industry has been in the developing world. In these countries tourism makes up a substantial portion of their gross national and gross domestic products as well as a major portion of their foreign earnings. Many scholars feel these countries show the greatest prospects for continued growth. However, tourism is not a panacea for the economic crises of the developing world although it has become an economic fact in today's society.

Government Policy in the Mass Market Era

Marketing is indispensable part of any substantive tourism enterprise. As the market is expanding, the role of marketing as a driving force in a business endeavour is also being recognized. With growing competition, organisations in tourism business have no option but to do organised and targeted marketing. An organised approach to marketing always helps, whether it is on the tour operator end or at destinations. Guides, escorts, restaurants, hotels, transporters, shops etc. compete one another to stay ahead. A proper tourism marketing strategy calls for close cooperation between the government, tourism industry and the local population.

Evolution of Marketing

Marketing as a concept has evolved in the last 30 years. Development of marketing has three distinct stages: Production Era, Sales Era and Marketing Era. Marketing era arrived when organizations began producing what they could sell rather than trying to sell what they manufactured. While planning and designing a product, customers' needs, tastes and satisfaction were considered. Growth of competition prompted organisations to frame marketing techniques.

Change in travelling trends also made it necessary to adopt new approach. The emergence of long haul traveller prompted the need for marketing research which studied market trends, consumer behaviour and ascertained procedure to make products which satisfied the users of tourism products. Gradual social and economic development culminated in segmentation of mass market into specialized target markets. Tackling these markets needed an approach which was in tune with new times.

Selling and Marketing

Selling and Marketing are different concepts. Selling focuses on the needs of the seller while marketing concentrates on buyers' needs. A marketing oriented organisation focuses on customer needs and earns profits through customer satisfaction. Several organizations in tourism field are product oriented. They emphasise on the available services of products but ignore consumers' requirements. A marketing oriented tourist organisation has a completely different approach. They offer services around the tourists' needs.

Marketing and Travel Industry

Marketing is an important part of any tourism agency. As the market is growing, the role of marketing as a driving force in a business endeavour is also being acknowledged. With growing competition, organisations in tourism business have no option but to do organised and targeted marketing. An organised approach to marketing always helps, whether it is on the tour operator end or at destinations. Guides, escorts, restaurants, hotels, transporters, shops etc. compete one another to stay ahead. A proper tourism marketing strategy calls for close cooperation between the government, tourism industry and the local population. Marketing as a concept has evolved in the last 30 years.

Development of marketing has three distinct stages: Production Era, Sales Era and Marketing Era. Marketing era arrived when organizations began producing what they could sell rather than trying to sell what they manufactured. While planning and designing a product, customers' needs, tastes and satisfaction were considered.

Growth of competition prompted organisations to frame marketing techniques. Change in travelling trends also made it necessary to adopt new approach. The emergence of long haul traveller prompted the need for marketing research which studied market trends, consumer behaviour and ascertained procedure to make products which satisfied the users of tourism products. Gradual social and economic development culminated in segmentation of mass market into specialized target markets. Tackling these markets needed an approach which was in tune with new times. Selling and Marketing are different concepts. Selling focuses on the needs of the seller while marketing concentrates on buyers' needs. A marketing oriented organisation focuses on customer needs and earns profits through customer satisfaction. Several organizations in tourism field are product oriented. They emphasise on the available services of products but ignore consumers' requirements. A marketing oriented tourist organisation has a completely different approach. They offer services around the tourists' needs.

The Growing Importance of Business Travel

Despite the economic downturn, the flight cuts and the reduction of business trips, business travel to Asia is experiencing continued growth. Several airlines are profiting from business travel to Asia.

According to *Air Transport Association* analyses compiled for The New York Times, *American Airlines'* revenue for flights to and from Japan and China grew 12.8 percent for the first three months of 2008, greater growth than in any other region. That region also saw the biggest growth in average fares paid, 12.2 percent.

The report shows that 996 nonstop flights a week were scheduled in the third quarter of 2008 from the United States to Asian countries, more than ever before. Los Angeles is the most popular departure city from the United States, with 180 flights a week. Narita Airport in Tokyo is the most frequent destination, with 380 arrivals a week.

Among the factors driving this growth, there is the economic boom in China and India translating to more business travel between East and West.

However, The New York Times reports, *Mary Tabacchi*, a *Cornell University* associate professor who has tracked airline trends for 15 years, attributes this growth also to another factor, the new bigger planes used for long-haul flights. They can carry more fuel, eliminating the need for extra landings and takeoffs, which use more fuel.

The newspaper says major airlines are asking the *Department of Transportation* to negotiate with Asian countries to open traditionally restricted rights to sky routes in the East.

Gary Dorman, an airline expert and senior vice president with NERA Economic Consulting, says: "If they (the airlines) can establish brand dominance now, they will be one step ahead of their competition as conditions improve". The importance of Business Tourism continues to expand around the world, with a growing number of destinations entering the market for Conferences, Exhibitions and Incentive Travel. In most countries in the developed world, income from Business Tourism now represents between one-third and one-quarter of all tourism spending. Destinations in the developing world have also understood the potential benefits of Business Tourism, and in such countries investment in facilities for Conferences and Exhibitions is at an all-time high.

The worldwide expansion of Business Tourism has been matched by increased interest, on the part of educators and researchers, in the phenomenon of business events as an academic subject and as a field of theoretical and empirical investigation. As a result, there has been considerable growth in the number of Universities offering courses related to Business Tourism and Business Events, and research in this field is increasing.

The All-inclusive Holiday

The all inclusive vacation has become one of the most popular ways for people to take a holiday in recent years. This type of vacation offers a few advantages and disadvantages, which we'll go over, but this can be a very cost effective way to enjoy a holiday. Depending on what you look for in a trip and what needs you have, this can be an excellent choice. On the other hand, for certain kinds of vacationers an all inclusive package might not be for them.

There are two primary types of all inclusive vacations – the all inclusive resort destination and the all inclusive cruise. There are fewer all inclusive cruises because typically there will be many extra costs for port fees and other travel costs. However, there is an abundance of all inclusive holiday packages that include airfare, hotels, food, and drinks, along with some activities that are offered to tropical destinations around the world. Bermuda, the Dominican Republic, Jamaica, and Mexico are among the many places that offer these all inclusive package vacations.

The best thing about these vacations is their cost and ease. There is no hassle in booking an all inclusive vacation package since it is all completed in one fell swoop; whereas, on a normal holiday you might have to book a flight, transportation to a hotel, living accommodations, pick out restaurants, decide which activities to participate in and more, but with an all inclusive resort that is all taken care of from the outset. Also, because of the package deal these holidays tend to be the most affordable way to go on vacation. Especially when you consider the cost of food and beverages into a holiday, you can save hundreds of dollars by going to an all inclusive resort rather than by booking a more traditional vacation.

The only downside is that you are somewhat limited to the resort, or you defeat the purpose of saving yourself that time and money. Many people simply want to lie in the sun and enjoy the pool or beach, and for them the all inclusive vacation is perfect. For those who like to get out and experience local culture and see the sites and sounds that are off the tourists' beaten path, the all inclusive vacation may not be for them. You also need to read the fine print carefully when booking your vacation. Some all inclusive packages will note that they only provide for one meal or a set number of alcoholic beverages, whereas others provide all meals and drinks regardless. Be sure you so, there are ups and downs to an all inclusive resort vacation, as there are to any type of vacation. For those who want to just enjoy themselves and to be able to afford a vacation they might not otherwise be able to, an all inclusive vacation package can be a great alternative. For travellers who prefer getting off the beaten path and immersing themselves in local culture, a more traditional vacation may be the way to go instead.

Planning a family holiday is a really difficult task, particularly when you have real money on the line. Plus, how many of us actually have relatives who work with travel agency, who will help us scout for the best holiday plan. I am sure many of us don't. Thus, it is always better for us to choose an inclusive package holiday to help us cut down the time required to do the planning.

A cheap package holiday is an all inclusive holiday and it is similar to buying items in bulk. The more you buy, the better value you will get for your money. When you are planning a holiday, it is very important that you know whether you are going to use a travel agent or you are going to do it yourself via online booking. Regardless of your decision, it is really important that you do your planning at least two weeks in advance.

When you are going on a trip, you should be thinking of its duration and how long you are going to stay. Taking the cheap buying in bulk approach, it is more beneficial for you to stay longer. But of course, the decision is yours to make. There are cheap package holidays that last for a weekend and there are some that last for at least a month. Make your judgment call. I will provide you an example of the duration of your trip and why it is better to stay as long as possible. If you take the weekend holiday packages, you will actually spend more for fewer activities, even though entertainment and leisure are covered by the package.

Accommodation is another issue. While accommodation is already fixed in most holiday packages, you can choose one that suits your needs. For instance, will you be staying in hotels or holiday villas? If you value privacy, staying in a holiday villa is better. The opposite is true if you would like to have more convenience.

The key here is to take affordable holiday packages as a whole. In fact, companies that structure the cheap holiday package deals are playing the number game. The bigger the turnover, the more they will make. These companies are also thrilled to accommodate a group for a longer duration because it is less risky. It is better for them to have a steady income over the long term than a sporadic one from some weekend holiday deals. Even though the weekend package is cheaper, travel companies run a higher risk of making less money in the long run. So, take advantage of this and make your trip as long as possible.

The rule of thumb is to stay for at least a week. This is the most efficient way to make use of a cheap all inclusive package holiday. You will have lots of fun and you will get the most bang for your bucks if and only if you give your vacation some time. You know what you're paying for before you book your vacation.

Mass-market Tourism in its Maturity

Introduction/Background

Accordingly, one of the most important developments in the tourism markets is the growing attention for service quality from such customer's perspective. This is the consequence of the increase of the degree of dominance of the customer in the service process. This degree of dominance is high if the customer can dictate his/her demands to the service provider and is low if the service organization can dictate its demands. The latter often occurs if the service provider has specific knowledge or know-how, or if he has the power to put the customer in dependent position. There is ample growth and encouragement issues pointing to the tourism ways as these issues involve addressing some of its economic perspective that stresses changes in its market conditions which affect people's motivation to travel and the factors which influence their ability to do so, for example increased leisure time and disposable income, improved technology and travel organization, as in tourism's ability to generate income, jobs and corporate profits, bring in foreign exchange, boost tax revenues, diversify the economy and aid regional development.

The successful integration of tourism development into such destination should make the development more acceptable to local residents and existing resource users than when tourism development is imposed in a segregated and unrelated manner. Successful integration can also be a much more efficient process. To most planners, developers and managers efficiency is a goal to be achieved, and steps and processes which speed the process of completion and acceptability of development are to be welcomed. The one importance is, the fact that successful integration can avoid problems that could otherwise materialize later in the operational phase of development through achieving synergy and even symbiosis with other existing activities and resource processes rather than competition.

In the real world very few economic or social-cultural activities are equal in priority. There is normally constant state of competition or at best uneasy alliance between activities in most communities, some being in the ascendance and others stagnating or being in decline. In many parts of the world in which tourism has been introduced, traditional primary activities have had long established priority, both in terms of economic importance and because of the intricate links with cultural patterns and behaviour. Tourism is often seen as being in direct competition with these traditional activities and in such situations integration rather than imposition is essential if development is to be successful. Thus acceptance may be difficult if tourism is not carefully and appropriately fitted into the existing systems. This situation is often compounded by the fact that in the case of large-scale tourism developments, ownership and control of these developments commonly lies outside the local community, and the element of external control can make acceptance of such development much more problematic. Lack of appreciation of local preferences, patterns of activities and priorities can exacerbate such tourism market situations. These market issues may be not so much how feelings towards tourism develop over time, but whether there are opposing views at any time. There need to be policies and practices in communities to determine views towards development and to enable the community to decide what type and scale of development can be accommodated in the community before development occurs, If such processes are in place and operational, then integration of the appropriate type of development should be much more easily achieved.

Globalization has transformed the tourism product over time from domination by mass tourism to a diversified industry catering more for the individual needs of travellers. Globalization has transmitted these ideas and practices worldwide, thus making the tourism industry more diversified and putting pressure on developing countries to create targeted, niche markets. Competition has become stronger and is based increasingly on diversification, market segmentation and diagonal integration, which involves the merger and conglomeration of related business activities. An important source of tourism revenue is now based on identifying, developing and promoting niche markets. New niche markets are constantly being identified in an attempt to diversify the industry further. The changing consumer preferences of international tourists constitute another aspect of globalization that is creating new challenges for developing countries. Providers of tourism services now try to gain a competitive advantage by catering for the individual needs of travellers. Tourists are actively changing the pace and direction of the tourism industry as they become more experienced travellers and change their behaviour and values. The increased travel experience, flexibility and independent nature of tourists have been generating demand for better quality, more value for money and greater flexibility in the travel experience. The new tourism also reflects demographic changes as well as changing lifestyles, thus creating demand for more targeted and customized holidays since travellers now belong to a number of different lifestyle segments. The changing values of tourists are also generating demand for more environmentally conscious and nature-oriented holidays, which means that tourism providers have to pay more attention to the way people think, feel and behave. In recent years, the niche market has become more important factor in the tourism industry, reflecting the need to diversify and customize the industry and ensure product sustainability. The main niche markets hold great potential and are developing rapidly. The transformations that have created new tourism put pressure on basic ways of doing business and on government strategies and plans for national tourism development.

Tourism has become a global industry and is widely considered to be one of the fastest growing industries, if not the fastest growing industry in the world (WTTC, 1995). It ranks as the largest industry in the world in terms of employment and ranks in the top two or three industries in almost every country on nearly every measure. Thus, tourism industry has become a major contributor to the gross national product of many nations, with marketing tourist destinations and its products becoming a widely recognized practice for both public and private sector organizations. It provides general models, concepts and techniques for strategic marketing but there is no academic analysis of their application to the marketing of a country as a tourist destination. It is important to distinguish between strategy to improve design quality and a strategy to improve the quality of service delivery. The process of improvement and innovation in Service Company is a continuous process. To improve this process managers must know what to do, how to do it and know the appropriate methods. Certain methods and techniques are more appropriate for improving the service delivery system such as continuous collecting and analyzing the delay time of flight departures and the waiting time on the phone, analyzing complaints, mystery shopping, etc. Other methods further innovation: e.g. brainstorming, brain writing, lateral thinking, mind mapping. In this article we will discuss three methods that further innovation of the service concept as well as incremental improvement of service delivery.

Amicably, market contribution to tourism maybe undervalued by policy makers and practitioners leading in misunderstanding of nature and value of marketing discipline designed for the powerful innovation within the tourism industry. Several authors have noted the lack of detailed work in relation to strategic issues in tourism marketing and distribution processes which require a more rigorous analysis of contextual factors. Similarly, other authors have argued that the marketing concept is based on a "long-term commitment" to the satisfaction of travellers' needs and motives and for a more strategic approach to marketing instead of relying on operational measures such as marketing communication.

There are three approaches to strategy that may be used by the tourism industry. The consumer-oriented approach dominates most current discussion of international marketing strategies. Another approach focuses on competition. However, these two approaches may be insufficient for they neglect the role of intermediaries in travel and tourism. Hence, a third approach to strategy, the trade-oriented orientation of intermediaries' desires, problems and demands needs to be investigated. Although each of these three approaches to strategic marketing will be discussed in turn below, they should not be regarded as alternatives, for they may be integrated into an overall strategy.

The Consumer-oriented Approach

Undifferentiated strategic marketing focuses on the average expectations of target markets: marketing efforts concentrate on the common interests of the target segments' needs and behaviour rather than their variances. In contrast, differentiated strategic marketing aims to identify the characteristics of diverse consumer groups through the use of marketing instruments directed at specific targets in order to create and implement a marketing approach and program that suits particular segments' needs and expectations. The extent of differentiation will vary depending on prevailing market conditions (1993).

The Competitor-oriented Approach

The next approach to strategy concentrates on competition. The tourism industry is undergoing a period of rapid change and uncertainty, with new technologies and more experienced consumers being some of the opportunities and challenges facing the industry.

The role of a competitive marketing strategy is to develop, maintain or defend the position of an organization. Public and private travel and tourism organizations may either strive for an overall cost/price leadership, or differentiate themselves to gain a product quality leadership.

Furthermore, a concentration on market niches may lead to a successful strategic position. As a tourism market becomes more mature it will continue to segment itself. With greater maturity, niche marketing approaches appealing to particular segment seem to become the focus of, in particular, travel and tourism organizations. In addition, airlines and intermediaries may specialize in sectors other than package holidays, that is, potential niches such as ecotourism may become more important. However, charter packages may also become increasingly popular due to their low cost, such trend suggesting the growth of the mass tourism market.

The Trade-oriented Approach

The third approach to strategy focuses on intermediaries and appears to be particularly relevant to the travel and tourism industry. The distribution of travel and tourism products/ services is a most important activity along the tourism chain. There are two main considerations which need to be distinguished: first, the degree to which organizations become involved in organizing and structuring the overseas distribution channel, and second, organizations' reactions and responses to marketing and distribution strategies of intermediaries in overseas markets. As a result of organizations' activeness or passiveness with regard to these two considerations, four trade-oriented strategies are possible: bypassing, cooperation, conflict, or adaptation. The tourism sector is probably the only service sector that provides concrete and quantified trading opportunities for all nations, regardless of their level of development. However, it is also a sector where there is clearly an uneven distribution of benefits, which is threatening the social, economic and environmental sustainability of tourism in some developing countries. For many developing countries tourism is one of fundamental pillars of their development process because it is one of the dominant activities in the economy, while for others, particularly by islands and some small economies, it is the only source of foreign currency and employment, and therefore constitutes the platform for their economic development. Against this background, part I presents an overview of the most important trends and features of international tourism and the most influential factors affecting the performance, efficiency and sustainability of tourism transactions in developing countries.

Part II presents an overview and examples of the main issues affecting the viability of tourism in developing countries, including (a) the impact of the leakage effect which is adversely affecting them in taking advantage of commercial opportunities; and (b) the anti-competitive practices affecting tourism viability and performance in different segments of the tourism sector, as well as in other sectors closely linked to travel and tourism. Part III presents some reflections about the GATS 2000 negotiations as a possible turning point for making effective the increasing participation of developing countries in international tourism flows in a sustainable perspective. In this connection, some comments are provided on the impact of the proposed Annex on Tourism on the economic, social and environmental sustainability of tourism.

Salient Trends and Features of the Performance of Developing Countries in International Tourism

Trends and features of international tourism: some indicators showing the sustainability of tourism in developing countries

Overall Trends in International Tourism

"International tourism highlights 2000" of the World Tourism Organization (OMT/WTO) reports that during 1998 total tourism receipts, including those generated by international fares, were the most important export revenue worldwide. Export revenue that year amounted to an estimated US$ 532 billion, surpassing all the other international trade categories. International tourism totalled to US$ 441 billion and the international transport of passengers US$ 91 billion, which corresponded to 7.9 and 1.3 per cent respectively of worldwide exports of good and services. According to the OMT/WTO *Tourism Economic Report 1998,* tourism is one the five top export categories and the main source of foreign currency for at least 38 per cent of them.

Figure 1: Worldwide export earnings, 1998

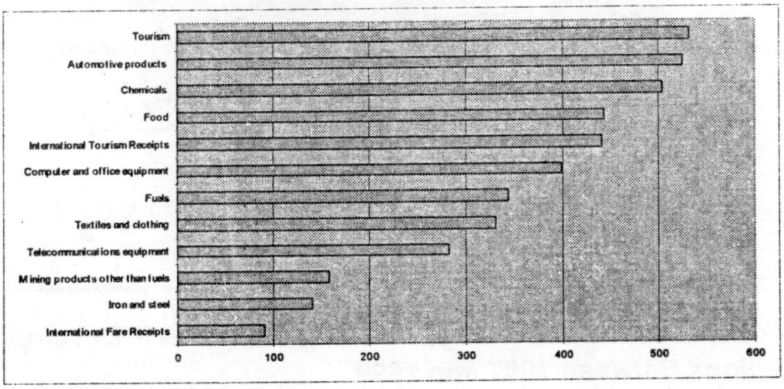

Sources: *Omt/WTO and IMF.*

Tourism Spenders

The world's top tourism spender during 1998 was by far the European Union, with an over US$ 160 billion. The most important spenders among its members were Germany (2nd world ranking), US$ 46.9 billion; the United Kingdom (4th), US$ 28.8 billion; France (5th), US$ 17.8 billion; Italy (6th), US$ 17.7; and Netherlands (7th), US$ 11.0 billion. The other members' expenses during the same year ranged between US$ 8.8 and 1.8 billion. During the same year, the United States (1st in world ranking by individual countries) spent US$ 56.1 billion; Japan (3rd), 28.8 billion; Canada (8th) US$ 10.8 billion; China (9th), US$ 9.2 billion; Russian Federation (13th) US$ 8.3 billion; Switzerland (14th), US$ 7.1 billion; and Australia, US$ 5.4 billion. Also during the same year 45 countries reported more that US$ 1 billion in international tourism expenditure

International Tourist Arrivals

Preliminary figures for tourist arrivals for 1999 show that these arrivals totalled 664 million. The distribution and share are presented in figure 2.

Figure 2

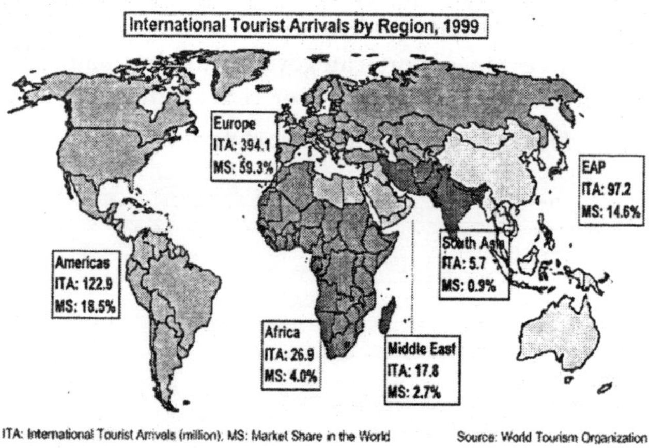

ITA: International Tourist Arrivals (million), MS: Market Share in the World   Source: World Tourism Organization

Tourism Trends and Best-performing Countries in Developing Regions Between 1997 and 1999

Africa. The African region showed a growth rate of 7.8 per cent in the number of arrivals, nearly twice the world average. There is a high concentration of international tourism arrivals in this region, bound for destinations in the north and south of the continent. The best-performing countries in terms of the increase in the number of arrivals included Morocco (18 per cent), Zimbabwe (11 per cent) and Zambia (26 per cent), while the important tourism destinations of Tunisia (3.4 per cent) and South Africa (6 per cent) continued to show steady gains.

Americas. The rate of growth for the whole region 2.4 per cent was lower than the world average, mainly owing to flat results for South American countries (-1 per cent) and Mexico (-2.9 per cent). Central America fared much better, especially Guatemala (29 per cent) and El Salvador (21 per cent). Results in the Caribbean were mixed, with Cuba (12 per cent) and the Dominican Republic (15 per cent) among the big winners and Puerto Rico (-11 per cent) among the losers.

East Asia/Pacific. After two years of decreasing tourist arrivals, East Asia and the Pacific bounced back strongly in 1999, attracting nearly 10 million more tourists than the previous record, set in 1998. Growth was widespread, with especially good results in Malaysia (43 per cent), Cambodia (29 per cent), Viet Nam (17 per cent), Singapore (11 per cent), Thailand (10 per cent), Republic of Korea (10 per cent), China (8 per cent) and Hong Kong, China (18 per cent). Europe. Overall, tourism to Europe grew by 2.7 per cent in 1999, with results mixed according to region.

In this region some economies in transition were affected by the Kosovo crisis and instability in the Russian market, which caused problems for mature destinations in Central and Eastern Europe such as Hungary (-14 per cent), Poland (-4.4 per cent) and the Czech Republic (-1.8 per cent). However, emerging destinations managed to attract the interest of travellers, for example, Estonia (15 per cent), Kyrgyzstan (17 per cent) and Georgia (21 per cent), as well as Russian Federation (17 per cent) and Ukraine (21 per cent).

Middle East. The Middle East is one of the world's smallest regions, receiving nearly 18 million tourists in 1999, but it also had the fastest growth rate with arrivals up by 16 per cent. Egypt, which represents a quarter of the regional total, recorded a spectacular growth rate of almost 40 per cent and a record number of tourist arrivals that far exceeds the totals achieved in its best year, 1997. Dubai, Lebanon and the Syrian Arab Republic also fared well, with arrivals increasing by 14, 12 and 9 per cent respectively. The Libyan Arab Jamahiriya registered an increase of 25 per cent.

South Asia. Tourism increased in most countries in this region, resulting in an increase of 8.3 per cent over the previous year's results. India registered an increase of 5.2 per cent, while arrivals in the Islamic Republic of Iran rose by 16.5 per cent, in Sri Lanka by 14.4 per cent and in Maldives by 8.6 per cent.

International Tourism Receipts

Figure 3: Tourism receipts market share (%), 1998

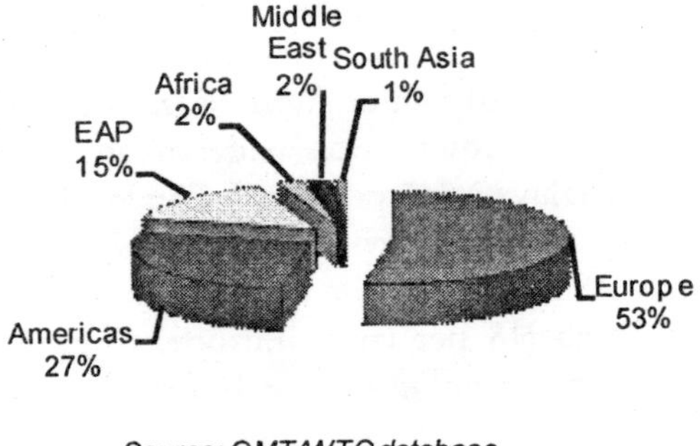

Source: OMT/WTO database.

Preliminary results processed by the OMT/WTO indicate that during 1999 tourism receipts worldwide amounted to US$ 455 billion and a further US$ 93 billion. In 59 countries the receipts amounted over US$ 1 billion. Figure 3 presents the receipts in different regions of the world during 1998.

Some Indicators about the Sustainability of International Tourism in Developing Countries

Importance and Impact of Export Revenues from Tourism for Developing Countries

During the period 1995-1998, tourism revenues were one of

the five leading sources of export revenue for 69 developing countries. Among the latter, tourism revenue was the main source of foreign currency in 28 countries, its share in total exports ranging between 79 and 20 per cent; in 27 countries it accounted for between 20 and 10 per cent; and in the 24 remaining countries it was around 10 per cent.

The contribution of export revenues to gross domestic product (GDP) was equally important and accounted for between 82.29 per cent (in Maldives) and 30 per cent (in Samoa). In the second group the contribution of export revenues to GDP is between 30 and 10 per cent and in the remaining countries under 10 per cent. One aspect to be underlined is that although the contribution of tourism revenues is important in all these countries, its contribution to GDP is declining as the economies become more diversified. The best examples of this are Mauritius, the Dominican Republic and Tunisia.

The Particular 'Situation of LDCs

Although only 0.5 per cent of the world's exports of services originate in the LDCs, international services are an important part of the economies of those countries. In 1998, services accounted for 20 per cent of the LDCs' total exports of goods and services. However, in 13 of the 49 LDCs services export receipts exceeded merchandise export receipts and in all but three of those the share of tourism services exports in total foreign exchange earnings was more than twice the share of merchandise exports.

The share of the LDCs in the world's exports of international tourism services was 0.6 per cent in 1988 (with 2.4 million international tourist arrivals) and 0.8 per cent in 1998 (5.1 million). During the 1990s tourist flows to the LDCs increased more rapidly than tourist flows to the rest of the world. This growth was particularly strong in seven countries (Cambodia, Mali, Laos People's Democratic Republic, Myanmar, Samoa, Uganda, United Republic of Tanzania), which hosted over 1.2 million visitors in 1998, in comparison with 0.4 million in 1992. During that period, tourism growth was much slower in several LDCs, while a decrease was observed in a number of countries that suffered socio-political and economic instability. The growth of international tourism receipts in the LDCs was also quite rapid during the 1990s: total receipts more than doubled between 1992 and 1998 (from US$ 1 billion to US$ 2.2 billion). There is a great degree of concentration in the distribution of tourism receipts among the LDCs: five countries (Cambodia, Maldives, Nepal, Uganda, United Republic of Tanzania) accounted for 51 per cent of the total tourism receipts of the group in 1998. Particularly strong, over the decade, was the growth in international tourists' expenditure in Cambodia, the United Republic of Tanzania, Myanmar, Bangladesh, Samoa, Uganda and Haiti. Tourism is the first source of foreign exchange earnings in the whole group of 49 LDCs, aside from the petroleum industry, which is concentrated in only three LDCs (Angola, Yemen, Equatorial Guinea): the combined tourism export receipts of all LDCs in 1998 accounted for 16.2 per cent of the total non-oil export receipts of the LDCs, thus exceeding the second and third largest non-oil export sectors (cotton and textile products) by 39 per cent and 82 per cent, respectively.

Level of Performance and Sustainability of Tourism in Developing Countries

The proper functioning of the tourism economy is linked to that of many other related economic activities, which accounts for the importance of its economic, social and environmental sustainability. As a matter of fact, the extent to which the business operations of international tourism, backward and forward are linked with other sectors will determine the level of performance and profitability of tourism, the extent of multiplier and spillover effects, and the retention of value added, i.e. the leakage effect. The sectors producing goods and services are linked backwards with tourism in catering for the needs of tourists and tourism operators, e.g. agriculture and food-processing industries, and other manufacturing industries providing furniture, construction materials and other articles required by tourism establishments. Similarly, many other services, such as transport, business services, financial services, professional services, construction design and engineering, environmental services, security services and government services, also ensure the efficient performance of tourism operators. Some of these sectors are also crucial for the proper linkage of tourism with foreign markets (forward linkages) because they constitute the platforms for "taking off" and for keeping the national tourism providers fully integrated with international tourism flows.

Many developing countries have found important to improve the linking of tourism (forward and backward) with the other sectors of the economy as one of the foundations of tourism development policies, so as to capitalize on the benefits of the globalization and internationalization of markets. Successful experiences of small economies and islands that have recently become emerging tourism destinations, such as Mauritius, Maldives, the Dominican Republic and other Caribbean islands, attest to the vital importance of the proper linkage of tourism with the rest of the economy, in their capacity of retaining value added, e.g., reducing leakages. Despite developing countries efforts to develop the most suitable domestic policy environment, the economic sustainability of tourism is being undermined by external factors beyond their control, notably the predatory behaviour of integrated suppliers which enjoy a dominant position in the originating markets of tourism flows.

Key Issues with Special Impact on the Social, Economic and Environmental Sustainability of Tourism

This part presents an overview and illustration of the main issues affecting the viability of tourism in developing countries, including (a) the leakage effect produced by their structural vulnerabilities and their difficulties in taking advantage of commercial opportunities; and (b) anti-competitive practices affecting tourism viability and performance in different segments of the tourism sector, as well as those in other sectors closely linked to travel and tourism.

Leakages from Tourism in Developing Countries

As a modality of international commerce, tourism involves not only inflows of foreign financial resources but also outflows, referred to herein as "leakages". When they exceed specific levels, these outflows can significantly neutralize the positive financial effect of international tourism. Leakage is the process whereby part of the foreign exchange earnings generated by tourism, rather than being retained by tourist-receiving countries, is either retained by tourist-generating countries or repatriated to them in the form of profits, income and royalty remittances, repayment of foreign loans, and imports of equipment, materials, capital and consumer goods to cater for the needs of international tourist and overseas promotional expenditures.

Leakages can be divided into three categories: internal leakage or the "import-coefficient" of tourism activities; external leakage or pre-leakage, depending on the commercialization mode of the tourism package and the choice of airline; and invisible leakage or foreign exchange costs associated with resource damage or deterioration.

Internal leakages can be measured by establishing "satellite accounts" within national accounting and survey procedures to detail all tourism-related economic activities. It is a normal effect present in both developed and developing countries. In principle, import-related leakages are highest where the local economies are weakest owing to sparse factor endowment or inadequate quality of goods and services. The average leakage for most developing countries today is between 40 and 50 percent of gross tourism earnings for small economies and between 10 and 20 percent for most advanced and diversified developing countries. Importantly for LDCs, tourism import-related leakages are often inferior to other economic activity leakages, including manufacturing and, in some cases, agriculture, thus confirming tourism as a choice sector of development for which they possess comparative advantages in many areas.

A first step in reducing internal leakage is to identify what levels are appropriate given the economic structure of a country and then to ensure that effective leakage remains near this objective range while strategies to build up the local supply capacity are put in place. Although restrictive trade policies can reduce the size of the market, it is important to note that import openness tends to facilitate the leakage effect unless the economy has already in place a structure capable of reacting to the competitive stimulus of imports, which is usually not the case in LDCs.

External leakage or pre-leakage is much more difficult to measure and relates to the proportion of the total value added of tourism of services actually captured by the servicing country. To the extent that developing countries have limited access to commercialization channels in their target markets, they can only offer base prices to intermediaries that capture the mark-up on those services. Observed differences between paid and received prices for developing country tourism services (lodging, food, entertainment, etc.) suggest external leakage or pre-leakage levels of up to 75 percent. In some cases, base prices do not allow for the economic sustainability of projects, and normally do not contemplate replacement costs associated with resource depletion. This leads to problems of infrastructure and environmental sustainability, which tend to be overlooked in view of the short-term importance of crucial foreign exchange inflows.

As a flow variable, leakage levels do not have a static effect. They vary in time depending on:

(a) The stage or cycle point of the tourism industry. For example, a nascent tourism industry tends to require large amounts of one-time imports, whereas loan grace periods may allow for a decrease in leakage during the first few years of operation. During a maturity phase leakage may increase as large sums are invested in marketing, rehabilitation of facilities and upgrading of products provided, etc.

(b) The evolution of the economy to provide new services and products resulting from demand from the tourism sector. The import of products and services initially not available should trigger enough entrepreneurial response to enable these to be provided locally, thus allowing for a lessening of leakage. It is therefore a main objective of leakage limitation to provide and promote these links between domestic industry and tourism. For example, in the Dominican Republic leakages diminished between 1990 and 1995 as local industry became increasingly interested in servicing the tourism market. The largest companies have now created subsidiaries specifically for this purpose.

Another factor to be evaluated in identifying appropriate leakage levels is the type of tourism being promoted. High-income tourism, because it requires the provision of very high quality and high priced goods, may actually result in increased leakage in some cases despite of the higher income it may generate. Mass tourism could have higher potential for leakage than ecological or adventure tourism because the latter value and consume local resources as part of the tourism experience. However, low-leakage tourism can also equate to low-income tourism, resulting in lower total income and therefore limiting the possibilities for expansion and development by other sectors of the receiving country's economy. In order to correctly evaluate the return on investments it is necessary to carry out a cost-of-opportunity study that will establish a "leakage break-even point" as a function of the country's economic capacity to serve different types of tourism and choose the type most suitable for a project or country.

Leakage effects on tourism net income levels are nonetheless offset by increased value added or volume. As an example of the positive outlook for LDCs, value added in tourism, measured as tourism income per tourist arrival (Yt/At) has grown by over 100 percent in 21 (almost half) of the LDCs surveyed between 1998 and 1992.

Interestingly, growth in income per tourist appears to bear no clear relationship to the level of or growth in arrivals. This suggests that growth in income per tourist is not a function of volume, and has therefore grown basically because of a favourable quality/price ratio. This also confirms the enormous diversity of situations present in LDCs and their tourism industries; but, in general, as value added grows, the *potential* for leakage lessens.

However, for varying reasons, including differing lengths of stay, very few countries have achieved income-per-tourist levels of above US$ 1000. The growth of the middle-income tourism category of US$ $500–$999 has been higher not only for arrivals (a factor of 2 versus 1.75) but also for combined income per tourist category (a factor of 4.9 versus 2). This indicates that the primary competitive segment for LDCs, as well as the segment where most opportunities for growth in value added exist, tends to be in this category of pricing.

Tourism policy should therefore be based on the premise that although leakage is an intrinsic element of international tourism, and increased value added will also benefit the economy, leakage-containment measures have multiplicative effects that will allow developing countries to maximize the financial benefits to be derived from an expansion of tourism.

A study on Indonesia showed that the tourism multiplier (1.59) was the highest of all categories, including final demand, and exhibited strong links to the agricultural sector, on which it had no direct effect at all.

To the extent that leakages lead to a definition of economic opportunities it can be useful as a strategic blueprint for further economic development. Domestic policies in developing countries against leakages from international tourism should include:

(i) the provision of incentives to reinvest profits and potential cash transfers that otherwise would be invested abroad;

(ii) the enhancement of the capacity of tourist destinations for intensifying the production of goods and services required by the tourism sector;

(iii) the provision of incentives to domestic investors to expand their participation in tourism and iv) the enforcement of domestic competition policy against anti-competitive practices by tour operators.

As regards external leakages, most issues address points of discussion under the GATS Annex on tourism in the WTO, such as:

(i) local and international competition policy, particularly with regard to market access issues and best business practices in relation to regulations on contractual practices; and

(ii) ecological and economic sustainability and the valuation and use of non-tradable resources.

Anti-competitive Practices Affecting Tourism Sustainability

The competition issue and the treatment of anti-competitive behaviour are at the core of the problems of efficiency, viability and sustainability of tourism in developing countries.

The latter's ability to deal with those two aspects and to counter their effects is a crucial matter. Firstly, this is because anti-competitive behaviour occurs largely in developed countries, as a result of the fierce competition among a few integrated dominant players with a high market share in their own market and in all segments of tourism industry supply, notably tour operators, travel agencies, hotels etc. Secondly, the pattern of globalization, which is the driving force of many of the developments in the supply of the tourism and air transport, also mostly originates and is controlled in the two leading developed economies, namely the European Union and the United States.

Consequently, what often appears to be a normal commercial relationship in a developing country may actually be the result of a network of anti-competitive practices arising from a globalized and highly integrated tourism trading environment, dominated by a few suppliers in the originating tourism markets.

Moreover, other non-behaviour-related industry issues, such as the inadequacy or absence of a domestic competition legal framework in developing countries, and the lack of multilateral disciplines and mechanisms within the GATS framework, also affect the ability of developing countries to deal with or prevent anti-competitive practices in their tourism sectors.

Why and how do anti-competitive practices threaten the viability of sustainable tourism in developing countries?

Introduction

The economic and social viability of tourism in developing countries depends on sustainable growth perspectives, in terms not only of absolute values, but also of their capacity for retaining more value added in their economies, i.e. smaller leakages, an even distribution of benefits in commercial operations, elimination of all barriers to tourism, particularly to commercial presence, and the movement of tourism suppliers in both origin and destination markets, and the effective implementation of provisions enumerated in Articles IV and XIX of GATS.

The foundations for sustainable tourism are already in place in most developing countries as a result of the autonomous liberalization of the tourism sector itself and the progressive liberalization of many other services sectors. However, for those countries highly dependent on tourism revenue, the benefits of the liberalization of tourism are being threatened by the predatory practices of a few dominant tourism suppliers in the world tourism market.

The evolution of the GATS disciplines, and the consistency of future commitments of developed countries with the economic, social and environmental sustainability of tourism in developing countries in the GATS 2000 negotiations, should mark a turning point favouring more profitable tourism for all WTO members, particularly the most vulnerable small developing countries.

The predatory practices and anti-competitive behaviour in international tourism have two main effects on the economic sustainability of the tourism of developing countries: unbalanced trade benefits, and the deepening of the leakage effect. Their combined impact minimize the positive impacts of spillover and multiplier effects inherent to tourism, and undermine the financial capacity of enterprises and the ability of countries to earmark necessary resources to maintain and upgrade basic infrastructure and quality standards in order to satisfy in an adequate way competitive conditions and international demand.

Moreover, in most vulnerable and small developing economies, particularly LDCs, the foundations of tourism are threatened by unbalanced results in their business operations, which are in turn threatening the social, economic and environmental sustainability of tourism. There is much documented evidence about the negative impact of anti-competitive behaviour of developed countries' dominant tourism suppliers on their own markets and overseas. Unfair practices, which confront developing countries' suppliers in their business operations with dominant suppliers in tourism-originating countries, are of a different nature and occur in different segments of tourism and related activities. One of the salient features that become evident in commercial relations is the uneven distribution of benefits, due to the dominant position and market power of integrated suppliers in their own markets and worldwide.

These suppliers have absolute advantages, because of their control of inbound and outbound operations in their countries and overseas, which allow them to keep consumers dependent on the offer of the products and services they supply, at the expenses of imposing onerous commercial conditions on suppliers in different tourism destinations. The huge supply capacity of dominant players in all segments of tourism, including transporters, CRS/GDS, tour operators, travel agencies and hotels, allows them to prepare holiday packages and retail them through their own business networks, as well as to impose prices and conditions on suppliers in tourism destinations.

How do the business operations of tour operators and travel agencies in the originating markets of tourism affect the sustainability of developing countries' tourism?

Tourism suppliers from developing countries e.g. hotels, inbound operators and land transport companies participate in international tourism mainly through the transactions of tour operators and travel agencies from developed countries in the developed countries' originating markets. As wholesalers of tourism products and services they assemble the holiday package by negotiating with destinations and operators in third countries.

They view the tour package as an attractive option with many advantages for them: (a) it ensures flows of tourists; (b) it reduces the international marketing costs of the destination; and (c) it increase the volume flow of package travellers, which is likely to increase investment by foreign construction companies, major tour operators and airline companies that wish to make the tourism product more attractive to consumers. However, tourism suppliers from tourism destinations in developing countries have very often underlined their weak bargaining position in business transactions, particularly with dominant suppliers of the most important originating tourism market from developed countries.

International Competition Among Tour Operators and Travel Agencies

Tour operators in originating countries manage business operations through (a) a subsidiary of a vertically integrated firm with a number of related travel interests; (b) an entirely independent firm that specializes in putting holiday packages together and selling them; (c) a subsidiary of an airline; and (d) an operator directly linked to a travel agent. The tour operator of each major market is dominated by a small number of national firms with a relatively large market share, which compete fiercely with each other.

For instance, four firms with a share of over 60 per cent dominate the United Kingdom market. This results in the larger operators having a dominant position with a very little competition, because the layer of the next competitor is too small. Consequently, the travel agencies (the retailers of tourism packages) in destination markets are almost entirely dependent on their linkages with the dominant tour operators. Also, consumers become captive in their choices of tourist package offered by dominant suppliers. The effect of this supremacy of integrated tourism suppliers in their own markets is mirrored in their dominant position in commercial relations with tourism suppliers in destination developing countries.

The benefits and costs of package tours to service suppliers in developing countries depend to a large extent on the nature and terms of the contracts between them and the tour operators from the tourism-originating countries. Accordingly, the bargaining powers of suppliers from developing countries are a central issue affecting the tourism sustainability of developing countries. Some examples of how the common practices in contractual arrangements affect the sustainability of tourism in developing countries are presented below.

Use of Monopsonistic Power Over Local Tourism Suppliers in Developing Countries

The contract between a tour operator from an originating country and the suppliers in the destination country involves a block reservation for a future period at a negotiated price and specifies the terms of risk sharing in the event that not all the packages are sold. The tour operator normally has the greater bargaining power during the contract negotiations; if it considers that the negotiating partner's offer is not attractive enough, it can choose another hotel in the same area or even another region of the same country. Tour operators thus often exercise a monopsonistic power over local tourism suppliers, such as local hotels, since for the latter the servicing of the package tour is a vital means of securing their occupancy rates.

The asymmetry of bargaining power is clearly revealed in the content of the contract. Often contracts last for one year or more, and the risk inherent in a long-term contract for a tour operator is reduced by negotiating various conditions favourable to the tour operator. A contract frequently contains the following provisions: a substantial discount is provided on rooms after the departure of the clients; no deposit is required for the booking; payment may be made long after the departure of the customers; and the tour operator retains the right to return unfilled rooms ("release-back clause") shortly before the arrival date, without any need to pay compensation.

Anti-competitive Practices Resulting from Vertical Integration

Vertical integration among tour operators and travel agencies, which is currently proceeding at a notable pace in Europe, threatens to reduce the actual number of tour operators in the market. As a result, a great deal of market power is being transferred to the intermediaries that direct consumers to specific destinations. The consequences of this should be a major concern to developing countries' tourism destinations. The increase in the degree of concentration in the travel market in favour of mega-operators puts developing countries' suppliers and the other competitors in local markets at a clear disadvantage. It also opens the door to unfair practices, which directly affect tourist destinations. An example of this is the travel agent's "racking policy", which refers to the decision about which brochures to put on display. This has a crucial impact on the tourism destinations of developing countries, because for them the travel agent's display rack is almost an essential facility, and denial of access to it can severely restrict consumer exposure.

The threat of "deracking" (i.e. removing brochures from the shelves) is used by integrated suppliers in attempt to negotiate larger commissions, by pressuring tour operators not to supply independent travel agencies on better terms or by pushing their own holidays through in-house incentive schemes. The lasting impact of this practice is more restrictive in originating countries where tour operators are the main distribution channels, such as in Europe, where more than 60 per cent of tour packages are sold by integrated suppliers. Conversely, in the United States the possibility of "deracking" is lower because about 70 per cent of travel agencies are independent, GDS/CRS are more important as distribution channels, and the Internet is becoming a primary source of information for consumers about tourism destinations.

International Competition Among Hotels

The international hotels sector is characterized by a considerable diversity in the modalities of services provision, and by a high concentration of a very small number of large hotel groups, including hotel consortia, integrated hotel chains and tourism lodging (second homes). Their scope and focus are very often limited, either by a focus on home markets, notably through the hospitality franchising systems, or by a concentration on business travel and destinations.

One important aspect to be noted is that the intensive use of the accommodation infrastructure, particularly hotels receiving international tourists regardless of the hotel's size, requires the continuous allocation of financial resources to maintain and upgrade the quality of accommodation to meet the standards of international demand. In most developing country destinations huge investments have been made in the hospitality and accommodation sector either through investment of domestic resources or attracting foreign investors by increase of different modalities, including management contracts and franchising brand names

As in all the other segments of tourism-related activities, the importance of competition issues stems from a mix of practices through the distribution mechanisms. Anti-competitive behaviour in those mechanisms is thus most likely to have a significant effect on the ability of destinations, and of their hotel sectors, to compete effectively and to gain a fair share of the rewards of attracting tourists and travellers.

The sustainability of this sector in developing countries' tourism destinations depends on the occupancy rates (affected by seasonality) and the level of profits, which are highly influenced by the results of commercial transactions between hoteliers and tour operators from tourism-originating countries. In this connection, it has to be underlined that the accommodation sector is the one most affected by the dominant power of mega-operators, whose stringent demands in terms of quality standards are not duly compensated for with fair commercial remuneration. Another, wider impact of this predatory behaviour in the tourism economy of receiving countries is the deepening of the leakage effect and the undermining of positive inherent multipliers effects of tourism. Depending on the magnitude of these unfair compensations from dominant tour operators, some tourism destinations in developing countries might be subsidizing tourists from originating countries.

Computerized Reservation Systems (CRS) Global Distribution Systems (GDS)

The development of international tourism relies on the effective commercialization of tourism products to consumers at tourism-originating countries. World information and distribution networks play a decisive role in the international tourism sector since they bring the buyers and producers of tourism products into contact. CRS, GDS and the Internet are the backbone of world information networks, which provide the infrastructures and networking facilities for airlines, tour operators, travel agencies and other tourism operators to process and obtain information, make reservations and market tourism products.

CRS have been developed by large air carriers since the 1970s to process flight reservations. They later evolved and expanded to offer further services related to air transport, such as the storage of information on a worldwide basis, the issuance of tickets, marketing (by displaying information on fares, discounts and conditions attached to them) or the sale of products and services.

Moreover, they cover not only services provided by airlines, but also land services supplied to tourists, such as package tours, hotels and vehicle rentals. With this enlarged range of services, they became known as global distribution systems. GDS have significantly improved the efficiency of travel agents' business operations and their use is growing rapidly. They have become the main marketing and trading tool of international tourism, as well as a major source of income for the carriers which own them. Through strategic alliances and other forms of cooperation or mergers in the most important markets, these systems minimize their costs and reduce the need for a direct commercial presence. A single GDS terminal provides immediate access to all services companies which have opted to market their products through this network.

The companies (air carriers or independent commercial companies) that control CRS and GDS either partly or entirely sell access to the system to tourism operators worldwide. There are many obstacles to and measures governing GDS networks. These include (a) unfair rights of access, (b) restrictions on display, (c) costs of services influenced by monopolistic practices, (d) neutrality and regulations, and (e) the technology gap among users.

Access problems: Despite their major contribution to the development of tourism, GDS are frequently considered a barrier to market entry, mainly because they are controlled by the major carriers and because of the unfavourable access conditions for competitors. While some East Asian developing countries have participated in the establishment of a major GDS (Abacus, complemented by the strategic alliance with Worldspan), other developing countries have not been able to do likewise, leaving their carriers and other service suppliers without privileged access to any GDS.

Additionally, countries not yet seen as attractive tourist destinations, or whose hospitality sector is underdeveloped (particularly in Africa and South Asia), tend to be poorly represented, if at all, on GDS. Therefore, access to information on their tourism products is limited, thus making it difficult for them to sell their tourism services. These difficulties have meant that many smaller carriers, especially some from developing countries, have been obliged to continue using the traditional SITA CRS, which leaves them at a competitive disadvantage compared with those what are represented in the major GDS. On the other hand, in many developing countries, particularly in Africa, GDS are present as a result of joint ventures with local partners but operate within a de facto monopoly. This leads to excessive user fees and hinders their potential for developing tourism.

Display. The GDS allows a travel agent to view a wide range of information, which sometimes requires several pages on a terminal screen. In most cases, however, travel agencies only consult the information on the first page (screen); the order in which screens are displayed is thus a crucial determinant in the user's selection of products. The display may discriminate against smaller carriers which do not own a major CRS, since controllers' own flights may be better displayed on the screens than those of their competitors (this is known as "display bias"). There may also be discrimination in favour of their suppliers of land services.

Cost: The cost of having services presented GDS may be prohibitively high for SMEs, leaving them with no access to this marketing tool. Even though all service providers have to pay a fee for having their services displayed in the systems, the costs of participation for the owners of GDS are fully or partly covered by the profits generated by the systems. The cost of hardware and user fees may prevent small users from using GDS; this puts some service suppliers (particularly SMEs) from developing countries at a disadvantage compared with their larger national or international competitors.

Neutrality and regulations: In order to prevent CRS from being used as an anti-competitive tool and to ensure their neutrality, the United States, Canada and the European Union have issued regulations in recent years on GDS operations related to air services, while the International Civil Aviation Authority (ICAO) adopted a code of conduct for CRS in 1991.

However, the regulations and code have not been sufficient to resolve completely the anti-competitive bias of the systems, and particularly to address the specific problems of carriers from developing countries. The ICAO code (the only multilateral one) is non-binding and therefore there are no mechanisms to ensure its enforceability. The relevant domestic regulations are binding, but only within the territories of the countries concerned. The European Union regulations apply to CRS from countries which have similar legislation to ensure neutrality. On the other hand, although CRS have been included among the "soft" air services rights included in GATS, the commitments do not deal with their anti-competitive potential.

Technology gap: Installing and maintaining a system poses a greater problem to travel agents in developing countries, owing to deficiencies in the infrastructure necessary for such an information network, and the shortage of professionals to manage, operate and maintain the system. This not only represents a technical hindrance to the use of modern technology, but also increases the associated costs, thereby putting travel agents in developing countries at a disadvantage compared with their counterparts in developed countries.

Electronic commerce: The expansion of the use of the Internet and other forms of electronic communication opens up significant opportunities for developing countries to develop their tourism and air transport sectors. Their service suppliers can reach consumers around the world directly, offering both package tours and individual air and land services. They thereby cut out the costs of intermediaries and transaction costs and avoid the need for a direct commercial presence and its associated costs. Nevertheless, electronic marketing and trading have their own costs in terms of human and physical capital requirements. In countries where these requirements are in relatively short supply, the cost of electronic marketing and trading can be reduced if individual suppliers pool their resources. This could be coordinated, for instance, by national tourist authorities. Moreover, modern technologies are likely to be increasingly used as institutional promotion tools. If there is a minimal critical mass of information infrastructure in a given country, the new technologies can offer substantial cost savings.

Air Transport

Air access in international tourism depends on the availability and conditions of air transport connecting tourist-generating countries and destination countries. Air transport is a major factor underpinning international tourism in the vast majority of developing countries, but its importance for tourism varies considerably from one region to another. It is the means of transport used by the majority of tourists arriving in developing countries. Air transport developed as a result of the increase in demand for tourism-related travel, becoming in turn the driving force behind the development of the tourism industry. In 1998, passengers were responsible for about 75 per cent of air traffic volume and for of the total operating revenues of airlines. It is estimated that up to 40 per cent of air passenger travel is for business purposes (as opposed to leisure or personal travel) and that business travellers account for up to half of airlines' income. Like tourism, the world air transport industry has expanded at twice the rate of world output growth, and is expected to continue to do so in the next twenty years. The main recent developments affecting air transport and the industry structure are the increased international ownership of airlines and their growing concentration, worldwide moves to liberalize and deregulate the sector, the privatization of airlines and the formation of strategic alliances among firms. The main benefits of the latter are the cost reductions and efficiency gains that can be achieved by rationalizing the joint use of resources (such as check-in facilities and ground personnel), creating synergies and providing "network value" without the need to physically expand operations. The large global alliances aim at world coverage by pooling the networks of their members. The main drawback in doing this is that the alliances can restrict compctition and thus negate some of these benefits, particularly if they collectively achieve a dominant position on given routes.

How the GATS 2000 Negotiations should Mark a Turning point to make Effective

How Negotiations could Support the Sustainability of Tourism Operations

The GATS 2000 negotiations mandated by the Final Act of the Uruguay Round provide developing countries with a unique opportunity to counterbalance the asymmetries imbedded in the outcome of the Uruguay Round services negotiations. In this perspective, it is the right time to take advantage of these negotiations to prepare and put forward negotiating proposals on how to make effective use of the provisions of Art IV and XIX, aimed at increasing participation of developing countries in trade in services and the expansion of their services exports including through the strengthening of their domestic services and its efficiency and competitiveness. The two-way process involves not only the refinement of offers, but also the preparation of requests from trading partners as one of the key ways to obtain substantive benefits as result of the GATS 2000 negotiations. Moreover, an active participation of developing countries in the GATS rule-making process is a contribution to building of an improved multilateral framework which would take into consideration existing asymmetries and the need for a predictable markets access for exporters of services from developing countries.

The viability of tourism, i.e. its economic, social, cultural and environmental sustainability, is at the heart of domestic policies and development concerns of developing countries. Accordingly, in the course of the present negotiations on trade in services, there is a need for similar focus on strengthening future substantive commitments on tourism by GATS members as was the case in other sector such as telecommunications and financial services. In this perspective the proposal for the Annex on Trade in Tourism Services (WT/GC/W/372), may contribute to providing a pro-competitive framework as a complementary tool which would ensure:

(a) *An adequate coverage and consistency of commitments in all tourism activities as defined by the Satellite Tourism Account:* This aspect is of paramount importance in view of specific characteristics and diversity of transactions linked to trade in tourism services, notably the heavy reliance of tourism on air transport and travel distribution systems.

(b) *The prevention of predatory behaviour and anti-competitive practices by dominant integrated suppliers in the originating markets:* This refers to disciplines to prevent anti-competitive conduct including from air transport and travel distribution systems, and to safeguard trade in tourism services from competitive exclusions, abuse of dominant and misleading or discriminatory use of information.

(c) *The effective access and use of information on a non-discriminatory basis:* It should include provisions on access to ensuring non-discrimination, transparent, reasonable and objective criteria; compliance with Art. IV of GATS and the truthfulness of the information on tourism distributed by governments (travel warning) and through GDS; the unbundling of travel distribution systems as a measure to counter vertical integration and conflicts of interest in travel agencies and the interconnection of CRS, through the portability of reservation numbers. Submitting GDS operations to effective multilateral disciplines and dispute-settlement mechanisms would have a substantial effect on trade and anti-competitive practices.

(d) *The implementation of an adequate framework for sustainable development of tourism:* Provisions on cooperation for the sustainable development of tourism are needed in recognition of the role of tourism in economic development; its need for infrastructure and development assistance; equitable trading conditions for economic sustainability; the relevance of enforcing internationally-recognized environmental and quality standards; the need for cooperation at all levels; and the importance of providing information on technologies required for competitive provision, regulation and sustainable development of tourism and all related-activities.

(e) *To preserve the environmental sustainability of tourism and the cultural heritage*: Guiding principles for national policies and trade commitments to preserve the ecological systems, the biodiversity, cultural patrimony and traditions.

Issues for Consideration by Developing Countries in Negotiating Specific Commitments in Tourism

The liberalization under the GATS 2000 will be determined on one hand, by the level of removal of barriers in the revised horizontal commitments (which affect all sectors) and on the other, the lifting of conditions and limitations applied to each sector at sector-specific level and in the four modes of supply. Accordingly the consistency between the two types of commitment is an important issue to be addressed by developing countries, seeking to obtain commercially meaningful commitments at specific sectoral level.

Improvement of Horizontal Commitments

In preparation of their positions in services negotiations, developing countries must assess to what extent the horizontal commitments of developed countries impede the liberalization of tourism and travel and related services. The major limitation in the horizontal commitments is in the lack of significant trading opportunities in mode 4, i.e. temporary movement of natural persons, since practically no commitments in this mode were made in specific services sectors.

The temporary presence of natural persons in all services sectors is undermined by the recurrence at the horizontal level to the economic needs tests, nationality and/or residence requirement and cumbersome administrative and visa procedures to be met by foreign nationals as services providers. The existing horizontal commitments by developed countries mainly refer to limitations for the establishment of the commercial presence by foreign providers to carry out the commercial operations.

Specific Tourism Sector Commitments

Majority of tourism originating countries are developed countries, which have undertaking commitment to liberalize fully or partially the supply of services in different tourism sub-sectors and modes of supply. Still, *the impact of commitments in commercial presence* in term of market value is nullified by restrictions to the commercial presence of foreign tour operators, travel agencies, restaurants and hotels, which are not listed there.

Also, the movement of natural persons engaged in the tourism supply of different services is precluded by limited horizontal commitments and the lack of specific sectoral commitments. For instance in many Members States of the EU the commercial presence of foreign tour operators from the third countries is precluded or allowed only in association with already established national firms therein. Similarly, foreigners are precluded from undertaking of the business operations in the restaurant sub-sector even for those specializing in typical national food from other countries. In addition, the level of restrictions on commercial presence is aggravated by the possibility of recourse to the economic needs test, cumbersome and discriminatory licensing requirements that foreign suppliers of tourism services must meet.

Temporary Presence of Natural Persons as Consumers and Providers of Services

It should be underlined that although the existing commitments on market access on *consumption abroad have no limitations* in the case of majority of the GATS commitments, including in the top originating countries; in real terms the freedom of movement for consumption abroad is restricted by the level of binding in other modes of supply, in particular the commercial presence of foreign suppliers in the tourism originating markets.

The movement of consumers in most of the top originating markets of tourism is captive, because the existing level of binding of commercial presence consolidates the absolute advantage of the dominant mega-tour operators and other national suppliers including the travel agencies, since the exclusive right of selling directly to travellers of holiday packages in their own markets has been consolidated in the existing commitments on commercial presence.

Moreover, under such commercial conditions, the consumers' choices are limited by the offers of holiday package by dominant tour operators, but not only them, also by the opportunities for suppliers from destination countries to reach consumer in the originating markets directly. In addition, the consumers' choices in these markets are restricted by unfair practices in the management of information systems and the "racking policies" by travel agencies, which are usually integrated with mega-tour operators.

To improve horizontal commitments on mode 4, developed countries should remove the application of the economic needs test with respect to the movement of professionals supplying tourism services. Not all the professions and occupations are equally important to the movement of persons in the context of trade in tourism services. For example, the possibility to have the waiver from the application economic needs test should be provided to individual tourism services suppliers involved in catering, maintenance services or in such areas where cultural affinities and close contacts with tourists may contribute to the quality of the services provided. To the extent that the remaining occupations would remain subject to the application of economic needs tests, efforts should be made to reduce the scope for arbitrary and discriminatory practices, provide greater transparency and introduce more neutral economic criteria. The issue of transparency in respect of the application of the GATS commitments is crucial as a tool in promoting trade in tourism services.

In that respect, commitments in mode 4 are closely linked to the implementation of the relevant immigration regulations, policies and procedures in a clear and transparent manner. Publishing of the legislation and implementing regulations which significantly affect ability of the foreign nationals or permanent residents move across borders to supply services is a general obligation, since this is the way to limit the room for discretionary and procedural rules. The lack of transparency, clarity in the existence, implementation and application of policy guidelines affecting application for and consideration of temporary work permits, residency requirements of visas impede market access, effectively violating key GATS provision.

2

Hospitality Training Management

Over time, an increasing number of destinations have opened up and invested in tourism development, turning modern tourism into a key driver for socioeconomic progress, through the creation of jobs and enterprises, infrastructure development, and the export income earned.

Tourism has become one of the major international trade categories. The overall export income generated by international tourism including passengers transport reached US$ 1.1 trillion in 2008, or US$ 3 billion a day.

Tourism exports account for as much as 30% of the world's exports of commercial services and 6% of overall exports of goods and services. Globally, as an export category, tourism ranks fourth after fuels, chemicals and automotive products. For many developing countries it is one of the main income sources and the number one export category, creating much needed employment and opportunities for development.

The most comprehensive way to measure the economic importance of both international and domestic tourism in national economies is through the Tourism Satellite Account (TSA) Recommended Methodological Framework, *approved by the UN Statistics Commission.*

Though many countries are in the process of implementing the *Framework,* relatively few have full, comparable results available. As data is currently still fragmented, it is not feasible to provide precise and detailed worldwide results. However, the knowledge and experience gained through the TSA exercise has certainly contributed to a much better understanding of the role of tourism in economies worldwide and allows for a tentative approximation of key indicators. Based on the information from countries with data available, the worldwide contribution of tourism to gross domestic product (GDP) is estimated at some 5%. Tourism's contribution to employment tends to be slightly higher and is estimated in the order of 6-7% of the overall number of jobs (direct and indirect). For advanced, diversified economies, the contribution of tourism to the GDP ranges from approximately 2% for countries where tourism is a comparatively small sector, to over 10% for countries where tourism is an important pillar of the economy.

For small islands and developing countries, or specific regional and local destinations where tourism is a key economic sector, the importance of tourism tends to be even higher.

In 2008, international tourist arrivals reached 922 million, up from 904 million in 2007, representing a growth of 2%. This overall growth builds on the strong results of the first part of the year, before the collapse of the financial markets and the subsequent recession. The second half of the year showed an abrupt shift in trend, with international arrivals flat or showing negative growth in each of the last six months of 2008. Overall, the 5% growth between January and June gave way to a 1% decline in the second half of the year. Though not immune to the economic woes, tourism has so far resisted the economic downturn better than other sectors, such as construction, real estate and car manufacturing.

All regions had positive growth except Europe, which suffered stagnation in arrivals (+0.3%). The best performance was seen in the Middle East, where international arrivals reached 55 million, a rise of 18% over the previous year. Africa grew at half the rate of the previous year, but still registered an above-average growth of 4%. The Americas grew 3%, boosted by the strong performance of Central and South American destinations and the strength of traffic to the USA in the first half of the year. Asia and the Pacific saw a significant slowdown in arrivals as compared to its previous bumper years, growing just over 1% in 2008.

International tourism receipts rose by 1.7% in real terms in 2008 to US$ 944 billion (642 billion euros). Receipts from international passenger transport are estimated at US$ 183 billion, bringing the total international tourism receipts including international passenger transport (i.e. visitor exports) to over US$ 1.1 trillion, corresponding to US$ 3 billion a day. This represents around 30% of the worldwide volume of service exports and 6% of overall exports of goods and services.

Purpose of Visit and Means of Transport

In 2008, travel for leisure, recreation and holidays accounted for half of all international tourist arrivals (51% or a total of 467 million arrivals). Some 15% of international tourists reported travelling for business and professional purposes and another 27% travelled for other reasons, such as visiting friends and relatives (VFR), religious reasons/pilgrimages, health treatment, etc. The purpose of visit for the remaining 7% of arrivals was not specified. Slightly over half of travellers arrived at their destination by air transport (52%) in 2008, while the remainder travelled over the surface (48%) – whether by road (38%), rail (3%) or over water (6%). Over time, the trend has been for air transport to grow at a faster pace than surface transport, so the share of air transport is gradually increasing.

Growth in Receipts Mirrors that of Arrivals

Visitor expenditure on accommodation, food and drink, local transport, entertainment, shopping, is an important pillar of the economies of many destinations, creating much needed employment and opportunities for development. More than 80 countries earned over US$ 1 billion from international tourism in 2008.

UNWTO estimates that worldwide receipts from international tourism reached US$ 944 billion (642 billion euros) in 2008. In absolute terms, international tourism receipts increased by US$ 87 billion, but only by 16 billion euros due to the depreciation of the US dollar against several world currencies and, in particular, the euro (in 2008 the US dollar lost 7% against the euro).

In real terms, i.e. adjusted for exchange rate fluctuations and inflation, growth in international tourism receipts corresponded to 1.7%, only slightly lower than the growth in international tourist arrivals. After the substantial growth in 2006 and 2007 – of over 5% in both years – this represents a considerable slowdown.

All regions shared in the increase in tourism receipts in absolute values. In real terms growth was in all regions much weaker in 2008 than the year before with the exception of the Middle East, which registered a doubledigit growth of 17%. Asia and the Pacific grew by 2.7% (compared to +9.8% in 2007) and the Americas increased by 5.0%, slightly less than 2007's 6.3%. Both Europe and Africa (-1% each), however, suffered negative growth in receipts in real terms. By subregion, the strongest increases came from North America (+7%) and South Asia (+6%). In Northern, Western and Southem/Mediterranean Europe, North Africa, the Caribbean and Central America, receipts declined in real terms in 2008. In the case of North Africa and Central America, the decline followed two years of very strong growth.

For destination countries, receipts from international tourism count as exports and cover transactions generated by same-day as well as overnight visitors. However, these do not include receipts from international passenger transport contracted from companies outside the travellers' countries of residence, which are reported in a separate category, 'International Passenger Transport'. Although the availability of comparable international data is somewhat limited, the export value of international passenger transport has in recent years been estimated at around 16% of the combined receipts from international tourism and passenger transport, corresponding in 2008 to some US$ 183 billion against US$ 164 billion in 2007.

This takes total receipts from international tourism, including international passenger transport, to US$ 1.1 trillion in 2008. In other words, international tourism contributes over US$ 3 billion a day to the world economy.

No Major Changes in the Top Ten

When ranked according to the two key tourism indicators – international arrivals and international receipts –it is interesting to note that eight of the ten top destinations appear in both lists, even though they show marked differences in terms of the types of tourists they attract, as well as their average length of stay and their spending per trip and per night.

There were only slight changes in the ranking of the 'World's Top Tourism Destinations' in 2008. The top three places – both by international tourist arrivals and international tourism receipts – were still occupied by the USA, Spain and France, albeit in a different order. France continued to lead the ranking of the world's major tourism destinations in terms of arrivals, but ranked third in receipts. The USA ranked first in receipts, earning US$ 110 billion and regained its second position in arrivals, which it lost to Spain after 11 September 2001. Spain dropped to third place in terms of arrivals but maintained its position as the second biggest earner worldwide, and the first in Europe.

China and Italy both held on to their 2007 positions in terms of arrivals and receipts, with China ranking fourth in arrivals and fifth in receipts, while the reverse was true for Italy. The UK ranked sixth in arrivals and dropped to seventh place in receipts, after being overtaken by Germany (which ranked ninth in arrivals). Turkey moved up one rank in both categories, occupying the eighth position in arrivals and ninth in receipts. Completing the top ten ranking in arrivals were Ukraine and Mexico and in receipts, Australia and Austria.

The top ten tourism earners last year accounted for 49% of the total estimated US$ 944 billion in international tourism receipts. Their respective share of international tourist arrivals was slightly lower at 45%.

Europe – Noting the Effects of the Global Economic Crisis

Out of all regions in the world, Europe's tourism sector, the world's largest and most mature, was the most severely affected by the global economic crisis that emerged in mid-2008. The region, which accounted for over 53% of the world's international tourist arrivals and 50% of international tourism receipts in 2008, achieved the weakest growth in international tourist arrivals (+0.3% to 489 million arrivals). The impact was even more severe in terms of tourism earnings – while international tourism receipts increased by 5 billion euros (US$ 39 billion), to 322 billion euros (US$ 474 billion), this represented a negative growth of 1% in real terms.

Both Northern and Western Europe posted weaker arrivals figures for 2008. The world economic crisis and associated fluctuations in exchange rates heavily affected arrivals in both subregions, with many of their main tourism destinations recording negative results: the Netherlands (-8%), France (-3%), and the United Kingdom (-2%). A few countries, such as Germany, Switzerland and Austria, the latter two co-hosting the UEFA Football Championship, were able to maintain positive growth, with the first two increasing by 2%, while Austria experienced a 6% boost in arrivals.

Central and Eastern Europe bucked the trend with an increase of 3% in arrivals in 2008. Still, there was wide variation from one destination to another, with various destinations, including Bulgaria, Ukraine, Kyrgyzstan, Georgia and Armenia, recording double-digit increases. Southern and Mediterranean Europe recorded only slight increases in arrivals (+0.8%) with destinations such as Italy and Spain registering declines in arrivals. One bright spot in the region was Turkey which, with its attractive exchange rate and relaxed visa regime, achieved an increase of 12% in arrivals over 2007.

Asia and the Pacific – Rising Cost of Travel Dampens Growth

Asia and the Pacific experienced a significant slowdown in the growth pace of international tourist arrivals in 2008. The deceleration from +9.6% in 2007 to +1.2% in 2008 can be attributed principally to a rise in the price of tourism caused by increases in aviation fuel prices during the first half of the year. Growth in receipts in Asia outpaced that of arrivals. Year-on-year growth in receipts for the region was 2.7%, to US$ 206 billion, with South Asia (+6%) reporting the highest growth rate in real terms. North-East Asia experienced a significant drop in arrivals growth, from 10% in 2007 to-0.1% in 2008. The dynamo for tourism in the region, China, experienced a 3% decrease in arrivals, which may be attributed to visitors' fear of congestion, higher prices and security concerns brought on by the 2008 Summer Olympics.

Playing host to the Olympics did, however, have a positive effect on China's tourism receipts, which grew by almost 10% (in US dollar terms). Arrivals in Japan stagnated in 2008, which can be explained in part by the Japanese yen's appreciation over the course of 2008. Destinations such as the Republic of Korea (+7%) and Taiwan (pr. of China) (+3%) bucked the trend and recorded above-average growth.

South-East Asia and South Asia were the strongest performing subregions of Asia and the Pacific, growing at 3% and 2% in 2008. In South-East Asia, countries like Indonesia (+13%), Cambodia (+7%) and Malaysia (+5%) grew at above-average rates. Arrivals in India, the dominant destination in South Asia, grew 6%.

Oceania reported the weakest arrivals figures in the region (-1%). The high costs of air travel – especially significant for distant destinations – coupled with the global economic environment and high exchange rates have negatively impacted international travel to Australia (-1%) and New Zealand (-0.3%). However, some of the Pacific Islands, such as Fiji (+8%), reported encouraging results in 2008.

Americas – Still Considerable Growth in Central and South America

International tourist arrivals in the Americas grew by 3% in 2008, to 147 million, where Central and South America led the way with above-average increases of 7% and 4% respectively. Growth in receipts in the region (+5%) tripled that of the world (+1.7%), with the strongest performance coming from North America (+7%). International tourism receipts for the Americas totalled US$ 188 billion in 2008, representing 20% of the world total. Arrivals in South America were up 4%, following 2007's increase of 7%. Strongest performers in the subregion were

Uruguay (+10%), Chile (+8%), Peru (+7%) and Ecuador (+7%). International arrivals in Argentina and Brazil, on the other hand, grew at more modest rates of 2% and 0.5%, respectively. In Central America, Panama had an excellent year, showing double-digit growth of 17%, and other countries, like

Honduras (+8%), Nicaragua (+7%), Costa Rica (+6%) and Guatemala (+5%), also enjoyed above average growth in 2008. The results for North America were mixed. Mexico was up 6%, as against a flat 2007. The USA's performance was very strong in the first eight months but the looming recession in major source markets brought growth to a halt, ending the year at 4%. By contrast, arrivals in Canada continued to slide (-4%), due to factors which include a poor exchange rate, stricter travel restrictions to/from the USA, and reduced airline capacity from important source markets in Europe and Japan. The Caribbean saw arrivals grow by 2%. Cuba (+9%) and Aruba (+7%) posted excellent results and destinations such as Jamaica (+4%) and Puerto Rico (+6%) also did better than the subregion overall. Weaker results in the rest of the subregion can be attributed in large part on high airfares and decreased airline capacity, as well as economic difficulties in the USA and Europe.

Africa – above Average Growth in Arrivals

Africa's growth of 4% to 47 million international tourist arrivals, though at half the level achieved in 2007, was still very positive when compared to the world's performance overall. International tourism receipts amounted to US$ 31 billion, signifying a decrease of 1% in real terms. It is important to note that this decline followed a series of previous strong growth years.

North African countries Morocco (+6%) and Tunisia (+4%) posted good results, which can be attributed to strong government support coupled with easy access and attractive prices compared to 'euro' destinations on the northern shores of the Mediterranean. A number of Subsaharan African destinations reported positive growth, with Angola, Ghana, Mali and Uganda turning in double-digit results. Boosted by increased funding for tourism and targeted marketing promotions, South Africa, the leading destination in the region, increased international arrivals by 6%, boosted by the build-up to the hosting of the FIFA 2010 Football World Cup.

Middle East – Sustained Growth Amid Turbulent Times

The Middle East has succeeded in sustaining the high growth rate of the past few years. International arrivals in the region as a whole grew an estimated 18% to 55 million, and receipts increased 17% in real terms, reaching US$ 46 billion. Lebanon, Syria (both +31%) and Saudi Arabia (+28%) led the way in arrivals growth, followed by Egypt (+16%), Oman (+13%) and Jordan (+9%).

Middle East Outbound Market Continues Dynamic Growth Trend

Majority of international travel takes place within the traveller's own region, with about four out of five worldwide arrivals originating from the same region. However, travel between different regions tends to grow at a somewhat faster rate than intraregional travel. In 2008, interregional travel increased by 3.1% as against a growth of 1.7% for intraregional traffic. Source markets for international tourism are still largely concentrated in the industrialized countries of Europe, the Americas and Asia and the Pacific. However, with rising levels of disposable income, many emerging economies have shown fast growth over recent years, especially markets in North-East and South-East Asia, Central and Eastern Europe, the Middle East, Southern Africa and South America. Europe is currently the most important source market, generating 55% of international arrivals worldwide in 2008, followed by Asia and the Pacific (20%) and the Americas (16%). All three regions grew at below average rates as the global economic crisis dampened growth in most source markets in the second part of the year. The Middle East, however, continued its dynamic growth, recording an annual increase of 16%. Outbound tourism from Africa also maintained growth at a rate of 5%.

International Tourism's Top Spenders – Virtually Equal to Last Year's Line-up

The ranking of international tourism spenders shows no

major changes in 2008 apart from the fact that the Netherlands re-entered after a few years of absence, taking the number ten spot. Among the world's top ten spenders, apart from China (+21% in US$ terms), the Russian Federation (+12% in US$ terms) did particularly well in 2008, as did France (+10%) and Canada (+8%). Just one market, Japan, recorded negative growth (-8%), while world's top spender Germany increased spending only by a modest 2% for the year. In spite of an overall cooling of tourism growth in the second half of 2008, emerging source markets again turned in some of the best performances, with many registering growth rates of over 15% – Brazil, Hungary, South Africa, India, Bulgaria, Ukraine, China, Saudi Arabia, United Arab Emirates, Egypt, Malaysia and Argentina.

Hospitality and Travel

The hospitality and travel industry is comprised of companies enabling you to get from points A to B comfortably, as well as have a meal and some fun along the way. These companies may offer lodging, foodservice, gaming, travel services, attractions, recreation, or passenger travel. The Hospitality and Travel industry is fragmented. The production in this industry is divided among a few different companies, however, no single firm has large enough share of the market to be able to influence the industry's direction or price levels.

Primary Demand Drivers

- Business and tourist travel, which is closely linked to the health of the economy
- Competitive market conditions.

Profitability Drivers

- Efficient operations since many costs are fixed
- Effective marketing
- Increase the development of services offering additional conveniences.

Industry Composition: The hospitality and travel industry is a collection of companies catering to the needs of people with leisure time and money. These companies provide a range of services or products. The bulk of the industry is composed of lodging, from campgrounds to five star hotels; airlines and charters; and foodservice establishments, including restaurants, cafes, and catering. The industry also includes travel agencies and services, such as car rental or tours; gambling; and recreation and attractions, including sporting events, amusement parks, and roadside attractions. These different services also merge to offer options such as resorts or cruise lines-a mix of lodging, attractions, and even transportation. In the United States alone, there are over four million guest accommodations available, and many billions of dollars are spent on travel; with global travel becoming more affordable and in greater demand, the hospitality and travel industry will become increasingly important.

Leaders: American Airlines (AMR Corporation), United Airlines, and Continental proved best able to weather the rough U.S. market and have emerged as leaders in the industry, along with Air France. Providing travel services, resorts, restaurants, and cruises, Carlson Companies is another big name in the travel industry. Other big travel services providers include American Express, Expedia, and Travelocity. In term of lodging; Cendent, Hilton, Marriott, and Accor have succeeded at dominating the world market. Lastly, the big names in the global foodservice market are McDonalds, Yum! Brands, Starbucks Corporation, and Darden Restaurants. In the entertainment industry, Time Warner, Vivendi Universal, and Walt Disney are the major players.

Trends: The Internet has changed the shape of the travel industry; it is no longer necessary to call a travel agent, hotel, and airline to arrange a trip. Increased competition among establishments in this industry has spurred many independently owned and operated hotels and other lodging places to join national or international online reservation systems. Computer reservation systems have enabled the consumer to have direct control over the price and quality of a trip.

The foodservice industry is also being affected by technology as point-of-service (POS) systems enhance efficiency by combining functions such as keying in customer orders, sending them to the kitchen, totaling and printing checks, authorizing credit cards, and tracking sales. In the lodging sector, customer demand has shifted, with budget chains and extended-stay accommodations, such as time-shares, rising in importance.

The lodging industry is moving towards a more limited-service properties mostly in suburban, residential, or commercial neighborhoods, often putting hotels near popular restaurants. Full service properties are limiting the food service business and choosing to contract out their food service operations to third party restaurants, including some long-term arrangements with chain restaurant operators.

Recently, security has become a major issue for travellers. Across the globe, restrictions on what may be brought onto passenger airplanes are mounting, as well as preflight security measures. In addition, passports are now required for U.S. citizens travelling to Canada and Mexico. These measures have somewhat decreased airline demand, as much of the population does not possess a passport or is simply choosing not to fly due to the increased hassles of this mode of transportation. Increases in government-imposed taxes, such as fuel duties, are also shaving away at airline profit margins.

Future Outlook: The airline industry faces several challenges. After the September 11 events, network carriers faced reduced domestic capacity and several still remained in bankruptcy. Airlines must focus on cost control, cash preservation, and cautious growth. In the long run, inexpensive tickets and increasing demand for seats will bode well for the industry. Demand for air travel is expected to continue in the future. Growth in the more mature domestic markets is expected to be moderate, while travel between the U.S. and foreign points is expected to be moderate to strong. International travel will be spurred by the emerging economies in and around Asia, and by liberal regulations that allow U.S. carriers to fly to more foreign destination.

In the food services industry, competition remains steep and profit margins low, but studies in the U.S. have shown people are eating out more often. Demand is expected at the least to remain stable.

These companies must remain focused on cost control, but with a rise in consumer confidence, growth may be expected to continue. Lastly, the lodging industry has done well the last five years. National chains have seen the most growth, as they offer predictable prices with a consistent level of quality. The general expectation is that with the effect of globalization, travel and hospitality services will continue to increase in demand.

Air Transport

Airlines will achieve less turnover growth in 2008 and should post a loss of USD 2.9 billion (using a consensus oil price of USD 106.5 per barrel in 2008). The world economic slowdown and high fuel prices (34 percent of their operating costs) will prevent many sector companies from recovering. This turbulence will affect American airlines in particular.

The year will be all the more critical with the companies still subject to strict controls on the safety of their aging fleets and a the acceleration of new plane deliveries that will undermine their profitability.

These elements confirm the return to red ink for American airlines, which have already reported initial losses for the first quarter this year. In this context the transatlantic open skies agreement in effect since April could prove less lucrative than expected with the airlines reluctant to continue to make the capacity reductions needed to restore financial health out of fear of losing their allotted take-off and landing slots the following season.

The number of flights out of Heathrow is even supposed to increase by 25° percent with the pressure on prices intensifying in consequence particularly in business class. That will particularly affect British Airways and Virgin Atlantic, both very dependent on transatlantic routes, but less so Air France-KLM and Lufthansa thanks to their more balanced networks. European companies overall will take advantage of a durably weak dollar to compensate for higher fuel costs. That will also be the case for Asian carriers, which will moreover benefit from the regional dynamic. The profits of Middle Eastern companies will remain low during the current period of frenetic investment.

Low-cost carriers, meanwhile, will continue to diversify to more profitable medium and long-haul routes. Although the leaders will fare better thanks their lower debt burdens and more reasonable labour costs, weaker companies focusing on domestic markets will encounter difficulties. In such conditions the development of alliances and mergers not only between major companies but also involving low-cost operators should continue in industrialised and emerging countries alike to the detriment of smaller companies.

North America: airlines suffering from rising fuel costs and the world economic slowdown. Passenger traffic in North America will grow 4.2 percent a year on average through 2011. American carriers are still the weakest in the industry according to Standard & Poor's. After returning to profitability just last year (USD 2.8 billion) they will likely slip back into the red in 2008 amid the ongoing rise of fuel costs and the marked slowdown of household consumption and corporate spending on travel. And American Airlines, United Airlines, Continental Airlines, and Delta Airlines duly reported first quarter losses.

Very Gloomy Economic Conditions for Domestic Airlines

Already contending with competition from low cost carriers (JetBlue, Southwest, AirTran), they will suffer from the slower growth of domestic passenger traffic.

Capacity Reduction

To limit the negative effects on profitability of the poor economic conditions, major airlines have already begun to reduce capacity. Even as many carriers decide to ground a portion of their existing fleets, the acceleration of new airplane deliveries will only increase the pressure on margins. With the transatlantic open skies agreement in effect since April moreover expected to trigger a price war, the airlines will likely maintain their capacity in that segment to protect their allotted landing and take-off slots for the next season.

A Fuel Bill Exacerbated by Structural Factors

Persistent shortcomings of air traffic control in the United

States and antiquated infrastructure at some airports — affecting all airlines but especially those operating in the domestic market — will continue to add about 12 percent to airline fuel costs.

Volatile Ownership and High Debt

Although the major American companies carry high debt, their positive operating cash flow will, according to Calyon Securities, cover their operating costs this year based on average barrel prices around USD 100. That is not, however, the case for smaller airlines like Frontier Airlines that went bankrupt recently due to a lack of credit.

Ongoing Fleet Renewal

In the current context airlines may partially postpone the heavy investments required in the very near term and through 2020 to modernise their aging fleets — about USD 750 billion by FAA (Federal Aviation Administration) estimates. They will not be able to delay them for long, however, with FAA inspections increasingly exposing fleet maintenance deficiencies, attributable to the cost cutting undertaken in past years.

This year began with the announcement of a far-reaching merger between Delta and Northwest that transformed Delta into the world leader. The two companies — partners to Air France-KLM — are thus expected to dominate the transatlantic sky with antitrust immunity granted to the Skyteam alliance by the Department of Transport. Continental Airlines may react by joining forces with British Airways and American Airlines.

Europe: Transatlantic open skies will give rise to consolidation moves and a price war.

Like in North America, passenger traffic in Europe is expected to grow five percent a year on average through 2011

Airline Profits in General will Slow in 2008

The transatlantic open skies agreement between the European Union and the United States in effect since April this year could weaken British Airways and Virgin Atlantic with both very dependent on flights between Heathrow and Washington: BA notably derives 60 percent of its operating income from that route. The open skies agreement means that European carriers can henceforth fly to any American city from any airport whatsoever in the European Union while American carriers can operate intra-European connecting flights to and from any EU airport. The agreement also increased from 25 to 50 percent the maximum stake a European carrier can hold in an American carrier. In the economic conditions prevailing so far this year, the agreement may prove less lucrative than expected. With companies reluctant to reduce their capacity on the routes involved out of fear of losing their allotted take-off and landing slots, prices could be subject to intense pressure particularly on the business travel segment.

To improve the profitability of those routes, the airlines have been forming alliances: Air France entered into a joint-venture with Delta Air Lines expected to generate USD°1.5°billion in additional turnover without requiring any major investments by either airline. In a countermove, British Airways may tighten its partnership with American Airlines or take a closer look at its British competitor BMI (British Midland Airways), also coveted by Lufthansa. The German airline has also shown interest in the 49 percent stake in Virgin Atlantic Airways put on the market by Singapore Airlines. And other moves are in the offing: With a view to a possible buyout of Iberia Lineas Aereas, BA has teamed up with the American equity fund TPG Capital while Lufthansa has joined forces with Apax Partners Worldwide. Spain's Spanair is also up for sale while Italy's Alitalia has yet to find a buyer.

The airlines will thus have to contend with profound changes while their margins remain under pressure from the rise of fuel prices and the need to continue renewing a portion of their fleets. In this context BA has announced having raised USD 1.7 billion in debt refinancing to cover payments for air plane deliveries over the next five years. And the turbulence has not spared European low-cost operators

Some fifty carriers, including subsidiaries of major airlines, have been waging a fierce price war with their margins squeezed as a result. With the leaders Ryanair and Easyjet likely to experience slower growth, weaker airlines like Spain's Vueling are expected to suffer significant declines in profits. The low-cost segment is also ripe for consolidations moves this year. The Lufthansa subsidiary Air Berlin, after having absorbed its fellow German operators DBA (Deutsche BA) and LTU (well positioned on long-haul routes), has its eyes on Condor, a Thomas Cook subsidiary, whose acquisition would give rise to a new low-cost heavyweight alongside Ryanair and Easyjet.

Asia: more intense competition likely in Japan; airlines often still weak in India and China.

Driven by regional economic dynamism, passenger traffic in Asia-Pacific will grow 5.9 percent a year on average through 2011. As a result of their investment efforts, however, airline profits will remain the lowest of the three regions with 0.9 percent expected by IATA estimates.

Japan's

National company Japan Airlines ended the 2007-2008 financial year with a EUR 100 million loss and will continue its restructuring programme this year with a view to restoring equilibrium. Conversely, its rival All Nippon Airlines will continue to capitalise on the regional expansion, especially in China. The Asia Gateway project up for discussion in 2008 for the purpose of opening Japanese airports up more to international carriers is expected to spur trade with strong-growth countries. But that could also complicate matters for Japan Airlines and its efforts to return to profitability.

China

Three large, majority state-owned companies share the sky: China Eastern Airlines, Air China and China Southern. And the major international airlines have been working to establish positions in the country: Singapore Airlines — momentarily outmanoeuvred by Air China — has regained the upper-hand in negotiations over acquisition of a stake in China Eastern Airlines. And Cathay Pacific already has a reciprocal agreement with Air China concluded through the Hong Kong airline's Dragonair subsidiary and has announced the creation of a jointly-owned cargo carrier. Discussions are underway, meanwhile between Air France-KLM and China Southern. The opening of new routes between China and the United States will likely spur consolidation moves in this highly competitive segment especially with low-cost Chinese carriers like East Star Airlines now successfully penetrating international routes. Bankruptcies could increase among smaller companies like Oasis Hong-Kong Airline, which went into liquidation in April. All these developments, underpinned by large investments in airports and fleets, nonetheless remain dependent on airspace management still largely under military control.

India's

Two national companies, Air India specialised in international flights and Indian Airlines in domestic flights, merged in July 2007. Concentration moves have also developed among private companies with Kingfisher Airlines notably just taking a 26 percent stake in the low-cost carrier Air Deccan to rival the two leaders Air Sahara and Jet Airways. Although the government has implemented financial incentives to foster development of regional routes, the regulatory framework continues to impede the expansion of private companies with Jet Airways alone authorised to operate internationally.

Middle East: Booming Economic Conditions have Prompted Companies to make Heavy Investments

Passenger traffic in the Middle East : is expected to grow 6.8 percent a year on average through 2011, buoyed by a booming regional economy and the opening of new routes. And regional airlines have become fierce competitors via massive investments in new planes epitomised by Qatar Airways order for twentyfour A350 and ten A380 airbuses. Airline profits should nonetheless remain low at USD 0.2 billion this year.

Latin America: Antiquated Airports Pose a threat to Brazilian Airlines

Latin America : are expected to barely break even after suffering slight losses in recent years. The Brazilian sky has also been in the throes of consolidation. For the first time, a low-cost airline — Gol, Brazil's second largest carrier and the world's second largest low-cost operator behind Ryanair — has taken over a traditional airline, Varig, which filed for bankruptcy in 2005. With the revival of Varig's international routes and USD four billion in turnover Gol is now a worthy adversary for the leader TAM. Brazil's airport infrastructure has failed, meanwhile, to keep pace with the soaring growth of air transport in recent years, which could undermine the development of carriers operating in the country. In Mexico, after the sale of Mexicana in 2005, the transfer of Aeromexico to a group of investors led by the Banamex bank completed the privatisation of an air traffic sector characterised by competition between a large number of low-cost carriers.

The Product

With beauty and diversity, New South Wales has a wide range of experiences for international and domestic visitors. Tourists enjoy the big city buzz of Sydney, its great restaurants and shopping, the beauty of its world famous harbour. They can then step away to soak up the local flavours of regional of New South Wales. Visitors can laze on a beach, hike in fresh mountain air, journey to the red outback, soothe their soul in one of the World Heritage national parks, take a leisurely drive through the State's lush farm regions or stop in the quirky towns and cosmopolitan centres. Along the way visitors will be amazed at what they find – fine food and wine trails, lively festivals, Aboriginal heritage tours, amazing landscapes and friendly locals.

As a result, tourism products come in all shapes and sizes – from five-star hotels to boutique bed and breakfasts or trendy backpacker resorts. They also include iconic attractions such as the Sydney Opera House and Harbour Bridge, activities such as horse-riding, sea kayaking and rainforest tours, not forgetting ski, surf or circus schools, museums and galleries, aquariums, wineries, zoos and lots, lots more.

One of the challenges facing the tourism industry (and in particular tourism operators) is to develop and package tourism products in a way that people want, maintaining New South

Wales' position as a premier tourist destination, as well as ensuring a viable business for the operator.

Tourism is Everyone's Business

Everyone gains from properly managed tourism. These benefits can be especially significant in regional areas by diversifying the area's economic base and expanding the employment market. In its broadest sense, the tourism industry is the total of all businesses that directly provide goods or services to facilitate business, pleasure and leisure activities away from the home environment. The chart below demonstrates the impact within our economy and community when someone goes on holiday. As you can see it is significant.

The Tourism System

Before developing a tourism product it is useful to understand how the tourism system operates. The following diagram shows the basic components involved:

The Consumer

In the tourism system the consumer is the most important element as the consumer is the reason tourism products and services exist. Everyone working in tourism must ensure that the consumer is fundamental to all business and planning decisions.

Consumers have many choices about how to spend their money and leisure time. If they choose to spend their money on a holiday, they will then determine their budget, decide how much time they have available and what types of activities they would like to do while away. Then they will begin to select a destination, decide how they will travel there and make reservations accordingly through a travel agent, wholesaler, over the Internet or directly from the tourism operator.

The Travel Experience

The travel experience relates to how the consumer travels to the destination and the experience they have along the way. The choices can include air, car, boat, coach, train, motorbike, hiking or a combination of the above. The mode of travel affects the type of experience, for example flying to a destination is a very different experience to driving.

A destination can suffer if transport options, links and support services are limited or below standard. Issues such as the variety of attractions, facilities and accommodation available en route, the road quality, signage and frequency of transport services, can all affect the quality of the travel experience.

The Holiday Experience

When consumers decide to take a particular type of holiday they have expectations of the experience they will have. This could relate to the quality of accommodation, service and food, the range and cost of activities available, the length of time they have, the weather, etc. Their satisfaction will be based on how well the holiday met their initial expectations or exceeded them.

Marketing Your Business

Marketing refers to a multifaceted, on-going process that any successful business is continually working through. It includes activities such as: researching the market, your consumers and products; evaluating research data; developing your business and products; developing your own skills; and promoting, advertising or working with the media to raise awareness of your product and generate sales. Marketing is often described as 'the four Ps': product, place, price and promotion.

The product includes the physical attributes of the product, branding and packaging. Place is about distribution: the agencies, channels and institutions used to give consumers easy access to purchasing your product. Price must meet both the consumer's and your needs. Promotion is explaining destinations, products and services to consumers to help them choose their holiday. Promotion can use a range of media such as print (magazines, newspapers, brochures, posters displayed on billboards, bus stops, the sides of buses, trains etc), television, radio, direct mail, Internet, etc. Providing a holiday package as a prize for a competition or even staying in touch with customers provides promotion of your product.

Consumer Decision-Making

The above diagram assists in understanding the process consumers work through in deciding about taking a holiday. It is important to understand this process because it influences all stages of the previously discussed model, especially the marketing/promotion element.

Needs – Going on a holiday allows people to take a break from their normal life, whether it's restful idleness in scenic spots or extreme sports in challenging terrain, on their own, with a partner or friends, or in a large group.

Awareness – Consumers may have a recognised or unrecognised need for a holiday. Promoting a holiday destination, product or service can help consumers recognise they need a holiday, then raise their awareness of the choices available.

Motivation – If the consumer is positively aware of a destination, product or service they are more likely to be motivated to visit.

Planning/Decision – Promotional information helps the consumer decide how to get there, and what they want to do.

Satisfaction – If a product delivers what has been promoted, the consumer is likely to be satisfied and have a quality holiday experience, and vice versa.

Word of Mouth – Consumers share their holiday experiences with friends, family and colleagues. Their word of mouth raises awareness of the destination, product(s) and service(s) with potential future consumers.

Tourism Growth

The 'Grand Tour' and the First Package Tours

In the early 19th century the aristocracy, and the 'new money' from trade were caught up in a fashion to show their refinement by educating themselves in the artistic treasures of Europe. Young ladies, especially, were taken on a 'Grand Tour' of Europe to complete their education.. and perhaps meet an eligible young man! Such journeys were complicated and expensive in the days before railways, and were restricted to the very rich. Later, English 'gentlemen' took skis to the Alps and strared the winter sports holiday!

Railways to the Seaside

It was the coming of the railways that gave Thomas Cook the opportunity to develop inclusive travel, where he started by inventing the return ticket. Day excursions gave way to travel with accommodation, and finally foreign travel. the link above tells the story.

The Middle Class go on Holiday

In the 20th century the better-off middle classes joined the rich in foreign travel. They had the time and the money for modest holidays, but most of their trips would have been organised by themselves, which involved skills not shared by the mass of the population.

The Rapid Growth of Tourism Since the 1960's

The great social upheavals of the Second World War saw most of the class barriers breaking down, saw service people travel the world and gain wider visions and appetites, and, in the 1950's onwards, exposure to television.. and travel programmes. With the additions of technical advances, such as the jet airliner, that could deliver holidaymakers to the Mediterranean in a couple of hours, and the computer, which would revolutionise bookings and accounting, the modern travel business has come of age.

Tourism is one of three growth sectors a recent study on Vanuatu's private sector has identified. Construction and agriculture are the other two.

"The number of tourists arriving by air rose by nearly 14% in 2007 and by over 16% in 2008," said a report called 'Sustaining Growth: A Private Sector Assessment for Vanuatu'. The study was commissioned by the Asian Development Bank (ADB).

"Remarkably, despite the global economic slowdown, tourist arrivals by air in January 2009 were 28% higher than in January 2008.

"Over the past few years, there has been a very large growth in the number of cruise ships visiting Vanuatu: the number of arrivals has tripled over the past five years.

"Anecdotal evidence suggests that these rose by nearly 40% in 2008 after increasing by 60% in 2007.

"A growing number of tour ship visitors later return as tourists, which bodes well for future tourism growth."

Vanuatu appears to have been successful too in attracting high-spending tourists, the report observed. In addition, improved policies towards the private sector contributed to growth in tourism, especially with the removal of the monopolistic hold of Air Vanuatu on international air services.

"Vanuatu recently opened its air transport market to international airlines, creating competition that has resulted in significantly lower airfares and higher tourism arrivals," said the ADB report.

"Recent figures illustrate the extent of this increase: international tourist arrivals were nearly 30% higher in January 2009 than in January 2008.

"These results reinforce the wisdom of opening the country to additional foreign airlines and demonstrate the benefits of greater competition.

"In another positive step—and as a result of pressures placed on the airline by greater competition—the government is considering options for restructuring Air Vanuatu."

Removing monopolies, the report said has also worked in Vanuatu's telecommunications sector. An overseas mobile phone operator—Digicel—was granted a licence to operate which immediately resulted - as it did with international airfares - in the slashing of phone tariffs.

Internet charges in Vanuatu, however, are said to be among the highest in the world, the ADB study found.

"However, government recently announced the issuance of three new licenses for the provision of internet and other telecommunication services which should lead to better service and lower prices." The bank urged the Vanuatu Government to continue its policy of liberalising the country's telecommunications sector, as well as push on with the restructure of Air Vanuatu and "franchise out the domestic air routes that require operating subsidies (as was done successfully in Fiji)."

Further, management, air traffic control services, fire-fighting and aviation security at the country's three international airports (Port Vila, Santos and Tanna) should be out-sourced.

Tourism in developing markets has grown at an average rate of 6-8% over the past decade, twice the rate of traditional markets such as Europe, according to new figures released by the UNWTO.

It added that with international travellers projected to almost double by 2020, the most significant increases are expected to take place in markets like China (recent host of the World Travel Awards, with reigning Miss World one of the hosts, pictured above), India and destinations in South-East Asia. The Gulf States and emerging Eastern Europe complete this picture, followed by the Latin American and finally African markets.

Many of these are becoming important outbound markets, backed by growing middle classes on the one hand, and liberalising policies promoting mobility on the other. Chinese tourists already spent about US$30 billion abroad in 2007, according to UNWTO figures.

The domestic travel potential of emerging markets – in 2006 China registered 1.6 billion trips and India 461 million-is a further proof of their long term importance for international tourism.

Between 1996 and 2006, international tourism in developing countries expanded by 6% as a whole, by 9% for Least Developed Countries, and 8% for other low and lower-middle income economies. Against this backdrop, the sector will be more and more recognized as a key agent in national poverty reduction strategies and in development financing. Investment in infrastructure and human resource training, as key issues to make this trend sustainable. He also discussed the importance of credible long term climate response strategies – which allow these countries to realize their tourism growth potential.

World Travel & Tourism is expected to generate close to US$8 trillion in 2008, rising to approximately US$15 trillion over the next ten years, according to the latest Tourism Satellite Accounting (TSA) research launched today by the World Travel & Tourism Council (WTTC) and its strategic partner Accenture.

Overall, the new TSA results reveal a moderate impact on the Travel & Tourism industry as a result of the global economic downturn, with its annual growth rate experiencing a slowdown in 2008, to 3%, in comparison to 3.9% in 2007.

Looking past this present cyclical downturn, the long-term forecasts point to a mature but steady phase of growth for world Travel & Tourism between 2009 and 2018, averaging a growth rate of 4.4% per annum, supporting 297 million jobs and 10.5% of global GDP by 2018.

WTTC President Jean-Claude Baumgarten explained "Challenges come from the US slowdown and the weak dollar, higher fuel costs and concerns about climate change. However, the continued strong expansion in emerging countries-both as tourism destinations and as an increasing source of international visitors-means that the industry's prospects remain bright into the medium term."

Regionally Africa, Asia Pacific and the Middle East are experiencing higher growth rates than the world average, at 5.9%, 5.7% and 5.2% respectively, while the mature markets, most notably the Americas and Europe, are falling below the world average with a growth at 2.1% and 2.3 % respectively.

The overall impact of this slowdown for mature markets is expected to be offset by the strength of the emerging markets explains John Walker, Chairman of Oxford Economics "In particular, China, India and other emerging markets are still growing rapidly, which will increase both business and leisure travel, while many countries in the Middle East are undertaking massive tourism-related investment programmes."

Moreover, even in countries where economic growth slows, there is likely to be a switch from international to domestic travel rather than a contraction in demand for Travel & Tourism.

Among the 176 countries covered in the TSA research, the United States continues to maintain pole position as the largest Travel & Tourism economy, with its total demand accounting for more than US$1,747 billion this year. With a growth rate at 1.1% in 2008 the credit crunch is leading to a marked slowdown in US economic growth and is likely to restrict the business travel of those working in financial markets.

Considerable ground has been made by the emerging markets which are experiencing rapid economic growth. In 2008, China will jump from fourth to second position above Japan and Germany and is forecasted to increase its Travel & Tourism Demand four-fold by 2018, accounting for US$2,465 billion, with an annual growth rate of 8.9%. Among the fastest growers in 2008, Macau leads with a growth rate at 22%.

3

Food and Beverage Control Systems

Work Experience Activities

Complete and submit the following Work Experience Activities for your Work Experience Kit. Remember, all activities must be completed using this electronic file, then printed out in black and white and submitted. This is a "Read Only" file and must be saved as a separate document before you begin. Refer to the following guidelines when completing all activities.

- Use complete sentences to answer all activity questions.
- Eliminate all spelling, grammatical, and typographical errors.
- Include all appropriate back up materials to substantiate your work.
- Make sure all activities are computer generated or in typewritten form.
- Make sure all required activities are included in your Work Experience Kit.
- Make sure your Inventory Checklist and Sign Off Sheet are included in your Kit.

Activity 1: Identifying the Benefits of the Food and Beverage Operation

Directions: Answer the following questions concerning the Food and Beverage Operation at your facility.

1. What different types of food and beverage services are available at your facility?
2. What is the total revenue generated by the facility and what percentage of total revenue does the food and beverage operation generate?
3. What percentage of members (or customers) continues to utilize the food and beverage services even though they do not utilize any other amenities offered by the facility? Why do you think this is so?
4. Do you think the food and beverage operation is highly valued by the members and/or customers? Why?
5. If you think the food and beverage operation is not highly valued by the members and/or customers, how might this affect the outcome of the overall experience your guests may have?
6. What value does the food and beverage operation lend to the overall image of the facility?
7. Is the image of the food and beverage operation consistent with the mission statement and the image of the golf operation as well as other departments?
8. What improvements would you implement to enhance how the food and beverage operation affects the overall operation?

Activity 2: Day-to-Day Involvement of the Golf Professional

Directions: Answer the following questions concerning the involvement of the golf professionals in the food and beverage department.

1. Discuss how the golf operation and the food and beverage operation work together to ensure a positive experience is had by members and guests who frequent the facility.
2. How is the head golf professional involved with the food and beverage operation on a daily basis?
3. What types of functions are held at your facility that require the services of both departments?

4. Which staff members from each department are responsible for the success of these joint functions?
5. What are the most critical food and beverage issues you deal with on a daily or weekly basis?
6. Do you think it is important, as a golf professional, to be involved with the food and beverage operation? Why or why not?

Activity 3: Conducting a Customer Survey

Directions: In this activity, you will conduct a survey to determine how important the food and beverage operation is to the members and customers at your facility.

1. Make 25 copies of the customer survey presented on page 8. If your facility uses a customized survey, you can use that instead.
2. Meet with the food and beverage director at your facility and identify several key places to leave copies of the survey.
3. Ask the food and beverage director to inform the appropriate service personnel about the survey and what to do with completed forms.
4. Allow a week to collect completed forms and then answer the following questions.

Survey Results

1. What are the four most cited reasons members and/or customers joined the facility?
2. What amenities or functions do the members and customers participate in most at your facility?
3. How important is the food and beverage operation to the members and customers?
4. What did the members and customers say they liked best about the operation?
5. What did the members and customers say they liked least about the operation?

6. Do the members and customers feel their expectations are being met? Why or why not?
7. Has your facility conducted other surveys in the past? If so, how has management responded to the information gathered from these surveys?
8. If your facility has not conducted surveys, do you think conducting one would be beneficial?
9. Include the actual surveys collected in your Work Experience Kit.

Activity 4: Identifying the Appropriate Levels of Food and Beverage Services at Your Facility

Directions: Lesson 3 discussed the wide range of food and beverage services offered by various golf facilities—from casual to formal and from banquets to off-site catering. Answer the following questions regarding your particular facility and the types of services provided. (For example: on-course concessions, carry-out, full service a la carte, formal fine dining, banquets, and off-site catering.)

1. Describe the type of facility you are currently working in and the specific food and beverage services offered to your membershi
2. Do you think the food and beverage services offered are appropriate for your particular facility and your clientele? Why or why not?
3. What are the current operational goals for the food and beverage service?
4. Do you think your facility needs to offer different food and beverage services to better fit the operational goals and the customers' expectations? Why or why not?
5. What other golf facilities in your area do you consider your direct competition and what types of food and beverage services do they offer?
6. If your facility is losing business to the competition due to an inadequate food and beverage operation, what improvements can be made to the operation to regain the customers?

Activity 5: Shopping Your Competition

Directions: After identifying local competitors to your facility, select two of these facilities to compare food and beverage services. If your facility or the competitors do not offer a particular service, do not check the box. After completing the comparison chart, answer the questions that follow.

Food and Beverage Services Offered

Your Facility	Competitor #1	Competitor #2
On-course concessions	On-course concessions	On-course concessions
Carryout	Carryout	Carryout
Full service, a la carte	Full service, a la carte	Full service, a la carte
Formal fine dining	Formal fine dining	Formal fine dining
Banquets	Banquets	Banquets
Off-site catering	Off-site catering	Off-site catering

Price Ranges for Each of the Above Services

On-course concessions	On-course concessions	On-course concessions
$	$	$
Carryout	Carryout	Carryout
$	$	$
Full service, a la carte	Full service, a la carte	Full service, a la carte
$	$	$
Formal fine dining	Formal fine dining	Formal fine dining
$	$	$
Banquets	Banquets	Banquets
$	$	$
Off-site catering	Off-site catering	Off-site catering
$	$	$

Directions: Select one food and beverage service above that is offered by all three facilities and list the major menu items offered at each club. After completing this chart, answer the questions that follow.

1. What similarities do all of the facilities offer for the selected food and beverage service?

2. What differences are there in the food and beverage services offered by all three facilities?
3. What are the hours of operation for each of the facilities' selected food service? Do they differ from the hours of operation of your facility? If so, why do you think so?
4. Have you experienced the food and beverage services of the local competition? If so, was your experience positive or negative? How might this have affected your "overall experience" at that facility?
5. Why might it be important to play golf as well as utilize the other services offered by your competition?
6. Is there anything you think your food and beverage operation as well as your facility as a whole could do to improve the service provided to the customers? If so, explain what your facility could do to improve the "overall experience" for the customers.

Activity 6: Developing a Labour Pro Forma

Directions: For this activity, you will complete a labour pro forma for a food and beverage service offered at your facility. To get an accurate idea, select full service a la carte, formal fine dining, or other similar service that would normally utilize a larger number of service and kitchen staff.

Meet with the Food and Beverage Director to review the past three months' labour preforms or other information summarizing staffing schedules and payroll costs for the service you have selected. Be sure to discuss any situations (holidays, special events, etc.) that may affect next month's staffing needs. Also, ask the food and beverage director for a projected total income for the month for the service you have selected.

Develop one labour pro forma for the service staff and another pro forma for the kitchen staff. Calculate the projected payroll costs for the service staff and the kitchen staff as a percentage of the estimated total income for the month. List any situations that may have affected staffing levels and payroll costs at the bottom of each pro forma (such as weather, increase in play, added tournaments or events, and holidays).

Meet with the food and beverage director at the end of the month to review your labour pro forms and answer the questions following the charts below.

If your food and beverage director is unable to give you actual payroll income figures, put together a hypothetical situation to complete this activity.

If you work at a facility that has minimal or no food and beverage services, research another local golf club to complete this activity.

Activity 7: Developing an Estimated Potential Costs Chart

Directions: Select a food and beverage service at your facility and obtain a menu from the food and beverage operation in order to complete an estimated costs chart for four appetizers offered. Fill in the appropriate lines on the chart with the help of your food and beverage director.

Keep in mind that the actual food cost of the items may vary by the number of items sold, spoilage, pilferage, and mix of items on the menu. Briefly summarize how close the estimates in your chart came to the actual cost and profit for the items you selected and explain any discrepancies.

1. Briefly summarize how close your estimated costs were to actual costs.
2. Discuss why you think there were discrepancies in the estimated costs versus the actual costs.
3. Relative to your experiences in merchandise purchasing and inventory control, what improvements if any, could be made to increase the gross profit and decrease the food cost percentages?

Activity 8: Receiving and Storage Review

Directions: Check off any of the following that you observe during the receiving and storing of a food and beverage order. Answer the following questions concerning receiving and storing food and beverage orders.

- The order was received during a slow time of the day.

- Each item was checked against the purchase order.
- All items were weighed and/or counted.
- The food and beverage director or other management staff reviewed the shipment invoice.
- The items received were immediately placed in storage.
- The storeroom was clean.
- The storeroom has good ventilation.
- The storeroom was cool but not freezing (except storage for the frozen items).
- Old supplies were rotated before the new supplies were put away.
- Items were stored on free-standing shelves.
- The storeroom was locked after the shipment was placed in storage.

1. How was the receipt and storage of the shipment similar to the procedures presented in this lesson?
2. Describe the different food and beverage storage areas utilized in the kitchen and bar area.
3. If the procedures practiced at your food and beverage operation differ, discuss how they are different.
4. What procedures followed by the food and beverage personnel would enhance this checklist, and what items on the above checklist would improve the procedures currently in place at your facility?
5. How does the receiving procedure in the food and beverage department differ from the receiving of merchandise for the golf shop?
6. What procedures used in the food and beverage department might improve how merchandise is received for the golf shop?
7. Do you think it is important, as a golf professional, to cross train with the food and beverage department? If so, what cross training methods are currently being practiced at your facility? If not, discuss your reasons.

8. How would basic knowledge of all of the departments enhance your image as a golf professional, as well as the overall experience of the members and customers who frequent your facility?

Activity 9: Food and Beverage Regulations in Your Community

Directions: Meet with your Food and Beverage Director to identify and discuss the licenses, permits, and certificates required to operate the food and beverage services in your community and answer the questions below.

1. What different types of food and beverage services are offered at your facility?
2. List and include copies of the licenses, permits, and certificates required to operate the food services and the agencies granting each.
3. List five key laws affecting how food is prepared, served, and sold.
4. Which government agencies inspect the food services at your facility and how often are inspections held?
5. After inspections have been held, what actions have been taken by management to correct any deficiencies in the operation?
6. List and include copies of the licenses, permits, and certificates required to operate the beverage (alcohol) services and the agencies granting each.
7. List five key laws affecting how alcohol is served and sold.
8. Which government agencies inspect the beverage services at your facility and how often are inspections held?
9. After inspections have been held, what actions have been taken by management to correct any deficiencies in the operation?

Food and Beverage

Growth of counterfeit food and beverages puts brand

reputations at risk and is potentially life-threatening. So what is the market like now, and what might be done over the next few years? Pira International investigates.

The food and beverage sector represents a significant part of many global economies, but the increasing problem of counterfeit food and drink is having a damaging affect on brand owners' image and profits.

According to the European Commission (EC), seizures of counterfeit food products entering the European Union (EU) increased by 77 per cent from 2002 to 2003, and the problem of counterfeit food and beverages is on the rise. In the EU more than 26,000 companies are directly involved in the food and beverage sector, employing over 2.7 million people-making it the EU's third-largest industrial employer and largest manufacturing sector.

The annual turnover for this sector is in the region of €600 billion. Within the 15 countries that were EU members prior to the latest set of additions in 2004, the food and beverage sector accounted for 13.6 per cent of the EU's turnover and 13 per cent of its employment. Counterfeiting therefore has the potential to damage a large section of society, both through health and the economy.

Methods

Counterfeiting food and beverages takes two forms: passing a product as a branded food or drink without permission to do so from the brand owner, and adulterating a product by dilution or substitution of inferior ingredients. In addition to the more dangerous forms of tampering or substitution, trademark or brand fraud both have an impact on consumer trust, and frequent or high-profile trademark infringements can seriously damage a product's or producer's market share.

Europe-Mmarket Size

In 2004, European food and beverage manufacturers' production costs rose by 1.5 per cent, while the cost of imports fell by nearly double that figure, and exports dropped by 3.8 per cent.

Among the changes the EC has promised is the reform of the Common Agricultural Policy in order to reduce food production costs, and therefore enable producers to compete more effectively at one level. At the same time the EC is implementing wide-ranging anti-counterfeiting measures, to increase protection against piracy from both within and outside the EU.

Under Attack

The food and beverage sector is particularly hard hit by counterfeiting. The Italian farming association CIA, for example, says that the amount of bogus Italian products seized by EU customs has trebled. It calculates that the global market for pirated foods is worth €52.6 billion, or roughly half the whole of the food market's value in Italy itself.

In Russia, Ros Potreb Nadzor, the Russian Agency for Health and Consumer Rights, seized food products worth €9.6 million in 2004, and issued 30,000 orders to destroy counterfeit goods after inspecting 132,000 food companies.

Investigations carried out by the Russian agency also revealed that one-fifth of all food, beverage and tobacco products in Russia are counterfeit. It estimates that in Western Europe and the US the figure is closer to 10 per cent. In addition, the agency disclosed that 75 per cent of the mineral water sold in Russia has fake labels on its bottles.

In terms of seizures, the EU confiscated a variety of food products, drinks and alcoholic items worth €4.4 million in 2004. Confectionery and bakery products were high on the list of items affected, while brands such as Lipton, Coca-Cola and Nestle were the biggest corporate victims of brand piracy. The figure represents roughly 4 per cent of the total counterfeited and pirated goods seized in that year, which amounted to €103 million. This total figure represents an increase in counterfeit goods of more than 12 per cent compared with 2003, and a 1,000 per cent increase compared to 1998.

In 2004 the amount of food and beverage products intercepted and seized at the EU's borders and deemed to be counterfeit grew by a massive 200 per cent. This was on top of a rise in

2002-03 of 77 per cent for food and medicines together, according to European Commission figures, demonstrating that the problem is not just growing but also accelerating at an alarming rate.

The profits to be made from food and beverage counterfeiting can be substantial and fake foods are not always easy to detect. The US Food and Drugs Administration estimated that, in one case, a Mid-Western orange juice producer defrauded its consumers of more than €37 million over 20 years. Another orange juice company and its president earned €1.2 million in two years by substituting invert beet sugar for frozen orange juice in concentrate. Yet another orange juice manufacturer saw its earnings rise from zero in the company's second year of operation to €46 million in its fifth year, before being convicted and sentenced for adulterating orange juice concentrate with liquid beet sugar.

In 2004, a Chinese soy source producer was found to be using human hair to make a 'blended' sauce. More seriously, Chinese officials admitted that in 2001, fake food products killed 146 people and hospitalised over 15,000. In 2004 a single batch of fake milk powder killed 13 infants in China and put another 171 in hospital. In 2005, about 40 companies were found to be producing fake baby formula that was so lacking in nutrition that 229 babies fed on the formula in the city of Fuyang were found to be starving.

Technology Solutions

The technological solutions being developed in the fight against counterfeiting include covert systems that alert purchasers of fake products through simple means. A tamperevident seal can alert consumers if someone has interfered with a product. In addition, vendors can implement systems to detect bogus goods by raising the cost, and make it difficult to produce credible copies of the original product.

Labels

Brand owners can use security labels to secure and authenticate food products. PulsLine is an intelligent label created by UK-based Stanelco, which provides evidence of tampering that can be detected both electronically and manually. PulsLine uses a special multilayer laminate construction, with a security thread similar to the one used for banknotes, which can be micro-printed with a company name or logo. The thread is revealed by the removal of a tab pull, but can also be felt by hand. Companies can use scanners to detect broken threads on items that have been tampered with.

Codes

Another way companies can authenticate goods is by using codes. DataLase and DataLase Clear from DataLase (formerly Sherwood Technology) have both overt and covert applications. They can be used, for example, to produce a Datamatrix code that can be sandwiched between layers of laminate in a clear label, or to put a mark in the label that can only be detected when it is exposed to energy from a low-power CO2 laser.

Promotions

International security company De La Rue won a contract with a local Indonesian food manufacturer that, like its bigger multinational counterparts, was suffering at the hands of fake goods. Indofood launched a multi-billion Rupiah promotion based on people collecting six different designed holograms to make up a key word.

The beauty of the promotion was that it would make consumers look for the genuine product so they could compete for a prize based on the completed word. The competition would also make the company more familiar in differentiating Indofood's product from the bogus product. The holograms also allowed hidden levels of security, to make sure the counterfeiters had not tried to copy the concept.

It was not the first time such a strategy had been attempted. To beat the UK consumer's weariness of constant product promotion, Nestle decided to launch a €1.45 million promotion for one of its chocolate bars. A single hologram ticket would be the customer's route to riches. Naturally such a large prize would require unprecedented security, something that was put into place for the Indofood contract.

Growing Trends

With a growing number of technologies on the market, more brand owners are integrating security into their products to protect against counterfeiting and theft. UK-based food retailer Marks and Spencer Simply Food range is using electronic article surveillance (EAS) security tags to prevent theft of wines, ready meals and poultry items in some of its most vulnerable stores.

The store managers in London, where the tags are primarily implemented, will decide onto which products they want to attach EAS tags. The managers will be able to decide which products to tag, depending on the items that are at a greater risk of theft. If someone attempts to steal a tagged product the tag will activate an alarm.

Brand owners can also use a laser technique that etches away ink on labels. A US-based food supplier is trialling a technology called Laser Sharp that etches away the ink on poultry labels to display information. US-based laser company LasX has developed the technology. LasX says the laser process is expensive and extremely difficult to replicate, because it is hard to remove the surface of the ink without damaging the base layer of the substrate. The technology can also be used to etch serial or security codes on a label.

Alcohol

In addition to food products, many leading alcoholic brand owners are also suffering from counterfeiting. The alcoholic beverage industry attracts higher tax prices, making it a prime target for counterfeiters to make a quick profit. Trade of alcoholic beverages is one of the growing markets and has an annual growth rate of around 10 per cent since 2000, which makes it more attractive for the counterfeiters to siphon profits.

The World Economic Forum estimates that spirits companies lose €244 million a year through counterfeiting, while the International Federation of Spirits Producers (IFSP), which includes Diageo, Pernod Ricard, Remy Cointreau and Bacardi-Martini amongst its members, estimates the global losses for all spirits to be between €407-570 million per annum. EU exports of spirits amounted to €5 billion in 2004, with wine exports of €4.5 billion. The European Spirits Organisation (ESO) estimates counterfeiting of spirits drinks at 5-8 per cent of total yearly turnover. This equates to a loss of €600 million a year for spirits, based on the production volumes of the large producers. The ESO points out that this ignores the effect of counterfeiting on smaller brands.

To governments and tax authorities around the world, counterfeiting is only part of a broader picture of fraud affecting the alcoholic beverages industry. The governments link it to a range of crimes, from smuggling and tax evasion (often involving organised crime, supply networks and sophisticated labelling fraud), through to smaller individual offences such as tipping or the substitution of more expensive brands with cheaper ones, mainly to deceive consumers.

In Europe, there is also the problem of the origin of products such as Champagne and Cognac. Producers count the use of terms such as 'sherry' for fortified wines produced outside the area designated for Jerez production, for example, as fake.

Whisky

The Scotch Whisky Association attempts to protect Scotch whisky from all forms of unfair competition, including the use of misleading names or devices associated with Scotland to fool a consumer that a product is a genuine Scotch whisky. The association has a team of five lawyers and, at any one time, they can be involved in 50 legal cases around the world to protect Scotch whisky.

In 2004 leading drinks company Diageo launched the Scotch whisky industry's first miniaturised spectroscopic portable testing kit, called the Authenticator, to help crack down on counterfeit Scotch whisky.

The kit uses ultraviolet technology to test the authenticity of Diageo's Scotch whisky brands. Previously, the industry standard for verification of Scotch whisky required laboratory-based analysis-a process that can take up to two weeks. The Diageo Authenticator has been designed to work in the field and cuts the screening process down to less than one minute. This brings obvious cost savings, but more importantly means that action against counterfeiters can be swift.

Diageo has been developing the whisky authenticator for over a year. Unlike white spirits, where colourless markers can be added to determine authenticity, legislation prohibits the use of any markers in Scotch whisky. Since spirits attract the highest levels of tax of all alcoholic beverages, they offer the greatest opportunities for counterfeiters. However, counterfeiting is generally moving down-market and is no longer restricted to premium or luxury goods. In the spirits sector this means that, where false labelling was directed at international brands, even 'cheapest on display' spirits are affected in relatively wealthy and discerning retail markets such as the UK. Russia in particular has the potential to be a very large market for anti-counterfeiting technologies.

Counterfeiting is also associated with illicit distilling, which is both widespread and carries a huge human toll. In Russia, the problem of counterfeiting has undergone an unusual reversal. There is widespread alcohol abuse in Russia, and between January and August 2003 more than 27,000 Russians died from alcohol poisoning. While cheap vodkas do masquerade as more expensive brands, a great deal of illicitly distilled vodka is labelled and sold as products such as aftershave, insecticide and hoof softener, in order to avoid tax.

The National Alcohol Producers Association says half the vodka on the market is illicit and up to a quarter of this is surrogate hooch labelled as something other than vodka. While legal vodka production was down by 9.4 per cent in the first five months of 2005, the production of bootleg vodka and surrogate drinks shot up 40 per cent, it says. According to the Interior Ministry, North Ossetia and Kabardino-Balkaria are the main sources of illicit vodka in Russia.

Future Outlook

Counterfeiters are becoming more and more sophisticated, which makes it increasingly difficult for consumers, and even some brand owners, to tell the difference between a genuine or a fake product. Brand owners are now implementing intelligent brand protection technologies that allow them to secure their products and make authentication of genuine food and drink products quick and easy. New security technologies are also being developed so that makes it easier for brand owners to verify products. Wafer-thin labels for food packaging that incorporate moving images are being developed by Siemens in Germany, and are expected to be available in 2007. The labels use electrochromic materials that change colour when an electrical charge is put through an extremely thin, miniature colour display made of conducting and semi-conducting plastics, printed on paper or foil.

Food and drink companies that are using security technologies are protecting their consumers against the risks of consuming counterfeit food and drink. Innovations in on-the-spot testing and security labels are beginning to reduce the influx of counterfeit products. New technologies such as laser etching and security labels could help crack down on counterfeiters, but companies still have a long way to go before their profits stop being diluted by the sale of fakes.

Packaging

Alcohol is a major counterfeit target, but brands do have a way to fight back as well as getting more sales. Here, Pira International discusses intelligent solutions with a major market player.

Brand differentiation is the only way brand owners can succeed in today's competitive market, and this is especially true of the alcoholic drinks market. Since the competition is so hot, anything that can put a brand owner ahead is top secret. Intelligent packaging and emerging technologies are some of the best tools a brand owner can use to gain an advantage and attract consumers.

With that in mind, Pira spoke to a leading alcoholic beverage brand owner about its future plans for intelligent packaging and its thoughts on technologies that are currently available and those on the horizon. Following the interview the brand owner did not wish to be named owing to the sensitive nature of the material.

Our unnamed source is an international brand owner that produces a range of drinks, including vodkas, cognacs, whiskies, wines and flavoured alcoholic beverages. The company has offices all over the world and is a major player in the alcoholic beverage industry. The company sells over 200 million bottles a year in nearly 200 countries, and is the one of the largest spirits companies in the world.

Thermochromic, UV and Fluorescent Inks

The unnamed brand owner discussed the many intelligent technologies available to brand owners, and, based on that discussion, the ones that appear most accessible are thermochromic and fluorescent inks. The source admitted that this technology will most likely be used in its trial brands, such as some cognacs, vodkas and whiskies, rather than some of its more traditional brands, because of the use of shrink sleeves.

The use of shrink sleeves on bottles opens up various promotional possibilities as they can be printed on with thermochromic and ultraviolet (UV) inks. The brand owner we spoke to is currently looking at using thermochromic and UV inks in some of its brands and expects to roll out promotional packs with the ink technology in the next year or so.

"Fluorescent and thermochromic inks are already on the market and easily accessible. These are the cheaper intelligent option at the moment and will be used in the immediate future [by spirits brand owners]," explains the source. UV inks could also prove successful in providing brand differentiation. According to the source: "This technology could be used for both brand protection and to draw attention to our brand's bottles behind bars."

According to the brand owner, thermochromic inks particularly lend themselves to vodkas, as these are often stored in the freezer. Brand owners have to consider when the customer is going to drink their product and how they are going to drink it. "Thermochromic inks creates theatre at home and offers brand differentiation," comments the source. "The inks could either be used in a promotional label that indicates temperature, or as a glitzy gimmick in a competition. Perhaps it could also only activate if vodka is put in the freezer and therefore change the way consumers drink the product."

Thermochromic and UV ink technologies certainly do the job of catching a consumer's eye and are already being utilised by some brand owners. International spirits producer Allied Domecq was planning to use fluorescent shrink sleeves in its Malibu brand of rum. Last year, the company intended to adopt glow-in-the-dark shrink sleeves for its new flavoured range of the rum to help both bartenders and customers locate the drinks in dark bars.

However, the brand has since been acquired by spirits brand owner Pernod Ricard and plans have been put on hold. Our unnamed brand owner says the thermochromic inks could be used on flavoured alcoholic beverages in its range to indicate when bottles are sufficiently chilled and ready to drink. These technologies offer brand differentiation without high costs, something that needs to be taken into consideration.

"The inks don't affect manufacturing processes as they can be integrated into current processes. If a technology can be integrated into production lines it can save money," explains the packaging development manager at the unnamed company. Thermochromic inks change colour to indicate temperature changes and could be utilised to indicate an optimum temperature to drink a beverage. The inks were first used on wine labels to show when wine was at the correct temperature for drinking and are the first example of graphic arts being used in a label as a consumer interactive medium.

Thermochromic inks are the leading method for detecting and indicating temperature change in packaging. The inks are based on dyestuffs and take up minimal space on the packaging. The inks can be printed onto packaging materials and labels by most printing processes including offset, letterpress, gravure, flexo and screen methods. Dutch distiller Toorank used thermochromic ink technology for the launch of its Petrikov Red and Blue range of vodka-based flavoured beverages. The back label on the bottles used thermochromic inks to create a time temperature indicator (TTI) that bears the message "OK! I'm cool! Drink me now!" This was visible when the bottle contents were chilled to 7-8uC. The drink was very successful when launched and the company puts this down to the market presence afforded by innovative labelling. However, since then the company received no extra sales, and it stopped using the technology on the bottles.

Despite the many applications shrink sleeves offer, the unnamed brand owner says this packaging will not be seen on its premium brands, as shrink sleeves would drive away the core customer base for these drinks, because they prefer print sleeves. Shrink sleeves, although suitable for flavoured alcoholic beverages, are seen as inappropriate for high-end brands. However, the brand owner does see a future for flexible displays with its high-value brands.

Flexible Displays

According to the unnamed source, flexible displays offer great potential for brand differentiation and customer interaction. "I think brand theatre is the way ahead, which leads to a greater merging of display and packaging and greater customer interaction. There are so many whiskies on the shelf today that customers' senses are getting dulled with regular advertising."

Flexible displays are being developed by companies including Siemens, and look set to be on the market in 2007. The displays are planned to be cheap enough to use on throwaway packaging such as cereal boxes, so should certainly find applications on high-value spirit bottles. The electrochromic displays being developed by Siemens can be printed onto paper or foil and have no size restrictions. Felix Scarlett, a partner at UK packaging design company Webb Scarlett deVlam (WSdV), believes flexible displays could be seen first on spirit bottles when the technology is launched.

According to Scarlett, the labels could be used to change the appearance of a bottle or emphasise luxury and can make the same spirit bottle look modern or traditional depending on the consumer being targeted. Despite the potential for display labels on spirit bottles, Scarlett says the labels are unlikely to be used on more traditional spirits such as cognac or whisky, but may be used on products like vodka that have a more modern image.

Programmable Bottles

Technologies that offer brand differentiation at low cost seem to be the big winners now, but promotional packs look set for takeoff in the future. The brand owner believes personalised drinks bottles are likely to take off in gift packs and could be something that it is interested in using in the future. The bottles would enable several flavours of the same drink to be incorporated into one bottle, which would cut production costs. According to our source it is likely to be a niche product that will only be used in certain brands and a small percentage of the business.

US-based innovation company Ipifini has developed a prototype of a programmable container. According to Ipifini, the programmable drink bottle could enable brand owners to introduce new flavours without alienating customers or having the expense of giving out free samples to entice customers. The new flavour would merely need an extra button on the bottle that the customer would be encouraged to try. The programmable drink bottle allows consumers to customise and choose ingredients for their drink.

Scented packaging could be used by brand owners on packaging of flavoured drinks such as alcopops or flavoured vodkas. The use of scented packaging in lids, closures and on shrink sleeves promotes the product, increases brand awareness and product value, and also increases consumer anticipation. Tactile varnishes that provide different textures on packaging also offer greater depth to packaging and offers brand differentiation. Again, these technologies are likely to be brought out first on promotional packs first to test success before a wider rollout by a brand owner.

Brand Protection

Product protection is an issue that every brand owner, and

especially those in the alcoholic spirits industry, faces. According to our source, the biggest areas of counterfeiting for our unnamed brand owner are Latin America and Eastern Europe. Companies such as Diageo and Allied Domecq use a chemical marker in drinks that is a sugar that is odourless, colourless and tasteless. A dipstick will change colour when the marker is present. Other brand owners also use special closures to prevent bottles from being refilled. A code is printed onto the closure, which identifies that it is genuine.

Brand owners are also looking ahead to other brand protection technologies such as UV inks, holograms and label encryption to protect its high-end brands. In mid 2004, brand owner Bacardi began using a smart closure supplied by Amcor in its Bacardi Bay alcoholic beverages. The Twist-off closures have a compound channel replacing the full compound, and this results in less product migration and retains the flavour more effectively. As well as protecting their brand, another issue facing brand owners is where and how their product will be sold.

Alcohol with intelligent packaging may prove more successful in airport shops rather than in supermarkets. Customers shopping in duty free or tax-free outlets at airports tend to shop for gifts and bargains, whereas in national supermarkets the brand is competing with the supermarket's own brand and people tend to buy what they have on their list. This makes it all the more important for brand owners to have packaging that catches a consumer's eye.

Future Outlook

So what is the future for leading spirit brand owners? The key is brand differentiation, and according to the brand owner in 5-10 years the future for spirits will be electronic packaging using printed batteries: "The future will be self-powered labels using printed batteries-this will make the bottle stand out on supermarket shelves and in bars." This concept has already been explored by the new Muscovy Company for its brand Ivan the Terrible.

Webb Scarlett deVlam developed a prototype for the brand-the label extended to the base and could be plugged in behind a bar to act as a display. Although this remains a concept at this stage, it looks very much a possibility for spirit brand owners in the future. Although radio frequency identification (RFID) seems to be on the agenda for other industries such as the pharmaceutical industry, it is not something that our brand owner is focussing on at this point in time. There are serious read issues with RFID and metal, and 50-60 per cent of its closures are metal.

"We are observing what other companies are doing with RFID. At the moment I cannot see what advantages RFID can offer us over barcodes, especially considering the cost of the technology," says the brand owner. Despite this, the source says the smart shelf concept employed by the Metro Future Store is an interesting one. Smart shelves contain an RFID reader that scans RFID tagged products on the shelf and can notify the back of the store when stocks are running low.

"If we were asked by a supplier such as Metro or Wal-Mart to be involved in a concept like the smart shelves idea, we would definitely consider it. It is important to stay ahead with technology and it is a good reason to innovate," the brand owner comments. Packaging is predicted to be one of the major markets for scaled-down electronics and battery technologies, which will be applied to substrates and integrated into polymers. By 2008, the value of global market for laminar electronics in intelligent retail packaging will be worth €148.8 million, matching the value of RFID technologies.

High-value spirits have high margins and therefore can afford to experiment with intelligent technologies. With the shelves of supermarkets and bars bursting with rows of attractive-looking spirits bottles, brand differentiation is the key to attracting more consumers and intelligent technologies such as UV and thermochromic inks and flexible displays can offer this advantage.

What is clear is that intelligent packaging looks set to grow in the alcoholic spirits sector. A recent Pira survey showed that 70 per cent of European brand managers across a range of industries confirmed they would be using intelligent packaging in some form on their products. With the high value of spirits, and the greater need for brand protection, brand differentiation and added value, the alcoholic spirits industry looks set to be one of the first to test and commercialise new technologies as and when they are developed. The days when a bottle of vodka markets itself could be here sooner than you think.

Developments in Biodegradable and Sustainable Packaging

In a market where sustainability is fast becoming the buzzword, the use of biopackaging seems set to continue its growth. But can it become the dominant force in its most popular market-fresh produce? Katherine Vine considers the challenges. The markets for biopackaging are expanding. The technology and capabilities of the materials are improving, the price is steadily falling and the applications are broadening. The worldwide manufacturing capacity for biodegradable resins has risen sharply over the past five years, and is predicted to reach 600,000 tonnes by 2008.

The area in which biopackaging is most popular is still the area in which it was first accepted for use: fresh, short shelf-life produce, such as fruit and vegetables, and particularly organic ranges. But how long will it be before biopackaging completely takes over this market? Biopackaging refers to packaging that is either biodegradable (it will break down or compost), or sustainable (it is made from a renewable resource such as corn). There are three main forms of renewable biopackaging: polylactic acid (PLA), polyhydroxyalkanoates (PHA) and thermoplastic starch (TPS).

A package made from renewable resources will often also biodegrade, owing to the type of materials it is made from (mainly starch), but renewable materials are sometimes mixed with oil-based to improve performance capabilities, rendering the package no longer biodegradable.

No industry or market has yet taken on the use of biopackaging to completely replace oil-based materials, but the indication is that if this is going to happen in any market, it will be fresh produce. At the moment biopackaging seems only to be able to occupy niches in the packaging market, and fresh produce is undoubtedly its biggest niche. There are various reasons for this; the performance properties of biopackaging are best suited to fresh produce, and it also creates a marketing opportunity.

There is a perception that the type of customer that buys fresh, organic produce will be the type of customer that cares about the environment, and may even be willing to pay a little extra to preserve it.

This article will focus on UK retailer Sainsbury's, one of the first to begin using biopackaging. It will look at the challenges involved in using biomaterials, and what obstacles will need to be overcome if biopackaging is ever to completely replace traditional packaging in the fresh produce market.

What is it Worth?

The fresh produce industry is worth a great deal to the biopackaging industry. The properties of biopackaging are best suited to fresh produce, and it is very popular in organic ranges, as this gives retailers the opportunity to target a specific, environmentally-conscious consumer group.

Sainsbury's use of biopackaging is mostly restricted to its organic range. According to James McKechnie, Recycling and Resources Manager at Sainsbury's, there is a variety of reasons for this.

"Firstly, despite the rising price of oil and oil-based plastics, it still works out to be three to four times more expensive to implement packaging made from biomaterials-but because the organic produce comes at a more premium price anyway, it means we don't end up passing the extra cost onto the consumer," McKechnie says.

"The second main reason is that it does seem that customers who buy organic produce are more interested in the environmental benefits of biopackaging, and are more likely to have home-compost bins where it can be properly disposed.

"A couple of years ago we trialled a compostable carrier bag, and the consumer response was nothing like it has been with the organics range-people just weren't interested. For this reason, I think fresh produce as a whole is of great value to the biopackaging industry, but organic fresh produce is particularly vital."

It could be argued that, if it hadn't been for the fresh produce industry, biopackaging would never have taken off in the way that it did. The demand for biopackaging created by the retailers using it for fresh produce has given it a route for entry into the packaging market.

The involvement of large supermarket chains is crucial to the development of the biopackaging industry. Supermarkets create the demand for a certain material, which in turn dictates the supply-if the demand from supermarkets is not there, there is little incentive for food and packaging manufacturers to develop and use biodegradable packaging.

Escalating demand from retailers, who are themselves driven by ever more stringent packaging waste legislation, and the marketing advantages of having a green image, is putting increasing pressure on large food companies such as Geest and Uniq Foods to use biopackaging materials.If a large supermarket chain like Sainsbury's were to make the change to biopackaging across its entire fresh produce range, this would have a significant effect on the biopackaging industry, pushing it further towards the mainstream.

This relationship also works the other way around-biopackaging can be worth a great deal to retailers. Not only does it afford them the marketing opportunities already mentioned but it can also save them money in packaging taxes and give them an easy way of disposing of fresh produce that is too old to remain on the shelves.

In the UK, retailers have to take responsibility for the amount of waste they produce, and have to pay tax on any over the weight they are legally allowed. According to McKechnie, for a large supermarket chain this can be an expensive business, so any alternatives to landfill are welcomed.

Biodegradable packaging for fresh produce allows supermarkets to compost old produce along with its packaging, saving the time and money spent separating the produce from the packaging-another reason why fresh produce is such a popular application for biopackaging.

Sainsbury's Use of Biopackaging

Biopackaging can be used in a wide variety of applications, including flexible films, bags, trays, punnets, netting, bottles, cups, labels, tubs and blister packs.

Sainsbury's uses biopackaging for various fresh products, including fresh fruit, vegetables and prepared salads. As part of its organic standards, the retailer packs approximately 30 per cent of its organic produce in compostable biopackaging, a figure it intends to build on.

In April 2006 Sainsbury's announced that it was trialling a fully compostable wrap made from renewable resources for use with organic apples and potatoes. If trials-which are taking place in 140 stores-are successful, Sainsbury's will roll out this packaging across its entire organic range in all stores.

According to McKechnie, when the trials were in their second week, results looked promising: "So far, so good-we haven't had any negative feedback as yet." A total rollout will mean that 70 per cent of Sainsbury's SO organic range of fruit and vegetables will be packaged in compostable wrap by the end of 2006.

The biodegradable materials used by Sainsbury's are starch-based, and are sourced from various suppliers based in Europe and East Asia. One of Sainsbury's suppliers is Innovia Films, a UK-based packaging manufacturer that produces a biodegradable plastic film called Nature Flex.

NatureFlex is a glossy, transparent film manufactured from renewable wood pulp, sourced from managed plantations and is certified to EU and US standards for industrial and home composting.

Sainsbury's is not the only UK retailer that is using biopackaging with fresh produce. Co-op uses biodegradable netting to package organic oranges and onions, and biodegradable trays and film to package organic tomatoes. It also uses biodegradable film to package fresh bread.

Asda has started to look at the options for using biopackaging, and has engaged in preliminary meetings with the US supplier of PLA Nature Works. According to Ian Bowles, Corporate Social Responsibility Manager at Asda, the retailer is considering using PLA to replace polyethylene terephthalate (PET) in the packaging of fresh fruit and vegetables.

Asda is taking its lead from its US parent company Wal-Mart, which uses PLA to package fresh-cut fruit, herbs, strawberries and sprouts, and is trialling the material with 20 additional product ranges, including fresh cream cakes.

Tesco's entire organic fruit range is packaged in biodegradable trays, film and plastic netting. Paul Bidwell, Tesco's organic fruit development manager says: "Biodegradable packaging and organic fruit go hand-in-hand as both are environmentally friendly products."

Tackling the Challenges

There are still a number of challenges relating to the use of biopackaging materials-as mentioned earlier, one of the main difficulties is cost. However, the price of biopackaging materials has now reached the point where it can be absorbed when used with high-end, premium price products, such as organics. Also, as McKechnie points out, the price of oil is set to continue increasing, which could eventually stand to make bioplastics the more economically viable option.

Another remaining challenge, despite technological advances, is the performance capabilities of biopackaging materials. Compared to oil-based packaging, biopackaging tends to have a very low barrier to gas and moisture, a lack of resistance to heat and a short shelf life.

However, these problems do not occur when biopackaging is used with fresh produce such as fruit, vegetables and bread, and in fact go some way towards explaining why fresh produce is such a popular application. A major advantage of using biopackaging for fresh produce is that it doesn't require high barrier properties, heat-resistance or a long shelf life. When is comes to fresh produce, many of these cited problems can actually be advantages. For example, biopackaging is ideal for use with fresh bread because its high moisture transfer properties mean that the bread can be placed inside the package while still hot, and the package will not steam up, meaning that the bread does not become soggy.

According to Pira International market report The Future of Flexible Packaging, a core problem remains with biodegradable materials: "Not only is plastics processing know-how essential to make full use of the development potential of biodegradable materials, but well-informed consumers with a positive attitude to the products are also needed to ensure a promising future."

McKechnie agrees with this: "People have to understand what they are buying, and its environmental benefits, in order for it to be valuable. If people don't understand about biodegradable packaging they will simply place it in the rubbish bin, to be taken to landfill, where it won't break down properly.

"The public needs to be able to recognise a compostable logo in the same way that they recognise a soil association logo, and understand what it means."

Sainsbury's attempts to address this problem by clearly labelling its products as GM (genetic modification)-free and home-compostable. "We have a strong preference for biopackaging materials that are home-compostable," McKechnie says. "Some biopackaging materials will break down in landfill, but take years rather than months, and also give off greenhouse gases such as carbon dioxide and methane."

The UK Government's Waste and Resources Action Programme (WRAP) is running a project aimed at increasing the number of UK households with home-composting facilities. According to McKechnie, this should mean that by the end of 2006 houses without compost bins will be in the minority.

Philip Ward, Director of WRAP, says: "In order for biopackaging to help the UK waste problem, it really does need the capability to break down in a home composting system."

According to the UK composting association, with the way research and technological developments are advancing, it should be possible for all biodegradable packaging to be homecomposted before too long

Do-it-yourself Composting

As we have seen, the performance properties of biopackaging materials make them ideal for use with fresh produce, so despite the fact that steps are being made-using nanotechnology and polymer blends-towards improving performance capabilities, these are not really relevant to the use of biopackaging with fresh produce.

According to McKechnie, the main technological advance that is still needed to make biopackaging ideal for use with fresh produce is to make all biopackaging materials home-compostable.

It should be noted that this particular issue cannot be applied globally. In the US where there is still plenty of space for landfill, but dwindling supplies of oil, the emphasis with biopackaging lies much more on it being sourced from renewable raw materials.

However, in the UK and most of Europe, where landfill space is running out fast, the emphasis is much more on what happens to biopackaging at the end of its life and whether it will break down properly, alleviating the waste problem.

Because there are very few municipal composting systems in the UK, biopackaging is most beneficial if it will break down in a home-composting system, which McKechnie says is not always the case. "Rigid biodegradable packaging such as punnets and trays tend to be too thick to fully break down in a home composting system," he says. These packages are still able to carry the European EN13432 certification for compostability, as certified materials are only required to break down in the conditions found in a municipal composting system.

If a biodegradable plastic that cannot be homecomposted is placed in a home-compost bin, when it breaks down it will leave some polymer behind, which will contaminate the compost. This can be very damaging, as it makes customers suspicious of anything that claims to be biodegradable. "Although biodegradable trays and punnets cannot be homecomposted at the moment, Sainsbury's is involved with some research looking into how this can be achieved, and we certainly don't think it's impossible," McKechnie says.

One possible way for this to be achieved may be through nanotechnology. Researchers at the University of North Texas, US, are developing a process whereby nanocompositing is used to aid and speed up the composting process of biodegradable plastics.

Research has found that when nanoparticles are added during the foaming process used in the manufacture of biodegradable plastics such as PLA, the resulting materials will break down faster because of increased water permeability.

McKechnie says he feels that retailers will be more willing to take on the use of biopackaging that will break down in homecomposting systems, as many do not see the point in investing time and money in these new materials when they are fairly likely just to go to landfill, where it will take years for them to break down, if indeed they break down at all.

Biopackaging Takeover Bid

According to Pira market report, The Future of Global Markets for Flexible Packaging, many brand owners and retailers view sustainable materials as the future direction for packaging. Around 15 per cent of brand owners expect to start using biopackaging within the next two years.

In 2002, the EU consumed 20,000 tonnes of biodegradable materials. By 2004 this had increased to 50,000 tonnes, and the market is expected to continue growing at a similar rate. According to the report survey, this market growth has been influenced by a combination of factors, including technical innovations, specific cultivation of renewable raw materials in agriculture for greater supply, consumer acceptance and EU Sustainable Development policy goals.

Fresh produce continues to be the most popular application for bioplastics, but will they ever fully replace oil-based materials in this sector? McKechnie says yes. "I can see a full replacement happening at Sainsbury's within the next two to three years. In the long-term, oil-based plastics are only going to get more expensive, and meanwhile the pace of technological development is amazing really," he explains.

McKechnie says that the only thing that could prevent this from happening is if the supply is unable to keep up with demand. Supply is a particular problem for retailers like Sainsbury's, who insist on the materials being GM-free. Most of the larger suppliers of bioplastics such as PLA are US-based, and because GM is not seen as so much of an issue in the US, suppliers like Nature Works do produce a relatively large amount of GM materials.

This is a problem recognised elsewhere. According to The Future of Flexible Packaging, the next five years of the bioplastics market will see wider application to sensitive shelf life products, but elsewhere there will be little change because of restricted input of raw materials.

Takeaways

- As the markets and applications for biopackaging expand, the area in which it is most widely used is with fresh, short shelf-life products.
- Fresh produce seems to be the sector most likely to take on the use of biopackaging to fully replace traditional, oil-based materials.
- Sainsbury's was one of the first UK retailers to use biopackaging for fresh produce, and it is continuing to expand its use, expecting to have 70 per cent of the organic fresh produce range in biopackaging by the end of the year.
- The fresh produce market is worth a great deal to the biopackaging industry, particularly organics ranges, and biopackaging also gives retailers a good marketing angle for these ranges.
- Sainsbury's, Asda, Co-op and Tesco all use biopackaging for fresh produce, as well as Wal-Mart, Asda's parent company and the largest retailer in the US.

- Many of the challenges that are experienced when using biopackaging for other applications are not a problem when it is used for fresh produce and some, such as the high moisture transfer rate, can actually become an advantage.
- Cost can be a problem, but the price of oil-based resins is rising steadily, and the extra cost attached to the use of biopackaging can be absorbed when it is used for premium price products, such as organic ranges.
- The main challenge to the use of biopackaging with fresh produce is what happens to it at the end of its life.
- Some biopackaging materials will not break down in a home composting system, and with very few municipal composting systems materials actually stand a good chance of going to landfill where they will not break down.
- A way of solving this may be through the use of nanotechnology. Researchers in Texas are developing a process whereby nanocomposting is used to aid and speed up the composting process of biodegradable plastics.
- According to Sainsbury's, biopackaging could stand to completely replace oil-based packaging for fresh produce in the next two to three years.

Legislation Driving Pharmaceutical Packaging Change

Packaging in the pharmaceutical industry is often seen as a means to an end, with the focus, rightly, being on the therapeutic values of the product itself. However in recent years legislation has greatly impacted the pharmaceutical packaging industry in a number of ways whether its the performance (in the case of child resistance or tamper evidence) or the graphics (in the case of information, warnings, font sizes and more recently Braille). This trend looks set to continue.

In the European Union, in addition to national legislation, the European New Medicines Legislation (NML) now covers a broad range of products. This means that Patient Information

Leaflets, Track, Trace and Authenticate, Child Resistance, Compliance (with on pack storage requirements as well as patient dosing) and Waste – all have to be addressed.

A quick example can be used to illustrate the problem of how Legislative factors can impact on a typical product:

A small product (above the minimum stipulated size requirement for Braille – e.g. an eye-care or topical cream) requires Braille on pack. But when sizing the pack against the required Braille characters, there is found to be insufficient space. The solution may be to increase the pack size.

The "waste element" of the packaging component is immediately impacted. Similarly, if you require a larger Patient Information Leaflet, will it fit in the existing carton? Again Legislation has an impact. It is easy to see how Track and trace and other legislative elements may similarly cause problems.

In an ideal world, legislation would merely endorse industry practice by formalising standards. However, in many cases regulation and legislation is driven to meet needs not yet addressed by the respective industries. This leads to many challenges.

Braille Packaging Legislation

A topical example of the impact of legislation is the requirement to place Braille on pharmaceutical and OTC (over the counter) medicine packs on all new products registered after October 2005.

In the absence of National and European Standards this, for much of the Pharmaceutical industry, has been an extremely challenging and costly exercise.

In this instance the EU Legislation preceded the industry's capability to implement a standard solution. There was also a significant lack of basic Braille information and knowledge (such as National characters) as well as production "dot height" limitations on packaging formats and supplier capability issues

Implications for the Manufacturer

Manufacturing and producer companies are often affected

by legislation change, be this the brand owners or the licence holders. These manufacturers independently try and find solutions to legislative challenges resulting in broad swathes of industry attempting to find a multitude of individual solutions. Whereas, it might be more cost and time effective to coordinate and jointly develop industry-wide solutions.

A historical example of this scenario is neck finishes when PET bottles were first introduced to the UK market in the late 1970s. These were developed to become industry standards by a leading packaging manufacturer on behalf of the soft drinks industry with test data shared with all the parties funding the joint development. Once the solution was accepted, it soon became the industry standard. The alternative would have been for each packaging manufacturer to develop their own solution and then recommend their own solution over others, which would have only created more confusion.

If industry could pre-empt or better anticipate legislation requirements then maybe their findings could be plugged into the development of the legislation standards, which would smooth the introduction of the required improvements.

Late Stage Customisation (LSC)

Innovative technologies have opened up new opportunities to meet the challenges of packaging legislation.. A good example of this is Late Stage Customisation (LSC), which has allowed businesses to implement effective strategies for a wide range of products that may have had long lead times or high costs if produced by conventional technologies.

New LSC technology permits businesses (particularly those dealing with pharmaceutical products or high numbers of SKUs) to have the benefits of medium to long production runs combined with the flexibility to produce low volume orders – exactly matching market's specific needs and customisation requirements demanded by their regulatory authorities.

Dynamic digital artworking systems can be used in LSC which allows for varied text and coding systems (2D datamatrix codes) as well as dynamic sequential numbering of packs. This in turn can lead to improved track and trace and product authentication capabilities. Lesson's garnered from adopting an LSC strategy can be applied to higher volume products. So, in the case of the pharmaceutical industry, the developing technology of digital art working is facilitating the alignment of packaging with specific legislative requirements while assisting in building supply efficiencies and access to medicine.

Different Packaging Markets Means Different Requirements

Legislation now requires more information to be included with pharmaceutical products. In the EU the 'Centralised Procedure' for registering certain products often means that more than one language might be included or that the full licence holder address needs to be shown for each country that the product is marketed in the EU. This could mean 27 different addresses. Change an address and all the leaflets across the EU for that product need to be changed. Given the order sizes of many products this could be a production and procurement nightmare.

Network Rationalisation in the pharmaceutical industry has resulted in specialist manufacturing centres supplying global markets. The variations required to meet local regulations has increased packaging complexity. As an example, in the 'old' Central and Eastern European markets (CEE), the same medication may need to be packed to meet 25 different market requirements. Not only may language vary but so might the approved indications.

Some countries such as Belgium also require leaflets in three languages. A strategy to have more multilingual patient information leaflets to ease supply logistics adds to this demand.

Text Size and Type Face Considerations

Product liability requires the Pharmaceutical Industry to ensure the integrity of all information passing into the hands of the patient.

Regulators are concerned that an aging population is able to both read and understand all patient information. However, more product data, larger type faces and more user friendly layouts all increase the size of leaflets. Recently EMEA has advocated that leaflets have the minimum font size increased from 8 point to 12 point, with headings being 14 point. Packaging supply sites are being requested by the markets to insert increasingly larger leaflets into the packs. Some supply sites are resorting to hand packing, due to the limitation of their packing equipment. In addition, leaflet suppliers are reaching the maximum print capability on their conventional printing equipment.

The shape of the type, in the case of numerals, can also be an issue. In certain 'closed' font types, numerals such as 6, 8 and 9 can be confusing. In text 1 and l can also be confusing, or 0 and O. Hence careful consideration must be given to communicating information to the intended reader.

Providing increasing patient information with each pack is driving the quest for alternative solutions to conventional leaflets. Meeting these challenges can lead to many innovative solutions and some added value at the same time, which may also drive patient compliance.

Solutions to Legislative Requirements

With the rapid development of digital systems the range of opportunities is enormous.

When the much heralded implementation of RFID at pack levels occurs this will further open up communication standards.

Both the United State's FDA and Europe's EFPIA are both recommending the implementation of technologies which allow products to be tracked through the supply chain and used to verify that the correct product is being administered to the patient. Whereas RFID might have been nominated as the preferred solution both authorities have chosen to outline the performance requirements rather than the technology itself.

The increasing use of the 2D datamatrix code will enable more packs to carry sequential numbers (or encrypted codes) providing digital imaging technology is used to apply the code. Using such codes will depend upon the use of suitable data management systems and having the full supply chain saturated with coded products. It may take the full shelf life of some products before the pipeline is completely coded.

Whatever the coding system used global supply networks will have the challenge to develop global coding which can be defined at the time of application and read with meaningful results at the point of administration.

Codes which mean something to the administrator of the medicine need to be applied to the patient pack. This is done on the filling and packing line which has no visibility of the end user. So, asking the filling plant to apply such coding data or coding technologies would seem to add production 'hassle'. However, if one could include data and coding technologies which enable a more efficient production cycle and effective supply chain network then these benefits can fund the patient level requirements which on their own would not justify the financial case, even though legislation may demand it.

Such an example is the use of RFID to monitor the temperature an individual pack is subjected to. Often this is a contentious issue in that no business wants it's consignment rejected because the transit temperature exceeded that specified.

Conclusion

It is doubtful whether any product can be packed to be truly 'anti-counterfeitable'. All products can be copied in some form to look similar to the original. These similarities can often confuse the end user into believing they have the real product. The challenge is to allow the end user to check if the product is real for themselves

By the use of appropriate coding systems and having suitable readers available through the supply chain those who are of a responsible disposition could verify that the product is from the right source and is in the correct place. This would require a 'secure' supply chain a challenge in itself.

There is a developing market for coding systems and particularly readers with RFID. The real challenge for any system is to have a globally consistent coding process and a suitable data management system.

Developments in Extrusion Coating for Packaging

The chemical and molecular structures of new enhanced polyethylene (EPE) products are opening up new application opportunities in extrusion coating. To make the most of this new category of products, says Bernard Fehr of Dow Europe GmbH, it's crucial that converters and brand owners increase their functional understanding of resin performance attributes. Brand owners may be overlooking a very small detail in their drive to develop differentiated packaging solutions. With so much focus on improvements in packaging aesthetics to satisfy consumer demand for convenience, quality and safety, some material science advances at the molecular architecture level have gone almost unnoticed.

This is particularly true in the case of polyolefin products for extrusion coating and lamination, with the emergence of a new generation of enhanced polyethylenes that offer greater conversion flexibility than traditional low-density polyethylenes (LDPEs). With no pun intended, the expression "good things come in small packages" might never have been truer for brand owners.

Beyond Butcher Paper

Extrusion coating is a continuous process for applying a thin film of polyethylene to a non-plastic packaging substrate such as paper, paperboard, metal foil, polymeric film substrate or even a non-woven or fabric.

There are typically three events in the extrusion coating process. First, polyethylene pellets are made molten by the blending action of an extrusion screw inside an extruder. Then the flux of molten polyethylene is forced through a flat die to extrude a film that is only a few microns thick. Finally, the film is laid on a substrate and cooled until adhesion is tight.

One of the first flexible packaging applications for extrusion coating was the use of LDPE on butcher paper in the 1950s. Because of its processability, adequate moisture barrier, heat-sealing properties, and relatively low cost, LDPE soon became the dominant material used in extrusion coating applications.

As recently as 2003, LDPE was still by far the most commonly used polymer in European extrusion coating, accounting for 90 per cent of the 600,000 million tonne market (according to Dow estimates). However, new packaging performance requirements and higher capacity demands, coupled with environmental and economic incentives to down-gauge materials and continuously reduce costs, are now challenging converters to extrude a wider portfolio of polymers.

New Polyethylenes

The good news for brand owners and converters alike is that material science advances have enabled the creation of enhanced polyethylenes that can deliver unique combinations of performance attributes and be extruded at high speed on systems designed for LDPE. These products have been designed to meet the differentiated conversion and application requirements of today's leading converters. While extruding closest to LDPE, they offer improved environmental stress crack resistance (ESCR) and water vapour transmission rates (WVTR), an enlarged hot-tack window, tailored barrier properties and high-performance sealability.

Dow has made significant progress with enhanced polyethylenes in recent years, principally by combining the high-performance attributes of its resins with INSITE technology, the company's proprietary approach for linking the science of catalyst, process and materials to address market needs.

This approach has allowed Dow to manipulate the molecular structure and viscosity of these products to achieve previously unattainable performance attribute combinations, such as low-temperature sealability and stiffness, high modulus and high puncture-resistance, as well as LDPE-like processability on high-speed lines.

Dow has discovered that the ability to adjust such performance variables can make an enormous difference to the manufacture and end-use performance of a packaging structure. These products are also potentially viable for use in different forms of conversion.

Unlike traditional autoclave LDPE extrusion coating products, which have been increasingly fine-tuned for processing on larger capacity lines, the excellent processability of Dow's enhanced polyethylenes might actually turn the tables on extrusion equipment. Whereas line speed is often limited by the processability of the material, these enhanced polyethylenes will allow conversion at the highest line speeds and with the thinnest possible web gauges, while maintaining normally experienced web stabilities.

Without compromising performance, these products are designed to offer significant down-gauging of packaging structures, helping brand owners meet new sustainability targets (reduced raw materials in packages) and cut logistics and handling costs (reduced warehouse space needs and reduced weight of shipped packages).

The development of these new products recognises that resins cannot succeed solely on the basis of their molecular architecture. In equal measure they must be able to take into account various delivery options, allow for ease of use on highly efficient and often existing conversion equipment, stay well balanced at lower gauges, and, of course, most importantly be optimised to meet end-use application requirements.

Conversion Benefits

A key characteristic of this new wave of enhanced polyethylene products is that they are being developed to exhibit controllable performance on high-capacity conversion equipment. This is a departure from what converters might normally expect, since hardware design in extrusion coating predominantly accommodates high-pressure LDPE polyethylene.

As an impressive demonstration of specific macro molecular architecture, the design of enhanced polyethylene products takes into account how high-capacity conversion equipment absorbs the viscoelastic behaviour of the converted polymer.

Because of their molecular architecture, the nature of the new products doesn't further heat up through shear heating in the extrusion system, exhibits stable edges even with controllable and relatively low neck-in, and provides extraordinary stable thin web curtains at line speeds up to 700m per minute. Surprisingly enough, the products don't exhibit more than about 15 per cent higher machine power use at slightly elevated pressures compared to autoclave high-pressure LDPE extrusion coating products.

In summary, and while recognising the need for some high shear in melting, the enhanced polyethylenes exhibit a fairly constant rise in temperature over a broad extrusion operating window. Their ramping rate (as judged by average melt temperature over a screw speed range experienced during production start-up) has little impact on extrusion control parameters or web curtain geometry (as judged by neck-in).

Another high-performance attribute of these enhanced polyethylenes is their capability for outstanding draw down without web defects (i.e. draw resonance or edge tear). Draw down is assessed by a specific method developed by Dow.

This method has been proposed, used and publicised in various previous papers and consists of accelerating line speed from a coating base of 15g per m2 at 100m per minute at set extrusion conditions. The total throughput and die settings are fixed and the line speed is accelerated in steps of 50m per minute until the first web defect occurs. The line speed or draw down value of 700m per minute for the new enhanced polyethylenes reflects a stable web with minimal coating weights of about 2.2g per m2.

Application Performance Benefits

Current linear polyethylene coating products don't have a considerable market share in their respective applications. The major obstacle to growth has been the limitations of converting LLDPE products on high-pressure polyethylene hardware. This began to change with the introduction of polyolefins based on constrained geometry catalyst technology.

Products began to emerge with properties designed to match new conversion and end application requirements. These products, together with the more recent success of polyolefin plastomers in extrusion coating applications, have demonstrated significant improvements in sealant, mechanical and sensory properties. For brand owners and end-users this translates into higher package integrity, extended shelf life and improved appearance over longer periods of time, as well as low-flavour ab-or adsorption of contact layers to the filling product.

Linear products (and specifically polyolefin plastomers) allow low heat-seal initiation temperatures, exhibit high seal strength forces, and show broader sealing windows (which is important for package structure flexibility). Samples of the new enhanced polyethylene exhibit these properties with product densities similar to LDPE or VLDPE. It is interesting to observe that some traditional linear property relationships to densities have been broken up and almost disconnected. A differential scanning calorimetry (DSC) melting point can also be widespread and offer excellent low hot tack and seal-initiation temperatures, even at high values.

The options in molecular architecture also allow property combinations such as a higher water vapour barrier at the same densities as current high-pressure polyethylene. Up to a 20 per cent reduction in water vapour transmission at similar densities has been measured. This translates to either thinner total gauges for the same performance or in reality higher transmission resistance at same thickness. Another interesting observation is the excellent stress crack-resistance properties of basically linear products. In the usual test, even with higher nominal densities, the behaviour of pure high-pressure polyethylene is outperformed by a factor of seven or more.

An aspect of permanent interest to brand owners and converters is the possible interaction of the polymeric product layer with the packed goods. This is where the benefits of products based on constrained catalyst technology come to the fore. Its homogeneous characters allow the creation of neutral and stable products with lower interaction behaviour. The metrics used to express such values are evaluated by taste and odour panels. It is of specific interest that the ultimate tensile strength as well as the high ultimate elongation values of the new enhanced polymers will contribute to excellent puncture and abuse-resistance, thus providing an opportunity for optimised economics in current laminate structures. This is very important for high-efficiency packaging lines with a variety of closure systems. Since the linearity and specific molecular structure of such new products react slightly differently to heat immersion, it has been proposed that careful investigation is needed to optimise set conditions of sealing systems. Depending on the targeted end-use, enhanced polyethylenes can be designed for use either as a core layer or as the outside skin layer of laminates. Accordingly, their functionality can be tailored to enhance particularly desired properties (i.e. mechanical, barrier or sealing properties) and optimise their use in the intended application. Apart from primary flexible packaging for food articles, the property balance is very interesting for industrial and consumer paper wrap applications too, where moisture barrier as a single property and highly efficient conversion create an excellent marriage. A thin layer of such products like ELITE 5810G will allow excellent product protection of various printer or photographic base paper packages.

Summary

The chemical and molecular structures of new enhanced polyethylene (EPE) products are opening up new application opportunities in extrusion coating. Dow does see interesting benefits for brand owners and end-users based on the improved and therefore extended integrity of package laminate solutions. To capitalise on this new category of products, it is more important than ever for converters and brand owners to increase their functional understanding of resin performance attributes.

Takeaways

- Some materials and science advances at molecular architecture level have gone unnoticed, while the focus has been on packaging aesthetics to satisfy consumer demand for convenience.
- This lack of attention has been especially true for polyolefin products for extrusion coating and lamination.

- One of the first applications for extrusion coating in flexible packaging was the use of LDPE on butcher paper in the 1950s.
- New packaging performance demands, allied to environmental and economic incentives, are now challenging converters to extrude a wider portfolio of polymers.
- Dow has recently made significant progress with enhanced polyethylenes, mainly by combining the high-performance attributes of its resins with INSITE technology.
- Unlike traditional autoclave LDPE extrusion coating products, which have been improved for processing on larger capacity lines, the processability of enhanced polyethylenes might actually turn the tables on extrusion equipment.
- The linear structure of the new enhanced polyethylenes does not excessively push the limits and allows most current equipment and settings to be used.
- The major obstacle to growth has been the limitations of converting LLDPE products on high-pressure polyethylene hardware.
- The options in molecular architecture allow property combinations such as a higher water vapour barrier at the same densities as current high-pressure polyethylene.
- Of real interest to brand owners and converters is the possible interaction of the polymeric product layer with the packed goods.
- The ultimate tensile strength as well as the high ultimate elongation values of the new enhanced polymers will contribute to excellent puncture-and abuse-resistance.
- The chemical and molecular structures of new enhanced polyethylene (EPE) products are opening up new application opportunities in extrusion coating.

Flexible Packaging in India

The growth of flexible packaging in India has only just started. Chantal Borciani discovers why In the last 10 years analysts have started to look at India differently. Gone is the image of a poor nation with limited prospects, and in its place a vibrant and increasingly profitable global economy has emerged.

Forecasts have been right so far-the growing economy has encouraged large investments from overseas companies and a changing social climate has meant the Indian market is now supporting tastes and demands seen more in Western cultures.

Indian consumers now expect a certain level of packaging with their goods, and as foreign investors take advantage of the cheap material and labour costs, Indian exports in flexible packaging are on the up.

The Indian packaging market grew by around 9 per cent in 2004, after a slight slow-down in growth in comparison to 2003. For the remainder of the decade, growth of 14 per cent is predicted in packaging sales, with the less developed plastic packaging sectors set to be the fastest-growing areas of the market with annual growth set for around 20 per cent year-on-year.

Food markets will drive consumption growth, with the food processing industry keen to double capacity in the medium-term-along with other consumer markets-as India becomes an increasingly attractive option for finished goods suppliers exporting to neighbouring countries.

Other key flexible plastics segments include HDPE-based flexible bulk bags, consumption of which amounts to around 44,000 tonnes, with around 75 per cent of total usage accounted for by sugar, with the remainder attributable to salt, rice and atta (6,500 tonnes), onions and potatoes (3,500 tonnes) and tea (1,000 tonnes). Traditional woven fabrics, however, continue to dominate in areas such as cement, pesticides and fertilisers.

As a consequence of the low purchasing power of the majority of Indian consumers, most consumer goods come in small, affordable packages. The rapid expansion of the Indian flexible packaging market has accelerated because of the conversion of the more traditional rigid packaging into flexible forms and a favourable government tax structure-the excise duty, which was 24 per cent, was reduced in 2001 to 16 per cent. A liberalisation of the Indian economy, coupled with globalisation and the influx of the multinationals, has improved the quality of all packaging, particularly flexible packaging. It is estimated there are 600-800 flexible packaging converters in India, and most are small operations with capacities of less than 250 tonnes per annum. However, at least 10 converters have capacities of more than 4,000 tonnes per annum and are on a par with the leading foreign operations.

These larger converters include:

- Flex Industries, Nodia;
- Packaging India, Pondicherry;
- Paper Products Ltd., Mumbai;
- Positive Packaging Ltd., Mumbai;
- Supreme Industries, Mumbai;
- VFC Ltd., Mumbai.

There is a developing middle income group in India that demands more Western-style convenience foods, and has an improved level of disposable income to purchase them. This demand is further supported by more women entering the workplace, leaving less time for them to prepare traditional home-cooked foods. In turn, this has led to a growing market for convenience products, both in the food and non-food sectors, requiring light convenient packaging compatible with microwave cooking. Other major drivers in the use of flexible packaging include:

- Increasing health consciousness-with a move away from traditional unpackaged formats to packaged, branded goods.
- The Indian economy is experiencing high levels of growth; Indian GDP growth was 7 per cent in 2004 to 2005-higher than for developed regions, and only marginally below that of China.

- Overall economic growth has stimulated the salary levels of the huge middle income group providing higher levels of disposable income proving beneficial for the consumer goods market.
- There have been escalating growth rates in agriculture, industry and the tertiary sectors.
- Increasing affluence and less time available for home cooking has increased the levels of eating at fast food outlets and restaurants. This has cultivated a taste for non-Indian foods-Italian, Chinese and European varieties-which in turn has caused an interest in the development of a range of packaged products such as pasta, soups and noodles for use in the home.

Market Sectors

Flexible packaging dominates food packaging, being used for a variety of food items including milk, biscuits, vegetable oil and rice. Fresh/pasteurised milk is one of the main end-use applications for flexible packaging and accounted for almost 30 per cent of total units in 2002. Bakery products were another sector of note using flexible packaging, mainly paper-based.

As consumer tastes develop further and conventional flexible packaging begins to be commonplace in India, more innovative designs are likely to take shape, as has been the way in the US and European markets.

However, cost is a major influence on pack types in India and lower-priced plastic pouches allow manufacturers to keep down the retail price of their products. The demand from rural areas has increased the use of sachets in many consumer goods markets where their low unit price has proved popular in smaller towns and villages where households cannot afford to buy larger packs.

Non-food sectors that have seen the wide-scale use of sachets are personal care and hygiene products such as shampoo, powder detergents, hair oil, toothpaste, hair colourings and fairness creams-a unique Indian preparation intended to lighten skin tones. Sachets are helping to improve the lifestyle of lower income classes by reducing the use of unpackaged, lower-quality products in favour of higher-quality branded items.

In the beverage sector, sachets were introduced to broaden the market for powder concentrates, with a variety of branded goods produced by multinationals such as Coca-Cola India and Kraft Foods.

Despite some good movement, markets such as the food and beverage industries still have more to offer. In a country with such a large population, both the markets and the demand is large. With this in mind, only some of the potential has so far been tapped.

Food

A thriving industry with a large untapped potential:

- Indian food industry is worth over $400 billion (€304 billion);
- Second largest producer of fruits and vegetables-but only 2 per cent processed;
- Largest livestock population but only 1 per cent of meat production is converted to value-added products;
- Largest milk producer with about 15 per cent of milk production processed in the organised sector;
- Over 8,000km of coastline makes it potentially, one of the largest seafood producing and processing countries;
- Around 30 per cent of the world's trade in spices originates in India;
- A rapidly growing bakery, soft drinks, confectionery and beer and alcoholic drinks market;
- Size of the semi-processed and ready-to-eat packaged food industry is over $1 billion and growing at over 20 per cent per annum;
- Lifting of quantitative restrictions in accordance with the World Trade Organization (WTO) regulations from April 2001 means freer import and export.

Pharmaceutical

Opportunities for growth in the post WTO regime:

- Indian pharmaceutical industry value: more than $5 billion;
- Average growth rate: 8-10 per cent;
- Share of global sales: value 1 per cent, volume 8 per cent;
- Global ranking: 4th in volume, 13th in value;
- Production costs: lowest in the world-40-50 per cent compared to developed countries;
- A fragmented industry with over 20,000 registered units looking at consolidation;
- Top 250 companies control 70 per cent of the market and top 10 companies cover over 30 per cent of the market;
- An industry that possesses excellent chemistry and process reengineering skills;
- Per capita, expenditure on healthcare in India is $93 where penetration of modern medicine is less than 30 per cent, making it a huge untapped market;
- A growing affluent class has opened up the market for lifestyle drugs, virtually untapped so far;
- Indian Pharmaceutical Policy 2002 limits price controls and encourages foreign investment;
- Well placed to seize the opportunity in generic drugs going off-patent in Europe and in the US between 2005 and 2009;
- Being the lowest cost producer combined with FDA-approved plants, Indian companies can become a global outsourcing hub for pharmaceutical products.

On the Factory Floor

India makes the majority of the equipment needed by the flexible packaging converting industry including rotogravure printing presses, laminators, slitters and pouching machines. Often based on European designs, these machines are often not as sophisticated as European equivalents, but in most cases represent value for money. The majority of the small-scale flexible sector runs these machines.

Typical of this use of sophisticated European technology has been the growth of the Indian film and vacuum coating industries. Originally based on second-hand equipment, there has been a major investment programme by vacuum coaters and film producers in state-of-the-art, modern vacuum coaters sourced from Europe, and in many cases complementing investments in modern film manufacturing operations. In addition, several companies have bought top-of-the line, sophisticated laminating and printing machines since the early 2000s, and are now in a position to supply converted flexible packaging laminates meeting international standards.

Leading names include Samarpan, Nichrome, Rollatainers, Wraptech, Mico-Bosch and AMP Rose. These machines are of high quality and are very competitively priced compared to imported European machines. Hence, Indian FFS machines have become a major export opportunity to developed countries.

In terms of raw materials, India is almost self-sufficient for almost all the raw materials required in the manufacture of flexible packaging.

BOPP, PET, PE granule and films are widely manufactured in India. These materials are of international quality and are exported to Europe and the US.

Unlike European and North American markets, the Indian market is not founded on BOPP films but on PET materials. In addition, while the use of films is steadily increasing, there is a considerable market outside the packaging sector-principally in textile threads.

BOPP manufacturers include Cosmo Films, Gujarat Propack, Biax, Max and Supreme Oriented Films. Between them, Cosmo Films and Gujarat Propack have almost 50 per cent of the market share. Exxon Mobil is also exporting OPP into India from Europe and is making inroads in the market. Jindal Polyester Ltd. also invested in BOPP film manufacturing capabilities in 2003 with the commissioning of a 15,000 tonnes per year line.

Garware, Ester, Polyplex, Jindal, MTZ and SRF are some of the manufacturers of polyester film, with the first four having more than 60 per cent of the market share. PET is widely used in India for many applications and is also exported to Europe and the US.

There are also ongoing investments at the major Indian film manufacturers:

- Jindal Polyester Limited commissioned an additional 25,000 tonnes per annum PET line in March 2004;
- Polyplex has expanded its ambitions outside India with Polyplex Thailand announcing an investment to double output at Rayong to 30,000 tonnes per annum by April 2004, and the announcement of the formation of Polyplex Europa AS (Polyplex Turkey) to construct a 24,000 tonnes per annum PET film line at a greenfield site in Corlu, Turkey.

In addition to film manufacture the leading film producers of BOPP and Pso include metallised variants in their product offerings providing a source of added-value product complementing their clear film offerings.

Takeaways

- The Indian packaging market is predicted to grow year on year by between 14 per cent and 20 per cent until the end of the decade
- Traditional rigid packaging industries are migrating to flexible packaging
- Changing consumer tastes across a range of areas are placing new demands on the packaging industry but are also providing new opportunities for growth
- Laminated products including form-fill-seal pouches, laminated tubes and Tetra Packs are growing at around 30 per cent per annum
- The large growing middle class, liberalisation and organised retail sector are the catalysts to growth in packaging

- Fast-changing food habits are likely to spur on the flexible packaging market, especially the pouch and microwave packaging areas
- Unlike in past years, Indian packaging manufacturers are now embracing state-of-the-art technology, which helps Indian packaging reach western quality
- Sachets are proving popular in some rural and poorer communities as foods can be packaged in smaller, and cheaper, quantities making them more affordable
- Milk, both fresh and pasteurised, is one of the principal end-uses for flexible packaging, accounting for nearly 30 per cent of total units in 2002
- Cost is a big factor on Indian pack types, with lower cost plastic pouches allowing manufacturers to keep down the price of products
- Even with some good movements elsewhere, the food and beverage industries still have more to offer flexible packaging than others
- India makes the majority of the equipment that is required by the flexible packaging converting industry
- Unlike European and North American markets, the Indian market is not founded on BOPP films but on PET materials
- PET is widely used in India for many applications and is also exported to Europe and the US.

Future of Smart Packaging

Intelligent and smart packaging can benefit many end-use sectors, but none more so than food, drinks, pharmaceuticals and cosmetics. Pira International takes a closer look.

The global food sector is the main market for smart packaging, not just because of its size but also because active and intelligent packaging can help to meet consumer demand for improved quality and safety of food products, as well as more convenience. Among end-use sectors, the biggest sales of active and intelligent packaging will continue to be generated by the global food market. The food and drink market will be the fastest-growing outlet for sales of intelligent packaging. This will be mainly because of increased demand for diagnostic packaging in response to consumer desires for more information about freshness of foods, and also because of the need for track-and-trace systems. Intelligent packaging sales in this sector are expected to rise by more than fivefold to over $250 million (€199 million) between 2005 and the end of the decade.

Rising sales of oxygen scavengers, and to a lesser extent UV blockers, will be helped by the continued rapid rise of PET as a bottling material. The growing problem of counterfeiting, which electronic tracking systems can help to combat, will be a strong impetus behind sales of RFID components in the pharmaceutical, cosmetics and apparel markets.

Alcohol and Beverages

This sector saw the first applications of active packaging methods, in some cases before modern packaging technologies evolved. Hence in many alcohol markets, glass has retained its centuries-old dominance.

Glass is a highly effective barrier against oxygen and-when coloured-light, which together are the major contributors to the deterioration of packaged drinks.

In the non-alcohol sector, however, glass has been losing ground to rival materials, although remains popular in some local soft drink segments. In the milk market, for example, glass bottles were first replaced by paper cartons with coated inlays, and now increasingly by plastic containers.

Glass, and to a lesser extent metal, are now under attack from plastic materials-in particular polyethylene terephthalate (PET)-across a broad range of both non-alcohol and alcohol sectors. Changes in lifestyles and consumer consumption patterns have been a major impetus behind a switch to plastics.

The poor oxygen and light barrier properties of plastics has provided opportunities for suppliers of active packaging components to improve performance. For example, the amount of oxygen entering a PET bottle without an oxygen scavenger can be six to eight times higher, in the first 60-100 days of the shelf-life of its contents, than in one with a scavenger integrated into polymer.

Alcohol

Arguably the oldest form of active packaging has been the use of wooden barrels to help continue the fermentation and flavouring of alcohols during their storage, in particular spirits such as whisky and brandy, and to a lesser extent wines.

As a packaging application, the barrels have releasing and absorbing capabilities to change and improve the organoleptic qualities of the drink. European Union regulators have decided that these traditional storage methods should be considered part of the manufacturing process rather than as a packaging system.

The traditional wine bottles were designed for the continuation of fermentation and flavouring. Corks considerably reduce oxygen permeability but do not completely halt it. Wine experts believe the cork helps the continued fermentation of fine wines by admitting small amounts of oxygen into the bottle. Recently this process has been reversed by the introduction of plastic corks and screwtops, mainly in response to the contamination of corks, which can spoil 1-5 per cent of wines. Alcohol remains the principal supporter of glass packaging in many parts of the world, not only because of its capacity to keep out oxygen, but also because it has the image of a premium packaging material, especially in North America and Europe. However, in some regions PET bottles have virtually taken over the market, especially in the beer segment.

Unlike in the established markets of industrialised countries, glass in many emerging economies has a reputation for poor quality and lack of cleanliness, owing to the way glass bottles were reused and not washed ,properly by bottlers in the past.

In the Russian beer market, for example, there has been a massive switch to PET bottles. In 2005, Russia accounted for 70 per cent of Eastern European sales of beer bottles with oxygen scavengers, and 56 per cent of the global total. Glass is held in similarly low esteem in China, where PET has been making inroads.

In these relatively new markets for PET bottles, the material has tended to be applied as a single-layer barrier in which oxygen scavengers have been incorporated to prevent quick degradation of the alcohol. Higher grade PET-often still requiring active packaging components-has begun to gain comparatively big shares of certain alcohol markets in North America and to a lesser extent Europe. PET now accounts for 20 per cent by volume of spirits packaged in the US.

Soft Drinks

The fast growth of carbonated soft drinks in many parts of the world has been driven by PET. Its weight, stackability and unbreakability have made soft drinks much easier and cheaper to distribute. Unlike with alcoholic drinks, particularly beer, PET bottles for carbonated soft drinks do not typically require oxygen scavengers because they often have an interior coating. The main purpose of this coating is to keep in the carbon dioxide, but it also acts as a barrier to permeation of oxygen.

There is, by contrast, a relatively big demand for oxygen scavengers in plastic bottles for non-carbonated drinks such as juices, sports and functional drinks, the ingredients of which can be sensitive to oxygen.

There is an increasing demand in areas such as North America for antimicrobial components in PET and other plastic bottles for water. This is mainly because the water is packaged in larger bottles than in other regions, such as Europe, which can precipitate the accumulation of bacteria.

Pharmaceutical and Healthcare

Traditionally, the main requirements from packaging for pharmaceuticals, diagnostic medicines and other healthcare products were, besides the provision of basic identification and safety data, protection against damage and quick degradation. Recently these needs have been extended to safeguard against tampering, theft and counterfeiting, helping with brand protection.

In some areas of the world, including Western Europe, pharmaceutical companies are looking for active and intelligent packaging solutions to the problem of parallel trading. This is a practice under which distributors or traders buy branded pharmaceuticals in a country with low drug prices and sell them in another with higher prices.

Smart packaging is also seen as having the potential to improve patients' compliance with dosage regimes. It could even provide a means for self-diagnosis of some conditions.

RFID and other electronic systems with data memories and transmission capabilities are increasingly being employed by pharmaceutical companies and distributors to track and trace medical products through the supply chain. In the US, the Food and Drug Administration (FDA) has been working on regulations to make such systems obligatory.

Cosmetics and Toiletries

Packaging of cosmetics and toiletries has similar needs to that of pharmaceuticals. Because of their strong brand value, many cosmetics, particularly perfumes, are counterfeited. Cosmetics and toiletries are also subject to tampering. Some are heat-sensitive, so require a certain amount of temperature control when stored. Certain types of cosmetics are also vulnerable to oxygen and other gases, and to the effects of light. In some hot climates they are even susceptible to microbes.

Counterfeit products are estimated to account for around 10 per cent of the global cosmetics and toiletries market. As with pharmaceuticals, fake cosmetics have the largest proportion of sales in developing countries, particularly in Asia. Nonetheless, even in Western Europe bogus cosmetics are thought to have a share of 7 per cent of the market.

A report by the Centre for Economics and Business Research (CEBR) for the Global Anti-Counterfeiting Group (GACC), representing leading multinational companies, has estimated that counterfeiting in the EU has cut revenues from perfumes and cosmetics by €3 billion annually. The profits of perfume and cosmetic companies were reduced by €555 million by the activities of counterfeiters in the EU alone. Along with the pharmaceuticals sector, the cosmetics industry has been one of biggest spenders on security measures to protect itself against counterfeiters. Some of these initiatives have involved adopting innovations in intelligent packaging such as electronic tagging, digital watermarks, electromagnetic components and thermochromic inks. Expenditure on intelligent packaging within the cosmetics and toiletries sector is predicted to grow by 75 per cent to $64 million between 2005 and 2010.

Other Sectors on the Move

Apparel Fabrics provide a small outlet for oxygen scavengers as an aid to the preservation of natural fibres in storage and transit. However, the sector has the potential to be a significant market for intelligent packaging systems, particularly because of increasing pressure on clothing retailers to improve the efficiency of their supply chains.

In Europe, the fast fashion segment of the clothing market, which responds rapidly to trends determined by catwalk shows, increased by almost half between 2001 and 2005. The Spanish retail chain Zara can now design, manufacture and have a piece of clothing on its shelves within 15 days. The speed of its distribution is helped by an IT infrastructure using intelligent labelling systems along its supply chain.

The UK retail chain Marks & Spencer is extending an RFID trial from nine to 53 stores from spring 2006. This is to improve the availability of clothing with complex sizing systems, such as bras and suits. The test with passive RFID tags was started in 2004, with the chip contained within throwaway paper labels. During the next phase the chip will be integrated into the existing paper barcode label and will have the words "Intelligent Label for stock control use". The tags are being trialled to see how much they help Marks & Spencer check deliveries and count stock in stores and depots.

Clothes manufacturers and retailers are looking for assistance from intelligent packaging technologies like RFID to combat counterfeiting, which increased swiftly in reaction to the popularity of designer label clothes, which are comparatively easy to emulate.

Sales of intelligent packaging in the apparel market are expected to more than double to $55 million between 2005 and 2010. Although EAS and to a lesser extent EMID are employed as anti-theft devices at the item level, much of the increase is likely to come from increased use of RFID in the textiles supply chain and as an aid to more efficient stocking within stores.

Music, Videos and Software

The music, audiovisual and software industries have been trying to find ways of using intelligent packaging to fight piracy and counterfeiting. Illegal music sales are worth €4 billion globally, or one-eighth of the value of the worldwide music market. In the five years to 2005, the number of pirated discs has doubled to more than one billion, equivalent to one in three of all music CDs, according to the International Federation for the Phonographic Industry (IFPI).

A number of components on packaging of CDs, DVDs and videos, including RFID and other electronic items, have been tested to make the detection of pirated versions easier. However, one difficulty has been expense.

Among the cheaper methods has been digital watermarking, which is an image, digital signal or pattern that is embedded into the packaging. They can be like logos so that they are visually recognisable, or can carry covert serial numbers to verify authenticity. CDs, DVDs and videos are also fitted with anti-theft devices by retailers because they are among the most frequently stolen items.

Electronics

The electronics sector is a major outlet for various active packaging systems for protecting electronic equipment from moisture during storage and transit, particularly in humid and tropical areas. Moisture or condensation can cause irreversible damage to highly sensitive electronic goods. The packaging techniques for safeguarding the equipment include desiccants, corrosive gas scavenging bags, vapour-phase corrosion inhibitors

(VCIs) and moisture-vapour barrier systems. Their level of application depends on costs, effectiveness and practicability. The use of films with moisture-absorbing components, such as VCIs, has been eliminating the need for desiccant sachets.

Another threat to electronic equipment in transit is electrostatic discharge (ESD). In the whole US electronics sector, ESD is estimated to be causing annual damage of as much as $15 billion. Carbon black-based compounds in packaging materials have been the main components for protection against ESD, but these active substances have been meeting new competition from conductive polymers like polyaniline. They have the advantage of not requiring the addition of fillers to be made conductive. Unlike carbon, black polyaniline can be used with transparent and coloured films. Its level of conductivity is also easier to control.

4

Delivering Excellence in Hospitality Sector

The contribution of tourism and trade industry towards a nation's economy is manifold. It not only makes its impact on the economic growth of the country, in terms of revenue generation and employment opportunities, but also in terms of the cultural enhancement of the nation and its people.

What differentiates one country from another is the kind of service that is offered to the visiting population; and also the customer-centric approach of the government and the natives to the influx of tourists to their country. The paper analyzes the position of India in terms of the various yardsticks that define any great tourist destination across the globe.

The paper is singularly India focused analysis of the potential way forward for the native travel and tourism industry. It critically examines the current scenario of the Indian tourism industry with its pitfalls and then strategizes for the future.

Importance of Tourism Industry

A strong travel and tourism network system spanning the entire nation has the potential to pull off a multiplier effect on the economic growth of the country. It necessitates employment opportunities in direct interfaces of tourism such as hotels, restaurants, travel agencies and related services. The industry is fundamentally responsible for diversifying the economic activities in the country and opening up new means of trade and commerce.

Corporate travel is the new buzzword and any amount of investment into the existing businesses and creation of new business will only favour the local economy in terms of increased trade through exports and internal job creation.

However, the biggest gainer in terms of travel and tourism industry is the mutual exchange of culture and ideas and most importantly, the way of life. A keen knowledge of another culture throws open a wide variety of prospects in terms of not only commerce, but also perspectives and practices of a group of people that is worthy of emulation by the visiting nationals. Besides, the natives incorporate foreign nuances into the ethos of the local culture.

The paper analyzes the performance and possible areas of improvement for the Indian tourism industry. It would objectively looks at a) domestic tourism b) international tourism c) medical tourism d) corporate travel. A nation's ability to provide a standardized tourist experience will reflect its ability to provide professional services to the visiting population.

Indian Tourism Industry–A Snapshot

India was ranked as the 42nd most desired tourist destination by the United Nations World Trade Organization {UNWTO} in the year 2007. The same report mentions India as the 6th best in terms of price competiveness and 39th in terms of safety and security.

The global tourism industry is expected to touch $7.2 trillion in the next two years in economic activities, together with a generation of 260 million jobs across the world. India is expected to command 1.5% of this mammoth figure by 2011. It has also been observed that although corporate travel has taken a hit, the tourism industry has not suffered heavily because domestic travel and medical tourism have been as buoyant as before.

Currently, tourism and travel contribute about 6% of the Gross Domestic Product of our country, while in the world the industry contributes an average of 10.2 % of the GDP. International tourism contributes 6% to the total exports of the nation, and 6.4 % of the total employed force of India belongs to tourism and related services. It is expected to jump to 7.2% in a decade's time. India Tourism Industry Forecast 2007-2011 reports some interesting facts about the nation's travel and tourism perspective. Some of the key findings are as follows:

- In India, inbound tourist expenditure per head is the third highest in the world and even more than the global average tourist spending.
- India has been promoting its healthcare tourism by providing the visitors with private healthcare facilities. It is expected that the number of tourists visiting India for the purpose of medical treatment will reach one million by 2012, representing a CAGR of 28.09% from 2007.
- Indian outbound tourist flow is expected to increase at a CAGR of 12.79% over the five-year period spanning 2007-2011.
- Tourist influx to India is expected to increase at a CAGR of 22.65% between 2007 and 2011.
- India's share in global tourism is expected to reach 1.5% by 2010.

There are several fear factors that inhibit tourism to a country. Some of those that could be potential threats to Indian tourism could be as follows:

A) Political instability: although the UPA government has come back to power, Indian politics has a long way to go before they stabilize into real governance and professionalization of politics.

B) Shock factors: Terrorist activities could be a major deterrent to tourism in any country. The 26/11 attacks in Mumbai targeted the foreign tourists who were residing in premium hotels such as The Grand Oberoi and the Taj Mahal Hotel. The fear factor could seriously create a dent in the image of the nation.

C) Corporate infrastructure: Considering that corporate travel is an indirect effect of general tourism and factors that are beyond immediate influence, it is imperative that India builds on an infrastructure that would facilitate corporate travel.

Strategies for Success

Five strategies that should propel India's tourism industry in to the limelight are:

1. Segregated Tourism: Although an emphasis can be made on the pan-India initiative, segregation of tourist types could be done in order to attract differentiated tourist base. India should concentrate on the following areas with specific advertising and promotion:

A) Medical tourism: although it has been touted as the next big thing for tourism, it has had a lacklustre performance so far. Even within medical tourism, orthopaedic-, neurological-, cancer-and cardio-treatment could be dealt with and promoted separately. This will also depend very heavily on the available infrastructure for stay; as well as the medical facilities available. Yoga could be promoted extensively. There could be two aspects to this. One, for the ailments and their treatments and the second, for rejuvenation-centric tourism.

B) Adventure tourism: To showcase the cascading waterfalls, the rocks and valleys, adventure sports could be a brilliant medium to promote. River rafting, Bungee jumping, trekking, rock climbing, paragliding amongst others could be focussed on, to attract sport enthusiasts from both within and outside the country.

C) *Coastal Tourism*: Amongst travellers, a majority have been found to love the sea. With a mainland coastline of 5700 kilometres and an added 1800 kilometres of coastline of the Andaman and Lakshwadeep, India has a huge coastline to boast of.

D) *Historical Tourism*: Steeped in rich history of a civilization older than 5000 years, India's march down the annals of history can be packaged interestingly. The forts of Gwalior, Jodhpur, Udaipur; temples of Madurai, Caves of Ajanta and Ellora are exemplary locations that attract tourists in herds. Tourism can also be segmented region wise.

2. IT-based infrastructure: Aimed at corporate tourism as well as high-end travellers for leisure, IT-enabled solutions could turn out to be a great service differentiator. India should especially, in mid-sized and premium hotels, enable Wi-Fi connectivity with good and robust bandwidth. Not only does it facilitates business decisions and deals but also allays work-related tensions that could possibly be communicated through the Internet.
3. Safety: The recent spate of incidents that question, in many ways, the strength of the police and safety infrastructure in the country has to be a prime area of concern. The 26/11 attacks on the Taj and Oberoi hotels had terrorists targeting foreign tourists. There has to be safety cells with greater decentralization and fast track courts that cater to tourism related incidents specifically.
4. Pan India Integration: The Incredible India campaign was a brilliant exercise which successfully roped in greater number of tourists to India. However India, being so diverse a nation, cannot be packaged into a single ethos that can be described by the word 'Incredible'. There has to be a differentiation in terms of pan India packages and regional packages.
5. Public Private Partnership: There are several advantages that can be listed about such an initiative between public sector involvement (for their available funds) and private sector (through professional management of services). Some of the advantages are:
   - Acceleration of Infrastructure Provision
   - Faster Implementation

- Value for Money
- Genuine Risk Transfer
- Performance-Related Reward
- Improved Quality of Service.

Conclusion

One of the obvious conclusions about the Indian Tourism industry is that it has great potential to be one of the best tourist destinations of the world. The need of the hour is to milk the opportunity and apply a two-pronged approach. One, for first time visitors of other nationalities, there could be India wide tours and two, a segmented approach towards niche category of tourists, who should be served according to the specificity of their needs. In an increasingly customer-driven approach, the training of professional staff for serving the customer, who dictates the needs and the delivery, is aptly rewarded.

It represents not just an opportunity to showcase the true hues of Indian landscape and culture but also an immense platform to break the jinx of India as the land of snake charmers and black magic to a land of true beauty.

Use by Industry

There are three essential conditions for revenue management to be applicable:

- That there is a fixed amount of resources available for sale.
- That the resources sold are perishable. This means that there is a time limit to selling the resources, after which they cease to be of value.
- That different customers are willing to pay a different price for using the same amount of resources.

If the resources available are not fixed or not perishable, the problem is limited to logistics, i.e. inventory or production management. If all customers would pay the same price for using the same amount of resources, the challenge would perhaps be limited to selling as quickly as possible, e.g. if there are costs for holding inventory. Yield management is of especially high relevance in cases where the constant costs are relatively high compared to the variable costs. The less variable cost there is, the more the additional revenue earned will contribute to the overall profit. This is because it focuses on maximizing expected marginal revenue for a given operation and planning horizon. It optimizes resource utilization by ensuring inventory availability to customers with the highest expected net revenue contribution and extracting the greatest level of 'willingness to pay' from the entire customer base.

Revenue management practitioners typically claim 3% to 7% incremental revenue gains due to revenue management activity. In many industries this can equate to over 100% increase in profits. A competent revenue management analyst with good decision support tools can generate $10,000 per hour. Yield management has significantly altered the travel and hospitality industry since its inception in the mid 1980s. It requires analysts with detailed market knowledge and advanced computing systems who implement sophisticated mathematical techniques to analyse market behavior and capture revenue opportunities. It has evolved from the system airlines invented as a response to deregulation and quickly spread to hotels, car rental firms, cruise lines, media, and energy to name a few. Its effectiveness in generating incremental revenues from an existing operation and customer base has made it particularly attractive to business leaders that prefer to generate return from revenue growth and enhanced capability rather than downsizing and cost cutting.

Airlines

In the passenger airline case, capacity is regarded fixed because changing what aircraft flies a certain service based on the demand is the exception rather than the rule. When the aircraft departs, the unsold seats cannot generate any revenue and thus can be said to have perished. Airlines use special software to monitor how seats are being reserved and react accordingly, for example by offering discounts when it appears that seats will remain unsold.Another way of capturing varying willingness to pay is to attempt market segmentation. A firm may repackage its basic inventory into different products to this end. In the passenger airline case this means implementing purchase restrictions, length of stay requirements and requiring fees for changing or canceling tickets.

The airline needs to keep a specific number of seats in reserve to cater to the probable demand for high-fare seats. The price of each seat varies inversely with the number of seats reserved, that is, the more seats that are reserved for a particular category, the lower the price of each seat. This will continue till the price of seat in the premium class equals that of those in the concession class. Depending on this, a floor price (lower price) for the next seat to be sold is set.

Hotels

Hotels use this system in largely the same way, to calculate the rates, rooms and restrictions on sales in order to best maximize the return too. These systems measure constrained and unconstrained demand along with pace to gauge which restrictions e.g.. length of stay, non refundable rate, or close to arrival. Revenue Managers in the hotel industry have evolved tremendously over the last 10 years and in this global economy targeting the right distribution channels, controlling costs, and having the right market mix plays an important role in Yield Management. Revenue management in hotels is selling rooms and services at the right price, at the right time, to the right people.

Rental Cars

In the rental car industry, yield management deals with the sale of optional insurance, damage waivers and vehicle upgrades. It accounts for a major portion of the rental company's profitability, and is monitored on a daily basis.

Inter City Buses

Yield management has moved into the bus industry with companies such as Megabus and BoltBus, which runs a low cost network in the UK and parts of the US, and more recently, nakedbus.com and Intercape, which have networks in New Zealand and South Africa.

5

The Sociocultural Impact of Hospitality Sector

Introduction

- The sociocultural impacts of tourism described here are the effects on host communities of direct and indirect relations with tourists, and of interaction with the tourism industry.
- For a variety of reasons, host communities often are the weaker party in interactions with their guests and service providers, leveraging any influence they might have.
- These influences are not always apparent, as they are difficult to measure, depend on value judgments and are often indirect or hard to identify.
- Impacts arise when tourism brings changes in value systems/behaviour, threatening indigenous identity.
- Changes often occur in community structure, family relationships, collective traditional life styles, ceremonies and morality.
- But tourism can also generate positive impacts as it can serve as a supportive force for peace, foster pride in cultural traditions and help avoid urban relocation by creating local jobs.
- Sociocultural impacts are ambiguous: the same objectively described impacts are seen as beneficial by some groups and as negative by others.

Negative Sociocultural Impacts of Tourism

Change or Loss of Indigenous Identity or Values

Tourism can cause change/loss of local identity and values by:

- Commodification,
- Standardisation,
- Loss Of Authenticity/Staged Authenticity
- Adaptation To Tourist Demands.

Negative Sociocultural Impacts of Tourism

Commodification:

- Tourism can turn local cultures into commodities when religious rituals, traditional ethnic rites and festivals are reduced and sanitized to conform to tourist expectations, resulting in what has been called "reconstructed ethnicity."
- Once a destination is sold as a tourism product, and the tourism demand for souvenirs, arts, entertainment and other commodities begins to exert influence, basic changes in human values may occur.
- Sacred sites and objects may not be respected when they are perceived as goods to trade.

Standardization:

- Destinations risk standardization in the process of satisfying tourists' desires for familiar facilities.
- While landscape, accommodation, food and drinks, etc., must meet the tourists' desire for the new and unfamiliar, they must at the same time not be too new or strange because few tourists are actually looking for completely new things.
- Tourists often look for recognizable facilities in an unfamiliar environment, like well-known fast-food restaurants and hotel chains.

Loss of authenticity and staged authenticity:

- Adapting cultural expressions to the tastes of tourists or even performing shows as if they were "real life" constitutes "staged authenticity".
- As long as tourists just want a glimpse of the local atmosphere, a quick glance at local life, without any knowledge or even interest, staging will be inevitable.

Adaptation to tourist demands:

- Tourists want souvenirs, arts, crafts, and cultural manifestations, and in many tourist destinations, craftsmen have responded to the growing demand, and have made changes in design of their products to bring them more in line with the new customers' tastes.
- While the interest shown by tourists also contributes to the sense of self-worth of the artists, and helps conserve a cultural tradition, cultural erosion may occur due to the commodification of cultural goods.

Culture clashes :

- Because tourism involves movement of people to different geographical locations, and establishment of social relations between people who would otherwise not meet, cultural clashes can take place as a result of differences in cultures, ethnicity, religion, values, lifestyles, languages, and levels of prosperity.
- The result can be an over exploitation of the social carrying capacity (limits of acceptable change in the social system inside or around the destination) and cultural carrying capacity (limits of acceptable change in the culture of the host population) of the local community.
- The attitude of local residents towards tourism development may unfold through the stages of euphoria, where visitors are very welcome, through apathy, irritation and potentially antagonism, when anti-tourist attitudes begin growing among local people.

Cultural clashes may further arise through:

Economic Inequality

- Many tourists come from societies with different consumption patterns and lifestyles than what is current at the destination, seeking pleasure, spending large amounts of money and sometimes behaving in ways that even they would not accept at home.
- One effect is that local people that come in contact with these tourists may develop a sort of copying behaviour, as they want to live and behave in the same way.
- Especially in less developed countries, there is likely to be a growing distinction between the 'haves' and 'have-nots', which may increase social and sometimes ethnic tensions.
- In resorts in destination countries such as Jamaica, Indonesia or Brazil, tourism employees with annual salaries of US$ 1,500 spend their working hours in close contact with guests whose yearly income is well over US$ 80,000.

Irritation due to tourist behaviour:

- Tourists often, out of ignorance or carelessness, fail to respect local customs and moral values.
- When they do, they can bring about irritation and stereotyping.
- They take a quick snapshot and are gone, and by so acting invade the local peoples' lives.
- In many Muslim countries, strict standards exist regarding the appearance and behaviour of Muslim women, who must carefully cover themselves in public.
- Tourists in these countries often disregard or are unaware of these standards, ignoring the prevalent dress code, appearing half-dressed (by local standards) in revealing shorts, skirts or even bikinis, sunbathing topless at the beach or consuming large quantities of alcohol openly.
- Besides creating ill-will, this kind of behaviour can be an incentive for locals not to respect their own traditions

and religion anymore, leading to tensions within the local community.

- The same types of culture clashes happen in conservative Christian communities in Polynesia, the Caribbean and the Mediterranean.

Job level friction:

- In developing countries especially, many jobs occupied by local people in the tourist industry are at a lower level, such as housemaids, waiters, gardeners and other practical work, while higher-paying and more prestigious managerial jobs go to foreigners or "urbanized" nationals.
- Due to a lack of professional training, as well as to the influence of hotel or restaurant chains at the destination, people with the know-how needed to perform higher level jobs are often recruited from other countries.
- This may cause friction and irritation and increases the gap between the cultures.
- Even in cases where tourism "works", in the sense that it improves local economies and the earning power of local individuals, it cannot solve all local social or economic problems.
- Sometimes it substitutes new problems for old ones.

Ethical issues :

- *Crime generation:* Crime rates typically increase with the growth and urbanization of an area, and growth of mass tourism is often accompanied by increased crime.
- The presence of a large number of tourists with a lot of money to spend, and often carrying valuables such as cameras and jewellery, increases the attraction for criminals and brings with it activities like robbery and drug dealing.
- Repression of these phenomena often exacerbates social tension.
- In Rio de Janeiro, Brazil, tourists staying in beachside

five star resorts close to extremely poor communities in hillside "favelas" are at risk of pickpockets and stick-ups. Security agents, often armed with machine guns, stand guard nearby in full sight, and face aggressive reactions from locals who are often their neighbours when they go home.

Child labour:

- Studies show that many jobs in the tourism sector have working and employment conditions that leave much to be desired: long hours, unstable employment, low pay, little training and poor chances for qualification.
- In addition, recent developments in the travel and tourism trade (liberalisation, competition, concentration, drop in travel fares, growth of subcontracting) seem to reinforce the trend towards more precarious, flexible employment conditions.
- For many such jobs young children are recruited, as they are cheap and flexible employees.

Prostitution and sex tourism:

- The commercial sexual exploitation of children and young women has paralleled the growth of tourism in many parts of the world.
- Though tourism is not the cause of sexual exploitation, it provides easy access to it.
- Tourism also brings consumerism to many parts of the world previously denied access to luxury commodities and services.
- The lure of this easy money has caused many young people, including children, to trade their bodies in exchange for T-shirts, personal stereos, bikes and even air tickets out of the country.
- In other situations children are trafficked into the brothels on the margins of the tourist areas and sold into sex slavery, very rarely earning enough money to escape.

Prostitution and Sex Tourism

- The UN has defined child sex tourism as "tourism organised with the primary purpose of facilitating the effecting of a commercial sexual relationship with a child".
- Certain tourism destinations have become centres for this illegal trade, frequented by paedophiles and supported by networks of pimps, taxi drivers, hotel staff, brothel owners, entertainment establishments, and tour operators who organize package sex tours.
- At the international level, there are agents who provide information about particular resorts where such practices are commonplace.
- Although sexual exploitation of children is a worldwide phenomenon, it is more prevalent in Asia than elsewhere.

How Tourism Can Contribute to Sociocultural Conservation

- Tourism can contribute to positive developments, not just negative impacts.
- It has the potential to promote social development through employment creation, income redistribution and poverty alleviation.

Other potential positive impacts of tourism include:

- Tourism as a force for peace.
- Strengthening communities.
- Facilities developed for tourism can benefit residents.
- Revaluation of culture and traditions.
- Encourages civic involvement and pride.

Tourism as a Force for Peace

- Travelling brings people into contact with each other and, as tourism has an educational element, it can foster understanding between peoples and cultures and provide cultural exchange between hosts and guests.
- Because of this, the chances increase for people to develop

mutual sympathy and understanding and to reduce their prejudices.

- For example, jobs provided by tourism in Belfast, Northern Ireland, are expected to help demobilize paramilitary groups as the peace process is put in place.
- In the end, sympathy and understanding can lead to a decrease of tension in the world and thus contribute to peace.

How Tourism Can Contribute to Sociocultural Conservation

Strengthening communities:

- Tourism can add to the vitality of communities in many ways.
- One example is that events and festivals of which local residents have been the primary participants and spectators are often rejuvenated and developed in response to tourist interest.
- The jobs created by tourism can act as a vital incentive to reduce emigration from rural areas.
- Local people can also increase their influence on tourism development, as well as improve their job and earnings prospects, through tourism-related professional training and development of business and organizational skills.
- The San of Namibia and southern Africa and the aboriginal peoples of Australia have recently regained management or ownership of traditional national park lands and conservancies, operating eco-lodges and serving as guides and rangers while maintaining their heritage.

Faciiities developed for tourism can benefit residents:

- As tourism supports the creation of community facilities and services that otherwise might not have been developed, it can bring higher living standards to a destination.
- Benefits can include upgraded infrastructure, health and transport improvements, new sport and recreational

facilities, restaurants, and public spaces as well as an influx of better-quality commodities and food.

Revaluation of culture and traditions:

- Tourism can boost the preservation and transmission of cultural and historical traditions, which often contributes to the conservation and sustainable management of natural resources, the protection of local heritage, and a renaissance of indigenous cultures, cultural arts and crafts.

"Tourism has forced the Balinese to reflect on their artistic output as just one cultural identifier. The presence of visitors who continually praise Balinese art and culture has given people a kind of confidence and pride in their art, and made them truly believe that their culture is glorious and thus worthy of this praise and therefore justly admired. This realization removed any possibility in the people's mind that their art was in any way inferior to the art of 'advanced' nations, and plays an important role in conserving and developing the art in general."

Tourism encourages civic involvement and pride:

- Tourism also helps raise local awareness of the financial value of natural and cultural sites and can stimulate a feeling of pride in local and national heritage and interest in its conservation.
- More broadly, the involvement of local communities in tourism development and operation appears to be an important condition for the conservation and sustainable use of biodiversity.

Conclusion

- These are some positive consequences of tourism that can arise only when tourism is practiced and developed in a sustainable and appropriate way.
- Involving the local population is essential.
- A community involved in planning and implementation of tourism has a more positive attitude, is more

supportive and has a better chance to make a profit from tourism than a population passively ruled-or overrun-by tourism.

- One of the core elements of sustainable tourism development is community development, which is a process and a capacity to make decisions that consider the long-term economy, ecology and equity of all communities.

Legislation and Guidance Protecting the Tourism Destination

Tourism is a rapidly growing phenomenon and has become one of the largest industries in the world. The impact of tourism is extremely varied. On one hand, it plays an important and certainly positive role in the socioeconomic and political development in destination countries by, for instance, offering new employment opportunities. Also, in certain instances, it may contribute to a broader cultural understanding by creating awareness, respecting the diversity of cultures and ways of life. On the other hand, as a tool to create jobs, it has not fulfilled its expectations. At the same time, complaints from tourist destinations concerning massive negative impacts upon environment, culture and residents' ways of life have given rise to a demand for a more sustainable development in tourism. Different parties will have to be involved in the process of developing sustainable tourism. This section focuses on what the tourism industry itself can do in order to increase its sustainability, defines three major problems, and suggests possible tourism initiatives to help solve these problems. Other problems should also be included in the discussion for it to become exhaustive.

Industry Initiatives for Sustainable Tourism

Problems

Decreased access to natural resources for the local communities and environmental degradation: Tourism is not, as many people assert, a clean and non-polluting industry. A major problem is the lack of a common understanding of what sustainable tourism or "ecotourism" means. This ambiguity leads to violations of environmental regulations and standards. Hence, the environmental problems evolving from tourism are manifold. First of all, the tourism industry is very resource and land intensive. Consequently, the interest of the tourism sector will often be in conflict with local resource and land use practices. The introduction of tourism will imply an increased stress on resources available. An influx of tourists into the area will lead to a competition for resources. Employees working at the tourist sites compound this competition. Almost as a rule, tourists are supplied at the expense of the local population.

Tourist activities imply an intensified utilisation of vulnerable habitats. Investors and tourists do not necessarily possess awareness on how to use natural resources sustainably, and subsequently this utilisation often leads to a degradation of resources. Tourism is also a major generator of wastes. In most tourist regions of developing countries, sewage, wastewater and solid waste disposal are not properly managed or planned. Lastly, tourism is also responsible for a considerable proportion of increased volumes and mileage in global transport and hence the associated environmentally damaging pollutant emissions. The tourism industry has not shown sufficient willingness to (internalise or) compensate the cost of conservation of biodiversity in, for instance, protected areas, even though they can profit from it.

Increasing Cultural Erosion and Disrespect for Human Rights

Tourism is a powerful agent of change. International tourism acts as a catalyst for the transition from traditional ways of life to so-called modern, Western forms of society. Accordingly, tourism often brings with it the introduction of new behaviour trends and norms. Very often, these are contrary to traditional norms existing in the host community, and can come into conflict with its cultural identity and threaten the traditional value systems there. The problem is that the investors seem to have a lack of cultural understanding of the invested society. There is a need for an increased awareness that establishment of new hotels etc. will have its consequences on the society and the people who live in it.

Tourism has become associated with violation of human rights. Many destination countries have experienced an increase in criminality, prostitution, alcohol and drug abuse as a consequence of tourism. Furthermore, child labour is commonplace in the tourism industry (particularly in the informal sector). According to estimates made by ILO (International Labour Organisation), between 3 and 19 million children and teenagers work in the tourism sector. A particularly abominable form of violation of human rights is child slavery and despicable abuse of children taking place in the booming sex industry in many countries. In these countries, tourism has led to an incredible increase in prostitution and also in the exploitation of children. The tourism industry has not yet come up with a general condemnation of these violations of human rights.

Unqualified Jobs and Foreign Exchange Leakage

The tourism industry is characterised by a high degree of monopoly, which implies a concentration of services and profits into very few big transnational corporations. In many countries, tourism facilities mostly belong to foreigners. Furthermore, in local host communities in many countries a relatively small number of people are involved in the tourism industry in host communities in many developing countries. Very often, there is a lack of qualified manpower in the locality. Hence, most employees are recruited form the big cities, neighbouring countries or even from the country of origin of the investors.

Multiplier effects from tourism are less significant than is often assumed. One reason is that tourism industries purchase most of their inputs (materials, products or services) in their country of origin. As a result, a considerable amount of foreign exchange revenues leaks from the destination countries. The more goods, services, physical capital and human capital a country must import for its tourism services, the higher the leakage. Very often the investors are not approaching the local community to see what it actually can provide. In addition to this, the General Agreement on Trade in Services (GATS), with its liberalisation of global trade and services, is increasingly undermining the possibilities of individual countries and regions to control their tourism industries and the possible economic gains from tourism.

Solutions

Decreased access to natural resources for the local communities and environmental degradation.

In general, the tourism industry should engage in promoting sustainability as a hallmark for investors. More specifically, investors in tourism should strive to adopt environmentally sound technologies or other measures to minimise the consumption of local ground water. In the case of water utilisation, such measures might be water saving equipment, desalination systems and collecting and utilising rainwater. Using other types of resources in a sustainable manner is, of course, also crucial.

There is a need to use ecological materials and installation of renewable sources of energy systems (solar energy) in all new buildings and new construction. Furthermore there should be an acceleration of installation or solar/wind power in all public work projects of communities where tourism will be introduced. To prevent or minimise the impact of chemical inputs in soil, water and health, one should start utilising sound ecological methods, including IPM (Integrated Pest Management). Ecological methods need to be applied in all areas utilised for tourism, including in the maintenance of golf courts, gardens and recreational facilities.

Pollution of ground and coastal waters must be prevented, and recommendations must be made (perhaps even legislation) for tourism investors to invest in proper sewage treatment facilities. Appropriate waste disposal systems and ways to separate garbage into organic and non-organic waste should be developed. Organic waste can be composed and possibly reused on hotel gardens or even for local farming. This could be done through collaboration with local residents. Residents could organise themselves and manage the allocated dumping sites, and hence benefit from the system in receiving payment from the hotel for services rendered. A system to separate the different materials, and recycle some should be in place at the landfill site, thus reducing the waste even further.

To avoid degradation of the natural environment, tourism projects can help finance protected areas and safeguard ecologically sensitive regions against further environmental deterioration. By empowering local populations and have them participating in the entire process, sustainability will be ensured as it becomes accepted by and adjusted to the local communities. Also, a protected area might certainly be a suitable tourist-attraction, where tourists can experience amazing nature and learn about conservation and traditional uses of natural resources in the area.

Investors in tourism should always respect the traditional land tenure system in the area and the traditional user-right systems of resources. In regard to this, the communication and consultation with the local communities about resource-use is important. Tourism investors should not exclude local people from using local resources, and thus take away what they depend on for maintaining their well being. The tourism industry can and must take initiatives to implement that polluter(s) pay a principle (or other forms of internalisation of externalities) for pollution related to tourism operations. This may be organised and carried out through local tax systems or through funds established by the tourism industry for local community development. However, the paid principle should be applied for minor pollution only and should not be developed into a possibility for investors to pay a symbolic fine for imposed irreversible negative impacts on the local environment.

Inaccurate and/or mild environmental legislation in destination countries may possibly attract more foreign investors contributing to fast economic growth and development, but with environmental damage as a consequence. To avoid the dilemma, destination countries will have to choose between economic development and environmental protection international. Multinational enterprises must be committed to follow the environmental standards of their home country should these be stricter than those at the destinations.

Increasing Cultural Erosion and Disrespect for Human Rights

The tourism industry should promote projects, which are compatible with the cultural identity of the local population's way of life. Furthermore, the tourism sector should always make sure it acts in accordance with the cultural heritage, and respect the cultural integrity of tourism destinations. This might be accomplished by defining codes of conduct for the industry and hence providing investors with a checklist for sustainable tourism projects.

Establishing and developing tourist training programmes could be one way of managing codes of conducts for the tourists. Here, tourists can be informed and educated about the destination for their travel both before and after their arrival at the site. At the site, tourist information centres can be established through funding from the investor. The information given to tourists should include codes of conduct regarding appropriate behaviour and clothing. It is reasonable to assume that people's offending behaviour is largely a consequence of ignorance rather than intention. Consequently, information and facts about the destination, ways of life, history, cultural heritage is crucial to help tourists get along.

It is an absolute must that tourism investors do not engage in or promote child labour and prostitution. Moreover, it is appropriate that the industry commit themselves to a global campaign against such and any other violation of human rights. Evaluating the sustainability of the tourism development, in regards to cultural and human rights aspects, is highly recommended for those responsible for the tourism projects. As with the case mentioned earlier of preventing environmental degradation, this must be carried out through communication and consultation with the local communities.

Unqualified Jobs and Foreign Exchange Leakage

By devising local training programmes and establishing

educational projects, the tourism industry can ensure that qualified local people are employed in their projects. One should train the local people instead of foreigners to become guides due to their knowledge of the area and resources. The investors should be responsive to the kind of knowledge, abilities and skills found in the local communities. Very often such knowledge and skills are well fitted to be used in tourist activities be it fishing trips, nature trails, souvenir sales or dancing courses for tourists etc.

To constrain foreign exchange leakage, those responsible for the tourism projects should ensure that local inputs are purchased for their projects. A proper examination of local resources available will be beneficial for both the industry and the local residents. Usually, there is considerable local willingness to start producing new products if a market for these products exists.

The tourism sector should also adopt measures to prevent foreign exchange leakage by a commitment to reinvestment of a fair share of the locally accrued profit. We have already mentioned protected areas, training programmes on codes of conduct for tourists, or possible training of local employees, as projects in need of funds. Initiatives towards more local community development projects should also be appropriate.

The tourism industry should promote the establishment of small and medium-sized tourism enterprises which, compared to large-scale hotels etc., have far more moderate impacts on the environment. It is the industry's responsibility to act as a model for communities to show that it is possible to do business whilst protecting natural resources. The industry should also promote and support local communities to start tourism-related businesses and grant access to low interest loans. It is the responsibility of the tourism sector to ensure total transparency in all transactions, and to prevent tourism projects from being used as projects for laundering illicit money, as well as to refuse using bribes as a means to obfuscate or avoid government rules and regulations. There should be a global boycott against those investors involved in such or other types of illegal activities.

General Recommendations and Possible Solutions which Concern all three Problem Areas

Empowerment of residents at tourist destinations, through local participation, may be facilitated by providing written and legally binding contracts between local people and tourism investors. The contracts will help to avoid broken promises, which too many examples and previous experience prove to be a huge problem. In addition to the mentioned examples (providing proper information for tourists and establishing training programmes for residents), the tourism industry, through for instance the WTTC or the WTO with NGOs in the selection panels, could issue awards especially for sustainable tourism projects as an encouragement for investors.

Agents and Partnerships for Change

In this section, the focus has been on what the tourism industry itself can do in order to augment and improve its environmental, cultural, social and economic profile and make sure this is sustainable. However, the industry's effort cannot be successful without a profound collaboration with all stakeholders.

Within the industry, it is important that both small and large-scale tourism operators are included in the collaboration and that they participate in solving problems related to tourism development. As mentioned, a sustainable development of the tourism industry can only be ensured through participation of all local residents in the destination countries. There is a need for a willingness and ability for the partners to work with this kind of bottom-up approach. In this context, both environment and social NGOs have an important role to play, putting pressure on the industry and facilitating contracts and local participation for community development. Governments in both destination and countries of origin of tourists and investors are responsible for providing appropriate legislation for sustainable tourism development, and to follow up the tourism projects with sufficient monitoring and appropriate sanctioning. Exchange of successful experiences of sustainable tourism projects is an important factor in this connection. Lastly, an interdisciplinary approach to the problem is necessary: using local, regional and/ or international consultative forums.

Influencing Consumer Behaviour to Promote Sustainable Tourism Problems

International tourism plays an ambivalent role in contributing to cultural exchange and sustainable development. On the one hand, it involves a highly buffered, short-term consumer experience of other locales. Tourists can pay and leave, remaining isolated from negative impacts at the local level. On the other hand, tourism may increase recognition of the importance of respecting cultural diversity and developing an identity as a world citizen. It offers opportunities to educate consumers regarding responsible tourism and sustainable development. Consumers can play a major role in the transformation of societies towards sustainability. While mass tourism in the past was rather producer-driven, the industry today is becoming increasingly consumer-driven. In highly competitive tourism markets, well informed, responsible consumers can put increasing pressure on the industry to behave more responsibly.

A number of official proclamations have affirmed every individual's right to rest and leisure including tourism. However, tourism remains an unobtainable luxury for the majority of the world's population. Tourists primarily originate from affluent industrialised societies where tourism has become a mass phenomenon. Tourists' values, attitudes and behaviour are determined by their social environment, cultural identity and way of life which may be in conflict with local customs. Tourism is heterogeneous in nature, made up of many different types of traveller, seeking a wide range of tourism products. Demand is influenced by irrational factors, e.g. fashion and trends. Demand depends on the availability of time and money, on images, perceptions and attitudes. Tourists have various needs, desires and motivations, both of a 'push' and 'pull' nature. While household incomes in major tourist-sending countries are declining, industry sales projections continue to grow, indicating increasing competition. The consumer mind is set on discount prices and "buy now/pay later" options. This poses serious threats, as prices already lag far behind any realistic accounting of tourism costs and impacts.

Many of the demand patterns in tourism reflect the unsustainable lifestyles of industrialised consumer societies. Tourism acts as an agent in exporting these life-styles and consumerist attitudes to less industrialised societies via demonstration effects and modelling. Tourism increases demand for imported consumer goods in the destinations, with detrimental effects on the environment, due to the ecological costs of transport and the high amount of waste generated. Increasing imports also reduce local/national economic gains, due to foreign exchange leakage.

The over-consumption of resources by tourists and tourism infrastructure (e.g. the excessive use of water, firewood or food) is incompatible with sustainable development. The carrying capacity of natural environments is often exceeded with the addition of tourism demands.

Tourist demand for resources (land, water, energy, food) may also compete with the needs of local people and may increase social inequality, gender inequality and injustice. Tourist transport, especially air travel, is highly energy intensive and causes pollutant emissions. Many tourism activities such as skiing, boating, mountain hiking, motorised water-sports (e.g. jet skies), and trekking represent stress for fragile ecosystems.

Tourists often lack information and awareness about their impact in a different culture and environment, about their impacts on socioeconomic and sociocultural development, and about the environmental costs of tourism. While tourists may be open to learning, they are often unaware of inappropriate behaviour and have little guidance on how to improve them. Others may refuse to adapt to local lifestyles (even when informed) insisting on their freedom to behave as they want.

While the tourism industry may be willing to improve their products and services, there is a conflict between the industry's pursuit of economic gains and social and environmental responsibility. The industry lacks information on the requirements of sustainable tourism and on how to integrate economic forces with environmental and social requirements. Tourists shopping for escapism generally abide by one fundamental consumer ethic: receipt upon payment. Consumer advocates may intervene where inferior customer service is delivered. However, the sustainability of corporate practices is self-regulated. This conflict of interest within the industry, and consumers' low awareness of tourism impacts, have led to a widespread abuse of 'green' labelling.

The mass media, especially television through films and reports about events, sights, etc. in other parts of the world, are increasingly influential on travel decisions and consumer behaviour in the destinations. However, these programmes often serve primarily as advertisements, painting images of destinations, rather than providing relevant information for potential travellers. There is a lack of reliable and appropriate (e.g. age and gender segregated) research data on the determinants of tourist demand, motivation and behaviour. Few countries, whether tourist-sending or tourist-receiving, collect such data that are helpful under sustainable development criteria.

Most studies of tourist behaviour focus on mainstream markets or market segments, rather than assessing or modelling sustainable alternatives. Governments in many tourist destinations and local communities have little or no information on what to expect from tourism and the incoming tourists, and how to influence and control tourism and guide tourist behaviour; They are controlled by international/global institutions, the industry and the consumers. Governments of the affluent countries are only beginning to look at the issues of outgoing tourism.

They are not yet sufficiently aware of their responsibility and methods to influence tourist behaviour by political and legal guidelines/criteria and appropriate planning and policies. Trade unions have fought successfully for shorter working hours and more vacation. However, they need to take more responsibility for helping to create a leisure industry that is more sustainable.

Solutions

Consumer behaviour can and must be influenced by:

- Fighting unsustainable forms and aspects of tourism, at the various levels, by sanctioning unacceptable behaviour and discouraging inappropriate consumer behaviour.
- Promoting responsible and sustainable patterns of behaviour, at the various levels, by promoting best practises and encouraging responsible consumer behaviour. There are different types of instruments and remedial measures available:
  * Legal measures (rules, regulations, sanctions);
  * Market based instruments, such as taxes to influence market prices;
  * Promotion of and (financial) support for best practice;
  * Industry self-monitoring/codes of conduct;
  * Information, education and research.

Governmental Action

- Introduce and enforce legislation to abolish child prostitution, implement effective control mechanisms, conclude judicial assistance agreements;
- Regulate tourist access to ecologically fragile or stressed natural areas;
- Tourist-sending countries: develop policies on outgoing tourism from a development perspective;
- Provide frameworks for ecologically appropriate pricing by strictly applying the polluter-pays-principle to internalise external costs. This includes ecological tax reforms including the taxation of aviation gasoline and oil, removal of subsidies/other economic incentives with negative environmental impacts.
- Improve conditions for sustainable consumer behaviour by providing/promoting sustainable tourism facilities;

- Promote environmentally friendly modes of transport and transport concepts, reduce tourism-related traffic, shift demand to less environmentally damaging modes of transport;
- Promote renewable sources of energy (such as solar power), reduce the use of non-renewable energy and of limited local resources, through more sustainable practices/consumption patterns.
- Develop information and education programmes in cooperation with local stakeholders ensuring all stakeholders' involvement (e.g. women's); provide information to tourists on appropriate behaviour (sensitivity, respect for/adaptation to local culture), e.g. by establishing information centres in destinations, or by including briefing material for package tours;
- Take into account the specific information needs of various market segments, provide information to the local population on the opportunities and risks from tourism and on how to influence tourist behaviour;
- Adopt, observe, implement and promote codes of conduct, e.g. the planned WTO-OMT 'Global Code of Ethics for Tourism';
- Integrate sustainable development education including tourism in the curricula of schools at all levels, universities and training institutions, involving all stakeholder groups, create and promote open networks for information and research on sustainable tourism, disseminate and implement results; 35. Tourism Industry Action
- Promote sustainable tourism products, using market related instruments and incentives, such as contests, awards, certification, model projects, culturally sensitive quality labels covering both environmental and social sustainability;
- Reduce inappropriate consumption, use local resources in preference to imports in a sustainable manner; reduce

and recycle waste, ensure safe waste disposal, develop and implement sustainable transport policies and systems, e.g. efficient public transport, walking, cycling in destinations;

- Provide tourists with authentic information, enabling them to understand all environmental and related aspects (e.g. human rights situation) of tourism when selecting any destination or holiday package; educate visitors in advance of arrival and give guidance on 'dos' and 'don'ts'; make tourists aware of their potential impact on and their responsibilities towards host societies;
- Provide information on respecting the cultural and natural heritage of destination areas; employ tour guides who portray societies honestly and dispel stereotypes;
- Ensure that the marketing of 'green' tourism reflects sound environmental policy and practice; use non-exploitative marketing strategies that respect people, communities and environments of destinations, dismantle stereotyping, integrate sustainable tourism principles when creating new marketing strategies;
- Train staff to foster tourist responsibility towards the destinations, encourage multi-cultural education and exchange;
- Actively discourage exploitative sex tourism, particularly sexual exploitation of children, and tourism which causes or contributes to social problems;
- Adopt, observe, implement and promote codes of conduct.

Cultural Transgressions

The Exploitation of Indigenous Populations

Indigenous peoples are paying a high price for tourism, says Raymond de Chavez. In their drive for profits, transnational corporations which dominate the international tourist industry have, with the complicity of governments (particularly those of the Third World), devastated the lives and lifestyles of indigenous peoples. The process of globalization will only exacerbate their plight.

Globalization and tourism have become a deadly mix for indigenous peoples. Tourism's impact on indigenous peoples' way of life and on their control of and access to their resources and environment has become more pronounced with globalization of the world economy.

For several decades now, tourism has been a major source of revenue for countries, specifically in the Third World. Its growth has been nothing short of phenomenal. In the 1950s, 25 million people travelled to a foreign destination. In the 1960s, this grew to 70 million. By 1997, 617 million tourists had been reported by the Madrid-based World Tourism Organisation to have travelled to foreign countries.

The World Tourism Organisation has even predicted that by the 21st century, tourist arrivals would have reached billions annually. It foresees that by the year 2010, 1 billion tourists would have travelled abroad and by 2020, this would have increased to 1.6 billion.

In terms of revenues, this would easily translate to billions of dollars yearly. In the 1960s, for example, tourism earned 'only' US$6.8 billion. In 1997, revenues jumped to US$448 billion. By the year 2000, the WTO predicts tourism earnings to reach $621 billion and by 2010, a whopping $1.5 trillion.

Tourism is also touted as a major source of employment worldwide. According to the World Travel and Tourism Council (WTTC), an aggrupation of more than 80 chief executives of the travel and tourism industry, tourism employs directly or indirectly more than 260 million. This translates to one out of nine jobs in the world economy generated by the industry. By the coming decade, the work force is expected to increase by 100 million more jobs, 70% of these in the Asia-Pacific region.

The WTTC in fact now considers tourism as the world's biggest industry and a 'key 21st century economic and employment driver'. Its growth for the past decades has been a constant 9% annually, in spite of the economic slowdown. While acknowledging a decline in tourism activities due to the Asian financial crisis, the WTTC recommended in February 1998 that governments give continued priority to tourism to assist Asian economic recovery.

Tourism as Export Strategy

It is no wonder therefore that cash-starved Third World countries view tourism as a shortcut to rapid development. Its potential to earn billions of dollars easily has resulted in it being viewed as a panacea for debt-ridden countries. But more than this, tourism has become part and parcel of multilateral financial institutions' package for financial bail-outs for countries in distress. Tourism is now being pursued as a serious development strategy for the Third World.

The International Monetary Fund (IMF) has included tourism as part of its Structural Adjustment Programmes (SAPs). The SAPs, which are preconditions for the approval of financial assistance, require the indebted country to:

- be integrated into the global economy;
- deregulate and liberalise its economy;
- shift from an agriculture-based to a manufacturing and service industry-based economy; and
- liberalise its financial sector. In essence, these preconditions link the Third World country to the world economy. The SAP opens up the local economy to foreign investments and multinational corporations, while eliminating subsidies and protection to local industries. Under IMF-World Bank prescriptions, tourism is classified as an export strategy. With its capacity to earn billions of dollars, tourism is being promoted by the IMF-WB as a means for Third World countries to repay their debts to them.

Third World governments have therefore tried to fulfil their commitments to these SAPs by large-scale investments in tourism-related ventures. In conjunction with financial multilateral institutions and travel and tourism transnational corporations (TNCs), they have launched infrastructure projects such as roads, hotels and tourist-promotion programmes. Worldwide, public and private investments have reached $800 billion annually, accounting for 12% of total worldwide investments.

But these IMF-WB conditionalities have proven to be insufficient to integrate and open up Third World economies. The World Trade Organisation has taken further steps to fully liberalise the world economy. The most important international agreement with direct bearing on tourism is the General Agreement on Trade in Services (GATS). Signed in Morocco in April 1994, this agreement '... sets up a legal and operational framework for the gradual elimination of barriers to international trade in services'. GATS is an offshoot of the Uruguay Round talks of the General Agreement on Tariffs and Trade (GATT), the World Trade Organisation's precursor.

In short, GATS makes it easier for big tourist and travel TNCs to invest in the local tourism industries of Third World countries. Among others, it removes restrictions on foreign corporations' abilities to transfer staff from one country to another; and enables them to use trademarks, create and operate branch offices abroad, and more importantly, to repatriate their earnings to their mother companies abroad.

Under GATS, protection to the local tourism industry would be construed as unfair practice and would thus have to be eliminated. TNCs now enjoy the same benefits as local travel and tourism agencies. This opens the local industry to competition from giant TNCs, which virtually means effectively transferring its control to them.

Other international agreements integrating the tourism industry into the global economy include the Agreement on Trade-Related Investment Measures (TRIMs), which removes the requirement for foreign companies to utilise local input. The proposed Multilateral Agreement on Investment (MAI) also 'secure[s] for foreign investors, unfettered rights to invest in all sectors of the host country's economy and to obtain for them the same treatment as investors from the host nation'. This proposal has, however, been shelved recently as a result of intense lobbying by non-governmental organisations, indigenous peoples' organisations included.

Threat to Indigenous Peoples

But what does globalization and tourism mean for the indigenous peoples? It is already an established fact that tourism had brought pernicious and long-term damaging effects on indigenous peoples even prior to globalization. The present economic order further exacerbates and hastens these impacts.

For one, indigenous communities, which have otherwise been left untouched by traditional tourism activities, have now been targeted for tourism ventures, most specifically, ecotourism. A relatively new variant, ecotourism is described as environment-friendly, sustainable and nature-based. It came about as a response to the growing environmental awareness worldwide these past decades.

Eager to cash in on this trend, the industry promoted ecotourism as an alternative activity, ostensibly to promote tourism while protecting the environment. This activity 'involves visiting relatively undisturbed natural areas with the aim of studying, admiring and enjoying the scenery, wild plants and animals, as well as any existing cultural aspects'. It includes spelunking, mountain climbing, scuba diving, bird watching, and whale watching, among others.

This tourism sub-sector has been met with remarkable success. Today, it has become the fastest growing sub-sector, growing at a rate of 10%-15% annually. Ecotourism now accounts for 25% of all leisure trips abroad. It is important to note that ecotourism destinations are more often than not in the Third World. Tourism here has been increasing annually by 6% as compared to 3.5% in developed countries. After all, it is in these areas that relatively undisturbed and preserved natural environments and exotic areas are located. But it is also in these countries that the majority of the distinct indigenous cultures can be found.

To a large extent, therefore, indigenous communities have become targets of ecotourism in this globalised economy.

In Africa, tourism's effects on indigenous peoples have been profound: widescale eviction from their lands, economic dislocation, breakdown of traditional values, and environmental degradation. Although ecotourism is a relatively new phenomenon internationally, it has long been existing in Africa.

In the 1950s, the colonial governments of Tanzania and Kenya under the British legalised the hunting and culling of wild animals by 'white settlers', thus paving the way for mass tourism. They set up zones for the exclusive use of hunters and prevented access to local inhabitants. Lodges and campsites were established near the preserves, making them major revenue earners. Some 70% of the protected areas and wildlife preserves, however, straddled lands of the Masai tribe.

Basically pastoralists, the Masai used these lands for their economic activities and traditional practices. The ban thus dislocated them economically. Forced out of their traditional grounds, they were left with little or no support from the government. And even after independence, the government failed to provide them with social services such as education and employment.

The Masai's traditional economic activity-pastoralism-has been attacked as primitive and destructive. Yet it has been noted that 'pastoralism and conservation of nature go hand in hand'. Alienated from their main economic activity and disadvantaged from job opportunities by a lack of education, the Masai were subjected to poverty. Even the Masai's traditional sociopolitical institutions have suffered as a consequence of tourism. Lands outside the preserves where the Masai have been resettled are considered communal. In these areas, residents are registered, and land and resources are to be distributed equally by a management committee.

However, corrupt officials have registered even nonresidents who have monopolised prime lands near the preserves. Land disputes have thus arisen. Elders, traditional mediators of conflicts, have become powerless against nonresidents who are often backed by powerful persons. Destruction of properties by wildlife has also been reported but the government has not given any compensation to affected residents. This has caused disruption in the relationship between the tribes and the animals, which are given priority because of tourism. As a consequence, the 'Masai...are coming to abhor the very wild animals they have successfully coexisted with for centuries'.

Tourism has not spared the environment and biodiversity. The rise in tourist arrivals in these preserves-more so with globalization-has increased deforestation, pollution and disruption in the ecological balance. In the Masai Mara National Park in Kenya and in the Ngorongoro Conservation Area in Tanzania, forests adjacent to lodges and camping grounds have been cut down due to the demand for firewood.

The massive influx of tourists and their vehicles has also caused destruction of grass cover, affecting plant and animal species in the area. Hotels have dumped their sewage in Masai settlement areas while campsites have polluted adjacent rivers.

Masai culture has further been threatened and commercialised. Negative Western values have influenced the Masai youth, leading to a loss of traditional values, prostitution, and the spread of AIDS.

Postcards portraying tribes in their traditional costumes abound in these preserves. It is in the interest of ecotourism to 'preserve' indigenous communities and their practices since exotic tribes with exotic practices serve as the main selling point to foreign tourists. 'There is rarely an acknowledgement-much less support-of indigenous people's struggle for cultural survival, self-determination, freedom of cultural expression, rights to ancestral lands, and control over land use and resource management.' In the Philippines, where tourism has long been considered as a major dollar-earner, ecotourism has also become a priority. Blessed with a rich biodiversity, the Philippines has developed ecotourism as a strategy to entice more foreign tourists and increase its share in world tourism revenue. Its Department of Tourism (DOT)'s Master Plan aims to develop 'sustainable' tourism while making the Philippines a leading tourist destination in Asia. In support of this thrust is the National Integrated Protected Areas System Act (NIPAS) of 1992, which classifies certain areas as protected zones. The DOT has identified 17 protected areas all over the country as suitable for ecotourism. It is important to note that the majority of these areas are territories of indigenous peoples.

In the Cordillera in the northern Philippines, tourism continues to affect adversely many of its 1.3 million indigenous population. Sagada in Mountain Province, home to the indigenous Kankanaeys, is known internationally for its cool climate, rice terraces, and caves, among others. Its people have maintained their indigenous way of life, subsistence economy and sustainable relationship with nature for centuries.

In recent years, tourism arrivals have grown tremendously, caused in part by ecotourism promotion packages advertising Sagada as a pristine community where one can commune with nature. Hotels and inns mushroomed, changing the town's landscape and straining its water resources. Pollution caused by littering and improper waste disposal has now become a major problem for the community.

Apart from environmental degradation, the influx of tourists has disrupted the Kankanaeys' traditions and practices. The solemnity and sacredness of rituals, such as those relating to the agricultural cycle and passage of life, have been affected due to the presence of curious tourists. Caves, traditionally their burial grounds, have been vandalised by graffiti, and some of the bones of their ancestors stolen.

Western influences have also taken their toll on the local community. These include the production, distribution and use of prohibited drugs such as marijuana and hashish. Taboos have been constantly broken by foreign tourists. Tourists, for example, have bathed in the nude in waterfalls, which is frowned upon by the local community. In 1995, the world-famous Ifugao Rice Terraces in Banawe, Ifugao province, was declared by the UN Educational, Scientific and Cultural Organisation (UNESCO) as a World Heritage Site.

This was part of the Philippine government's campaign to sell Ifugao as a major tourist destination in the world. The influx of tourists over the decades has similarly affected the Ifugaos, the indigenous inhabitants of the province. Foremost is the disruption of traditional economic practices of the community. The builders of the world-renowned rice terraces, the Ifugaos for centuries have subsisted on crops planted in their terraces. With the entry of tourists and hotels, the lure of money from tourist-related businesses such as selling of woodcarvings, became more attractive than subsistence farming. This has left many terraces untended and in danger of deterioration.

Commercial production of woodcarvings has also affected nearby forests. Trees have been cut down to support commercial woodcarving activities that cater to foreign as well as domestic tourist demand. This has led to the drying up of water sources much needed for irrigation.

Joan Carling of the Cordillera Peoples Alliance aptly summed up the effects of tourism on the indigenous peoples in the Cordillera when she wrote: 'The tourism industry has facilitated the further disintegration of the peoples' indigenous way of life. Cash production for the tourism industry has led to commercialism and individualism in contrast to the indigenous ways of simple living and mutual cooperation. Likewise, the commercialisation of their culture has led to undignified ways of seeking a livelihood such as allowing themselves to be photographed as souvenirs or to do their indigenous dance for a fee. This practice was never part of their culture.'

The pervasive effects of globalised tourism can also be seen in the way it has affected other indigenous peoples all over the world. In the Cook Islands in the Pacific, a 204-room hotel was built on land sacred to the local people.

The construction has caused environmental damage amounting to US$1 million. In the Russian Federation's Providenskij and Tchukogskij regions, home to the indigenous Tchukchi peoples, the development of tourism in the past years has affected their source of livelihood. Known areas of walrus concentration such as those in Rugor's Bay and the isle of Arykamchechen have become ecotourism destinations. Sightseeing tour groups ride on motorboats to walruses' breeding grounds.

But a rise in such tours has affected the walrus population. Visitor arrivals have caused stress among the walruses, causing a decline in their population. This has in turn affected the quality and quantity of walrus catch, traditionally the Tchukchi peoples' source of livelihood.

Tourism's High Cost

Indigenous peoples are paying a high price for tourism. In their desire to cash in on the billion-dollar profits from this industry, governments, specifically in the Third World, and transnational corporations have disregarded the interests of indigenous peoples.

The effects have been devastating. Indigenous peoples have been evicted from their traditional lands, their control and access to their natural resources compromised. They have suffered social degradation brought about by foreign influences and the commercialisation of their culture. Even the rich biodiversity of their natural resources has suffered from pollution and environmental damage, unable to support the growing number of tourist arrivals. What few benefits indigenous peoples derive from tourism are far outweighed by the damage it has caused them. They have been made to bear the brunt of an industry over which they have neither say nor control.

With globalization, these threats have been exacerbated. International agreements that open up access to the local tourism industry by big travel and tourism TNCs will only speed up exploitation of the natural resources, culture and way of life of indigenous peoples. Ecotourism, which has been touted as the fastest growing form of tourism in the Third World, has not proven to be sustainable at all. Rather, it has targeted indigenous communities as areas of destination and exploitation in the guise of being environment-friendly.

Unless indigenous peoples have a direct participation in the planning, implementation, and regulation of tourism activities that affect them, and unless benefit-sharing mechanisms are put in place, tourism can never redound to their interest. Indigenous peoples will continue to be mere cogs in the wheel of this billion-dollar industry.

Managing Social Impact of Tourism

As one of the world's largest industries, tourism carries with it significant social, environmental, economic and political impacts.

Although tourism can provide significant economic benefits for some destinations, the image of tourism as a benign and environmentally friendly industry has often been challenged. There is a clear and growing body of evidence that suggests that the effects of tourism development are far more complex than policy-makers usually suggest and that the impacts of tourism occur not just at the destination but at all stages of a tourist's trip.

Furthermore, tourism does not exist in a vacuum. Broader social and environmental changes also shape the form, growth and experience of tourism development.

Bringing Economic Benefits to Locals

* Tourism generates jobs and income, and contributes to the economic health and vitality of a community or county.
* Like any development activity, tourism also generates social, economic, and environmental impacts.
* Communities often focus on only one type of impact, usually economic, that a development project might generate.

The accurate assessment of both costs and benefits helps communities avoid problems and maintain community support for growth. Planning discussions allow communities to put the whole range of impacts on the table, assess who will and will not benefit, and facilitate a compromise that results in mutual benefit. The following cost and benefit framework from the University of Minnesota Tourism Centre's Community Tourism Development Manual provides information on the "common economic, social and environmental impacts that communities face as a result of hosting visitors, as well as community strategies that can help mitigate costs."

Economic Impacts of Tourism

Economic Benefits

- Brings new money into the community.
- Helps diversify and stabilize the local economy.
- Attracts additional businesses and services to support tourism industry.
- May be a catalyst for other industries and bring capital investment to area.
- Creates local jobs and new business opportunities.
- Increases expansion and retention of existing businesses.
- Contributes to the state and local tax base.
- Helps support local businesses that might not survive on resident income alone.

Economic Costs

- Imposes organizational and operational costs to develop tourism.
- Places demands on public infrastructure that may exceed what the local tax base can support.
- May inflate property values and the price of goods and services.
- Requires customer service training of employees, business owners, and community residents.
- May be cyclical and impacted by forces outside the community's control.
- Reduces local economic benefits if developers come from outside the community.
- May cause economic and employment distortions if development is not geographically balanced.

Techniques to Minimize Economic Costs

- Use tourism development as a supplement to, not a substitute for, other sources of economic activity.
- Use local capital, goods, services, labour, and expertise whenever possible.

- Involve both public and private sectors in development process.
- Provide financial incentives and training to foster local business ownership.
- Implement tourism awareness programs for local businesses.
- Establish programs to ensure affordable housing for residents.

Environmental Impacts of Tourism

Environmental Benefits

- Fosters conservation and preservation of natural, cultural, and historical resources.
- Increases local environmental awareness.
- May encourage community beautification, revitalization, and environmental quality.
- May improve local urban/rural landscapes through facilities development.
- May simulate improvements in infrastructure (airports, roads, water, waste, sewage).
- May be cleaner than other industries.

Environmental Costs

- May cause environmental hazards due to poor land use planning and facility design.
- May create land use problems, add to urban and rural sprawl.
- May degrade quality of natural and historic sites.
- May increase water, air, and noise pollution.
- May result in visual/architectural pollution.
- May create solid waste problems.
- May bring overcrowding and traffic congestion.

Techniques to Minimize Environmental Costs

- Implement land use planning and zoning laws prior to tourism development.

- Design hotels and tourist facilities to reflect local architectural styles.
- Set standards for water, sewage, and power supplies that encourage conservation.
- Establish guidelines for local carrying capacity and limits of acceptable change.
- Implement visitor use and management plans for cultural, historic, and natural attractions.
- Organize proper building, park, and landscaping maintenance for public areas.
- Establish conservation/protected areas to prevent growth in ecologically sensitive areas.
- Execute environmental public awareness programs for visitors and residents.

Social Impacts of Tourism

Social Benefits

- Supports development of community facilities and other local improvements.
- May enhance community's "sense of place" through cultural/historic celebration.
- Encourages civic involvement and community pride.
- May help maintain cultural identity of minority populations that are dying out.
- May facilitate renewed interest in traditional lifestyles among younger residents.
- Provides cultural exchange between hosts and guests.
- Promotes peace and understanding.

Social Costs

- May introduce lifestyles, ideas, and behaviours that conflict with those of residents.
- May create crowding, congestion, and increased crime.
- May encourage "trinketization" of local arts and crafts.

- Brings residents new competition for services and recreation opportunities.
- May create conflict among residents if benefits are unequally distributed.
- May produce a "demonstration effect" (Imitation of visitors' behaviours and spending patterns), resulting in loss of cultural pride.
- May create racial tension and resentment between hosts and guests.

Techniques to Minimize Social Costs

- Inform residents about both the benefits and costs of tourism.
- Establish quality controls to maintain authenticity of handicrafts and cultural activities.
- Plan tourism based on goals, values, and priorities identified by residents.
- Ensure residents have convenient access to tourist attractions, facilities, and services.
- Strictly control drugs, crime and prostitution.
- Use selective, target marketing to draw the right kinds of tourists.
- Educate and train local residents to work at all levels of tourism.
- Have ongoing public awareness programs about tourism.

The application of sustainable tourism in practice means understanding and addressing the costs and benefits of tourism: This also means that a community has to find the means to balance economic, social and environmental needs while minimizing negative impacts. In practice the goal is to maximize benefits and reduce the costs that tourism, like any industry, can bring to a community.

The Impact of Travel on Tourist Health

Until 19th century, travel for recreation was only undertaken by the elite. With the advent of rail, mass travel was available for the first time and destinations such as Brighton, UK and Coney Island, NY developed. Status was then defined by the mode of travel. In 20th century status was revealed by the nature of the destinations. Travel and tourism has been going on since time immemorial, and for the 'twentieth century tourist, the world has become one large department store of countrysides and cities'. By 21st century, travel became a new economy-*tourism*-available to all with enough money.

The focus of the tourism industry has shifted from air travel, overnights, meals and so on to total experiences or fantasy worlds associated with specific destinations. This new tourism phenomenon is not only influenced by economic factors but also by new cultures and a new generation of tourists. In tourism, the different destinations compete worldwide through globalization. The paradigm shift from mass tourism (also known as *Fordian Tourism*), which was the norm for more than three decades, no longer suffices to achieve competitiveness in tourism enterprises and regions. A new paradigm, or new tourism, is gathering momentum owing to its ability to face prevailing circumstances. Modern information and communication technology development in symbiosis with the transformation of tourism demand gave rise to a *new tourism.* This paradigm shift is not easy to define but is indicative of a new type of tourist who wants a new or different product. The new tourists are more experienced, more educated, more "green", more flexible, more independent, more quality-conscious and "harder to please" than ever before. Furthermore, they are well read and know what they want and where they want to go.

The different approach of the new tourist's creates a demand for new products. The small, medium and micro entrepreneurs within the tourism industry are dependent on major tourism developments. It is essential role of these small entrepreneurs be increased to deal with the changing demands of the new tourists. In Canada, 20% of the population is truly entrepreneurial while in South Africa the role of entrepreneurs is still extremely small. Only about 4% of the South African population is truly entrepreneurial.

What is New Tourism?

New Tourism is characterised mainly by *supersegmentation of demand*, the need for flexibility of supply and distribution, and achieving profitability through diagonal integration and subsequent system economies and integrated values, instead of economies of scale. This paradigm permits the tourism industry to offer products adapted to the increasingly complex and diverse needs of demand, while being competitive with the old standardized products. These markets of experience have become global, affecting the demand as well as the supply side of the tourism industry.

The tourism industry has undergone profound changes, which have been categorized by Poon (1993) in the following groups: (a) new consumers, (b) new technologies, (c) new forms of production, (d) new management styles, and (e) new prevailing circumstances.

As a result of the super segmentation of demand there is a very strong need for *in-depth knowledge* of the market in order to identify the *clusters of consumer traits and needs*. This knowledge will enable the tourism enterprises to develop those products that will give a greater competitive edge, and to place them on the market using efficient methods of communication and distribution. *Flexibility* is also a very relevant factor since it can assist the enterprise in adapting to the new demand requirements. This factor is relevant in several areas: flexibility in the organisation and in the production and distribution of tourism products; flexibility in reservation, purchasing and payment systems; and flexibility in ways in which the tourism product is consumed. New technologies are fundamental in this respect and, in particular, in the expansion and development of new systems of tourism information.

Diagonal integration is the final basic element. Compared with vertical and horizontal integration, which characterise the mass-standardised production paradigm, this is a process by which the tourism enterprise can develop and compete not only in one activity, but also within a wider framework, seeking profitability on the basis of system economies, obtaining synergies between different products and offering services well integrated in the value systems of consumers.

Key shifts in global tourism market trends are as follows:

- In the long term, the average standard of living in western developed countries will increase, as will the amount of discretionary money available for travel;
- Rising affluence will bring with it increases in the amount of free time available. Longer weekends and increased paid holidays have helped to stimulate expansion in attraction visitation;
- There is a shift in emphasis from passive fun to active learning;
- Activity or special interest holidays are likely to gain at the expense of conventional sightseeing, visiting and other passive experiences;
- There is growing concern about the impact of modern industry, including tourism, on the physical and social environment;
- There is growing awareness of risks to personal health and safety;
- Leisure time will be used more actively, for mental development as well as physical exercise;
- People aged 45 to 64 years of age will be growing significantly in number to the year 2010. In the United States alone, this age group is forecasted to grow by 31% by the year 2000;
- The potential visitor of the future will be: older, more affluent; more demanding; more thoughtful and discriminating; and more active physically and mentally;
- Timeframes for decision-making windows will be smaller. Hence, one-stop-shopping for all-inclusive packages will continue to be appealing; and
- Consumers will increasingly seek low impact tourism facilities, consistent with environmental values and the desire not to contribute to negative impacts.

The New Tourist

The travelling consumer of today (let alone in the future) is very different from any other time in history. The most successful businesses in the travel industry are those that respond to the challenge through the use of technology, innovative marketing programs, better training of staff and by developing a closeness and understanding of its customers/guests.

The differences in travel patterns in the next century will be more related to what consumers are seeking in a travel experience than in how they travel. Today's traveller, the well-heeled or footloose back-packer, is usually informed, educated, and more often than not, fully aware of what he or she wants from their travels. For them the optimisation of time and money is the key and they prepare for their trip by researching their destination through the Web and the experiences of friends and fellow travellers. Mass media has responded to this shift and further fuelled the search for experiences through the promotion of a vast range of lifestyle/adventure programs which have evolved more recently into experiential voyeuristic docu-dramas referred to as reality programmes. Attention is being turned to exploring new frontiers or daring to go where traditional thought did not allow.

In *Tourism, Technology and Competitive Strategies,* author Auliana Poon speaks about the changes in consumer behaviour and values which are the critical driving forces for the new tourism. The new tourist is experienced, more flexible, independent, quality conscious and harder to please. "New" tourists however, are increasingly being seen to be environmentally sensitive, displaying respect for the culture of host nations and looking to experience and learn rather than merely stand back and gaze. "New" tourists are participators not spectators. Things that would never appear on the list of the "mass" tourist such as adventure, getting of the beaten track and mingling with the locals are now the foundations of the new tourist experiences. Typically these tourists are turning away from travel and prefer to have a high level of involvement in the organisation of their trip.

Comparison of Old and New Tourists

Old Tourists		New Tourists
Search for the sun	=	Experience something different
Follow the masses	=	Want to be in charge
Here today, gone tomorrow	=	See and enjoy but not destroy
Just to show that you had been	=	Just for the fun of it
Having	=	Being
Superiority	=	Understanding
Like attractions	=	Like sports
Precautions	=	Adventurous
Eat in hotel	=	Try local fare
Homogeneous	=	Hybrid

Travel is no longer a novelty to the new tourist. Studies support what industry executives have been noticing for the last few years. People expect more out of their vacations than they used to and they are more adventuresome. Surveys done by the Canadian Tourism Research Institute indicate a high degree of interest in getaway vacations, ecotourism, cultural tourism and combining a business trip with a pleasure trip.

Over the next ten years, tourism products and attractions will have to cater to visitors who are more demanding and discriminating, as well as more active and more purposeful in their choice of destination. There will be a shift in emphasis from passive fun to active learning, and the quality and genuineness of visitor experiences will be crucial to future success in a competitive market. An Acronym that is relevant to describe the 'new' tourist is REAL, which stands for:

- Rewarding,
- Enriching,
- Adventuresome,
- Learning Experience.

A key underpinning concept for REAL tourism is authenticity of experience, which is often related to the environment and culture and seen to be unaffected by "mass" tourism. The New Tourists prefer to be regarded as travellers and not tourists. Some specific points which need to be kept in mind while dealing with the New Tourist are:

- This type of traveller requires a completely different marketing approach. They avoid conventional glossy marketing mechanisms and prefer to use reliable sources such as *word of mouth referrals,* their own independent research and trusted publications;
- They desire *experiences* as opposed to products and services;
- They can be called *experiential travellers,* they extend across all age groups and traditional market segments;

New Tourism for the New Tourist

To enable new tourism attractions to stand the test of time and satisfy the demanding requirements of the evolving 'new' tourist, the following criteria should be applied to existing and proposed attractions:

- That the attraction offers a distinct, unique experience that cannot easily be replicated by competitors;
- That the attraction is value added through 'best practice' interpretation, which preferably utilises a 'human element' such as interpretive guides, seasoned veterans and/or local characters;
- That, where possible, the experience is externalised within the natural/actual setting rather than internalised within a false/reproduced setting;
- That the attraction offers an exciting, authentic, interactive and educational experience;
- That 'comfort' should not compromise the authenticity of the experience;
- That the attraction adheres to ecologically sustainable development principles;

- That the attraction avoids the over reliance on technological interpretive devices that will become quickly outdated; and
- That the attraction offers a choice in the form of interpretation offered.

Responding to the shift in market dynamics towards a "New" style of tourist, a number of initiatives need to be taken so as to fuel the growth of experiential tourism these include:

- Network tourism initiatives;
- The development of interpretive highways;
- The explosion of interpretive centres;
- The latest trend towards regional base camps.

Network Tourism Initiative: Tourism experience consists of a large number of factors, which have different levels of importance dependant on the perspective of the visitor. For experiential travellers, the experience may be strongly influenced by the experiences between attractions such as the expert commentary provided by a trained guide or the friendliness of locals along the way.

The aim of Network tourism is to package a diverse range of products and services throughout a broad region to create a quality experience that capitalises on a region's strengths and comparative advantages. This principle recognises that the combination of discreet experiences within the network creates a greater attraction than its individual components and serves to increase economic benefits and market profile for the entire region. To satisfy the diverse experiential requirements of the "new" tourist, it is imperative that a strong referral system is developed between attractions contained within the network. This therefore goes beyond current promotional attempts by the tourism agencies to promote the entire network, and rests with the individual attractions within the network themselves and the need to actively cross promote between attractions.

Interpretive Highways: Travel is seen to be a part of a network of experiences as opposed to the mere mechanism for going from point A to B. Interpretive highways have been a successful device to link a number of disparate experiences to provide a more comprehensive visitor experience. Whilst principally a tool for satisfying the travel desires of self-guided travellers, a framework should be developed that has also serves to assist experiential requirements of commercial guided tour operators. This is primarily attributed to improved interpretation offered along the travel path to break the monotony of long haul travel between attractions.

The Explosion Of Interpretive Centres: The purpose of the centre is to educate the general public and children in particular on the importance of a particular tourist site, historical monuments, natural resources, wetland ecosystems etc. These centres can contain permanent and evolving exhibit galleries, meeting space, a classroom and teaching laboratory, an auditorium, and a gift shop, along with offices and other support facilities. Indoor exhibits on natural history and other objects of tourist interest can be complemented by regular showings of multi image presentations.

The Wildlife Institute of India: United States Fish and Wildlife Services and Madhya Pradesh Forest Department collaborative programme aims to achieve long term conservation of the park by increasing awareness and appreciation towards Panna National park among visitors as well as local people through the use of interpretive centres. The main components of the programme are:

Outreach Programme: It is aimed at sensitizing the local community about the benefits of the programme to the park and eventually to them.

Resource Material: In the form of books, brochures and CD-ROMs would be developed to highlight the conservation needs. An exclusive website on Panna National Park is also planned for attracting international attention.

Interpretation Centre and Visitor Centre: They are an important component of the project and would comprise of exhibits on Panna National Park and its conservation needs. This is a means of education mainly targeted to the tourists, School children and local community.

Capacity Building: Training of local youths as guides, Park staff and tour operators on Interpretation and communication skills to enable them to run the programme.

The Latest Trend Towards Regional Base Camps: While the traditional centralised awareness centre can be thought of as a strategic hub located at a major strategic travel point, it is proposed that a 'hub and spokes' approach be the next evolutionary step. The hub can be thought of as the 'base camp' for regional exploration and provides advice, essential services, orientates the visitor, provides all the necessary supplies and equipment to enable the visitor to safely and sensitively explore the region. In delivering these services, the hub can also become an important community asset by encouraging mixed use. The spokes visit important remote sites and recognise that where possible, interpretation should be undertaken in the authentic setting. The 'hub' attempts to put the heart back into a township and revitalise the local economy.

Politico-cultural Impacts

- o Political stability and political relations influences the image of destinations in tourist-generating regions.
- o Media portrayal: books, magazines, newspapers, satellite and cable links has a substantial influence.
- o Examples of political strife that cause problematic concerns in the attraction of visitors are:
  - * Warfare.
  - * coups.
  - * political strikes or protests.

"Any evidence of domestic turmoil is likely to result in a decision not to visit that country. " Ankomah and Crompton.

What is Political Instability?

- "Political instability is described as a condition of a country where a government has been toppled, or is controlled by factions following a coup, or where basic functional prerequisites for social-order control and maintenance are unstable and periodically disrupted".

- Multifaceted and complex character.
- Impact in various countries worldwide is multilevel and multidimensional.

Relationship between politics and tourism

- "The political aspects of tourism are interwoven with its economic consequences...tourism is not only a "continuation of politics" but an integral part of the world's political economy. In short, tourism is, or can be, a tool used not only for economic but for political means".

Unwillingness on the part of many decision makers both in government and in the private sector to acknowledge the political nature of tourism.

- Lack of official interest in conducting research into the politics of tourism.
- Tourism not regarded as a serious scholarly subject.

" Tourism is by now too important and a pervasive activity for governments to ignore.".

The Reasons Behind the Neglect

China-Tiananmen Square, June 4 1989;

- Prime time news coverage showed army tanks threatening the civilian population.
- After the Tianamen Square incident Hotel occupancy rates in Beijing dipped below 30 per cent.
- Tourism earnings declined by $430 million in 1989 alone.

Has tourism been affected by political instability?

Effects of Political Violence

Effects of Military Coups ;

Fiji-1987: As a result of a mainly non-Fijian government being elected.

- Two military coups occurred within four months.
- Qantas imposed a two-month ban on flights to Fiji, following the hijacking attempt of an Air New Zealand Boeing 747.

- Travel Insurance cover was withdrawn after negative Australian government travel advice.

Effects of Revolutions

- Ejtrcito Zapatista de Liberacion National (EZLN) initiated an armed rebellion against the Mexican government.
- The revolution resulted in 145 to 500 deaths.
- 1994 visitation to Mexico dropped by 70 per cent.

Effects of Civil War

Yugoslavia – 1991, Army attacks Slovenia ;

- Conflict continued for 10 days before moving to Croatia in 1991, and Bosnia-Herzegovina in 1992,
- Tour operators for Yugoslavia lost over one million bookings in 1991,
- Two years after the war, figures for Slovenian tourism are still far behind prewar figures.

Sub Saharan Africa

The most extensive of Sub-Saharan colonial wars was fought in Angola, Mozambique and Guinea Bissau. Nigeria had five successful coups since gaining independence in the 1960'

- In total, more than 20 major wars have taken place on the sub-Saharan region of Africa since the 1960s.
- Zimbabwe (formerly southern Rhodesia) was the scene of a fifteen years Liberation War of Attrition between Africans and white settlers.

Effects of Civil War

Effects of Civil War ;

- IPRA targets included senior British government officials, British military and police,
- Visitor arrivals fell from a 1967 peak of 1,080,000 to 321,000 in 1976,
- Ceasefire which began on August 31 1994 was observed until February 9 1996 when a bomb exploded in London killing two bystanders and injuring 43 people,

- 18-month ceasefire recorded a 59 per cent increase (from previous year) in inquiries, 11 per cent increase in hotel occupancy, 18 per cent increase with out-of-state visitors, and a 68 per cent increase in holiday visitors.

Effects of Terrorism

Turkey – 1974, PKK Seeks to Establish Southeastern Marxist State;

- Kurdistan Worker's Party specifically targeted Turkey's tourism industry between 1991 and 1996.
- Bombed tourist sites, hotels and kidnapped foreign tourists.
- Foreign visitor arrivals dropped eight per cent from 1992-1993.
- After self-imposed ceasefire, international arrivals reached record levels (9.5 million) in 1996.

Peru –Formation of Maoist Terrorist Group;

- Aim of replacing existing Peruvian institutions with a peasant revolutionary regime.
- Attacks led to a steep decline in tourism from 350,000 international visitors in 1989 to 33,000 in 1991.

Egypt – Late 1970s, Islamic Extremist Group Activity;

- Egyptian Islamic extremist group works toward establishing an Islamic state.
- Specifically targeted and launched attacks against Egypt's tourism industry since 1992.
- Egypt removed from programs of international tour operators.
- Experienced a 22 per cent drop in international visitors, 30 per cent drop in tourist nights and 43 per cent decrease in tourism receipts.

6

Tourism as Placement Sector

Tourism is an economic tool which, when planted in a community expresses its positive presence through the jobs that spring from it. It then also contributes to the particular place's exposure to its external world drawing attention to it and with its visits that create the establishment of the logistics to address the needs of the visitors while they are there; food, drinks, transportation, communication, friendship, souvenirs.

Tourism is therefore a tool for poverty alleviation and social cohesion. The abject poverty in our rural areas could be reduced if tourism is developed.

This is because most of our attraction sites are dotted in the rural areas where poverty is prevalent. Tourists spend on accommodation, food, souvenirs and so on at places visited. However, the fact that tourists embark on return visits and sleep in the urban areas after visiting the sites does not augur well for poverty reduction.

The provision of social amenities in such areas will therefore go a long way to open up these areas to entice tourists to spend days at the attraction areas.

Tourism also orientates the community towards new introductions which may be positive or negative or both. Tourism never leaves a place without planting its footprints in there. It also makes a people conscious of their environmental cleanliness, and good conservation practices in a very sustainable way, because so long as the community area is acceptable to the visitors, they will continue to arrive and drop some benefits to the host community.

It addresses the social and cultural issues of the community in a very positive way. In Ghana, tourism as a tool for poverty alleviation is not in doubt. What is in doubt is the understanding of the industry because not much by way of education as to what it is and is not is brought home to the Ghanaian society. Tourism enjoys a lot of global attention due to its economic power to generate huge incomes to nations and its massive job creation base. The potential of tourism to transform developing economies and leapfrog them into middle income economies within record times has never been doubted both by economists and politicians.

The advanced countries commit so much budgetary allocations to the tourism industry and they receive the biggest chunk of business travellers who have all the money to spend. In recent times, developing countries especially those in Africa have taken to tourism as one of the possible panaceas for their economic challenges. Notable among nations that have given priority to tourism on their developmental agenda are Malaysia, Morocco, Mauritius, Kenya, Egypt and Singapore. These countries invested so much into developing tourism and are making gains.

We are told that Ghana's tourism makes almost $1.1bn USD in foreign exchange earnings, contributing four percent to the national Gross Domestic Product and creates about 220,000 direct formal employments across the country.

Tourism Development

Tourism has become a major global economic activity. In many countries it has overtake agriculture and manufacturing. The diversification of Ghana's economy in 1985 and the need to shift focus from the over-reliance of the economy on the traditional commodities brought the tourism sector into the front line as a major economic activity that has the potential of resuscitating the ailing economy. Ghana offers a wide range of unique and exciting natural, cultural and historical resources which are highly undeveloped but must be developed. As a traditional export, tourism has the potential to become a powerful tool in pro-poor development strategies. It has the ability to create jobs and wealth. This potential can be realized if sound economic and social development strength of tourism is effectively mobilized to create wealth and fight poverty in the communities in particular and the country at large. The positive impact of tourism can be assessed in terms of foreign exchange earnings, employment and income as well as a conservation of the biodiversity and also a catalytic tool for the growth of other businesses. Indeed, the tourism sector in Ghana is experiencing some significant growth since 1996 with tremendous positive impact from the year 2000. The growth experienced re-emphases the government's commitment to the development of the tourism sector. This statement has been re-echoed by President John Agyekum Kufuor in his 2005 sectional address to parliament when he said, "tourism is a gold mine that must be tapped." Tourism in Ghana is indeed the untapped gold mine of the economy.

Even though about 80 percent of the tourism potentials of the country remains untapped it is the fourth foreign exchange earner of the country after remittances from abroad, Cocoa and Gold. However, the Ministry of Tourism and Diasporan Relations is the least resourced. This has led to little publicity, poor marketing, sites are not properly developed, no promotional materials, and hence, tourism is relegated to the background. Looking at the fact that tourism is the fourth foreign exchange earner in Ghana's economy without any efforts, imagine what will happen if it is given little push with funding and support.

Though the country is blessed with pristine beaches stretching over 500 kilometres, these beaches are left undeveloped while portions have been turned into places of conveniences. Our habitual littering is also anathema to tourism development. How do we expect tourists to repeat their visits if we are misusing our tourism assets? We are renowned for our hospitality but when it comes to providing services we are not up and doing. Tourism is a very competitive business as people demand value for money if we wish to make the requisite gains then we should put our house in order.

Tourism Development and Poverty Aliviation

The Tourism Ministry in Ghana recently adopted a new approach to tourism development that maximizes the net benefit of tourism to the poor. This concept "Pro-poor Tourism" enhances the linkage between tourism businesses and poor-people so that tourism's contribution to poverty reduction is increased through the active participation of the local people in the development of the tourism product. The travel and tourism industry is itself human-resource intensive due to the service nature of the industry. Additional, one job in the core tourism business creates about two additional jobs (indirect) in the tourism-related economy. Available statistics indicate that in the area of employment, between year 2000-2003, total employment in the tourism sector in Ghana increased from 90,000 (direct-26,000; indirect-64,000) to 127,645 (direct – 37,283; indirect-90,362) representing 42 percent increase. Of those employed 56 percent were males and 44 percent females. It is projected that by the year 2009, tourism will employ about 300, 000 people. The gender dimension here is very important: according to the United Nations Development Programme empirical evidence which suggests developing countries with less gender inequality tend to have lower poverty rate. The implication for us is that gender equality through creating opportunities for women, as is typical of the tourism industry, has much stronger effect on poverty and the national economy.

Ghana is certainly endowed with a wide range of unique and exciting natural, cultural, historical and heritage resources, majority of which are located in the rural areas of where poverty is endemic. These resources are however, underdeveloped to harness the fullest potentials for the benefit of the communities within which they are located. City, district, municipal and traditional authorities who make efforts at developing the tourism resources within their localities are making gains from their investment.

This effort offers a wide range of service providers in the community economic and social benefits. It enriches members of the community, thereby enhancing their social life since they could afford the very basic necessities of life through descent work. Tourism is said to have a multiplier effect, once it is well developed and promoted. A case study is the Hohoe Municipal Assembly that declared its highest revenue coming from their investment in tourism. About 19 ecotourism sites around the country are not exceptions.

Tourism is also a catalytic tool that boosts growth in the other sectors of the economy which equally employs a good number of people. The agricultural sector employs about 60 percent of the country's total labour force. The tourism sector provides ready market for farmers at the restaurants and traditional/indigenous restaurants thereby helping to sustaining farmers in their trade. It is an undeniable fact that, tourism also sustains the industrial sector by patronizing their product likewise the manufacturing sector. Producers of local textiles, that is, tie-dye and batik fabrics have their products highly patronize by tourists as unique identification of "been to" a destination.

The vision of the Tourism Ministry to support and promote the achievement of the overall vision of the Government of Ghana aims at achieving a per capita income of USD$1,000 by 2015 through the realization of the sector's full potential in contributing to economic wealth creation, employment generation, poverty reduction, environment conservation, as well as national and international cohesion. To achieve this vision, the Ministry seeks to attract about a million tourists which imply a corresponding growth in the expansion of tourism plants across the country including restaurants, pubs, night clubs, tourist receptacles, and the like. With the current incentives available to attract investors L.I. 1817 when effectively implemented there is the likelihood to realize the continued and fast growth in the expansion of tourism plants that create more descent jobs for the citizens.

Challenges Facing the Tourism Industry

The tourism industry is beset with scores of challenges. These include; poor marketing of Ghana as a destination; lack of Ghana Tourism Brand; low awareness of the potential of tourism as a viable economic sector; poor infrastructure especially poor condition of access roads to tourist sites; inadequate funding from government for the sector; and inadequate skilled manpower as well as lack of professionalism to enhance service delivery. Paucity budgetary allocation, lack of logistics, poor human resource base, lack of domestic awareness and patronage, waste management, lack of corporate support, lack of favourable credit facilities, the perception of tourism as a high risk sector, quality products and services, lack of branding, marketing and a respectable attractive tourism image abroad, rampant road accidents among others are myriad of problems that the Ghanaian tourism sector has to contend with. Other challenges include poor institutional commitment, collaboration and support for tourism development at the District level; slow private sector investment in the sector; limited capacity and access to credit especially women entrepreneurs such as caterers and local fast food vendors; poor waste management and sanitation especially in the major cities; Ghana perceived as a high cost destination in the sub-region due to relatively high air fares and hotel tariffs; and low budget allocation

Justification for Government Support to the Tourism Sector

The vision of Government is aimed at achieving a per capita income of USD$1,000 by 2015. This implies that all sectors of economy must ensure growth to aggregated meet this target. The tourism sector has the magic to attain the overall vision of the country. A simple statistical calculation as follows proves this magic. Considering the fact that, the average spending of a tourist as at 2006 is US$1,985 and average length of stay is 10-days. Ghana attracted 497,129 tourists. Mathematically, revenue accrued in 2006 total US$986,801,065. This imply that tourism per capita in Ghana is US$41.12 with the assumption that the population at then stood as 22 million. However, the ratio of international tourists to domestic tourist generated is 1:7, meaning each international tourist arrival has a complimentary seven domestic tourists. Conventionally, both tourists have the same expenditure pattern, it signifies that total receipts from the tourism sector is approximately US$ 6,907,607,455.00 and holding constant the total population, it's very convenient to conclude that the per capital income of tourism is say US$ 314.

Given that the Ministry is adequately resourced and all other factors favouring growth of the sector are conducive and we attract a million tourists as targeted it is very comfortable to say that the tourism sector could drive the growth Ghana needs to become a middle level income country. Therefore, we need a tourism fund, and serious talk on this is very important factor for tourism development. Financing and management are the most critical factors for tourism development.

Everything including product development, training and human resource development as well as marketing and promotions are directly dependent on financing and management. The financing factor or lack of it has had the most debilitating effect on our tourism development: the terms of banks for long-term financing are quite prohibitive and tourism projects tend to have long gestation periods. The solution to this palpable situation is the National Tourism Fund, whether it takes the form of a special bank or a revolving fund for the private sector tourism service and plant operators.

Tourism marketing starts with the products that we are promoting. Financing will determine how well we add value to our tourism resources. Financing will also determine how accessible our tourist products become to both our domestic and international markets. We need money to develop our attractions where value-adding is necessary. The Metropolitan, Municipal and District Assemblies need to invest in tourism and support tourism investments. Financing is necessary for reaching the markets that we find lucrative to tap and exploit. Marketing and promotions has become a complex, competitive and highly technology-based activity, not aided at all by the facts that tourism is highly competitive and has a highly elastic demand. The industry needs soft financing to support facility development, to provide infrastructure at our tourism hot spots, to do good maintenance on existing facilities and amenities, and to start new projects in an expanding industry. We need to use the opportunity to as a matter of urgency review outdated and archaic legislation and regulation that regulate our tourism industry, since the sector is very robust and dynamic. Sadly the Ghanaian sector is being regulated by laws as old as thirty years and above. The Ghanaian sector deserves better attention, since each and every hamlet, village, town, city, district or region in Ghana has one unique tourism plant or facility that are scattered around the country, whose potential is crying for exploration and development, which has the potential to ensure an even development of the country to above all stop the rural-urban drift, in search of non-existing white collar jobs.

Tourism thrives on good roads, portable water. Electricity and effective telecommunications apart from the attraction itself. Unfortunately, most, if not all, of our attraction sites are in their raw state and the only way to exploit this gold is to develop them to meet international standards. If the Ministry of Tourism and Diasporan Relations target of attracting one million tourists annually is attained, tourism will rake in $1.5 billion with the corresponding 300,000 employees in the sector.

Indeed, Ghana is endowed with a lot of natural resources, and there is enough we can do to compete with the International Community in terms of development. What we have, no country has, as far as Tourism is concerned. The industry is the only area that brings in foreign exchange earning without export It is an indisputable fact that Ghana has today emerged as a special African tourist destination, drawing people and visitors to experience not only its fascinating cultural diversity, history and natural endowments, but all that there is to go with peace, stability, good governance and a hospitable people.

It plays a central and decisive role in promoting the development of responsible, ?sustainable and universally accessible tourism, paying particular attention to the ?interests of developing countries.? Ghana's opportunity to use tourism as a major pillar for its economic growth is realistic. Globally, Tourism today, is the second largest industry, which employs the most people and it is still growing. It is the major foreign exchange earner of more than 60 countries. It creates jobs at all levels. From shoe shine boys and porters, through receptionists, tour guides, accountants, managers, and the like, tourism also creates micro and small enterprises. Tourism will create jobs, jobs, jobs-attractive jobs; productive jobs and for that matter reduce poverty.

Customer-Driven 'Green' Tourism

In its efforts to diversify the nation's economy, the Government of Trinidad & Tobago has identified tourism as an area of potential growth. In this respect, we may consider ourselves fortunate that several of our Caribbean neighbours have many years experience in the Tourism Industry. Barbados and Jamaica, for example, have been established tourist destinations for many decades. Even in the relatively new ecotourism thrust, Belize and Dominica have more experience than we do. Thus, the opportunity presents itself for us to learn from the experience of our neighbours. In particular, we can identify problems which they have experienced, and study how they sought to solve those problems.

This paper discusses the issue of Customer-driven Green Tourism, which is increasingly becoming an issue in neighbouring Caribbean islands. There are those who would consider Green Tourism to be a benefit to our countries, but anecdotal evidence suggests that the demands of the Green Movement are posing significant problems to the owners and operators of tourist plant. Specifically, questions have been raised about:

* The criteria applied by the «Greens»,
* The sources of data used to evaluate individual facilities,
* The transparency of the process, and
* The lack of recourse by facility owners/operators.

Each of these issues will be addressed in this paper, but first there is a brief introduction of the concept of «Green Tourism».

Green Tourism

Customer Discretion

Of all industries, Tourism is the one in which the customer has absolute discretion. The tourist may choose one destination or another, or none at all; applying any criteria he sees fit. Destinations and individual facilities must therefore seek to provide a product which will satisfy the requirements of a suitably large number of customers, or they will face financial ruin. After all, in this industry the Customer is Always Right!

Environmental Concerns

There has been a growing trend of environmental consciousness among tourists, particularly those from Europe. This has led to two trends:

* Ecotourism, and
* Green Tourism.

The Eco-tourist is one who has a keen interest in nature, and seeks a vacation which will maximize the naturalist experience. Ecotourism is the fastest-growing segment of the tourist industry, and Eco-tourists tend to spend more at their destination (per person, per day) than other types of tourist (Final Report on the Feasibility Study for the Bloody Nature Project, Tobago, prepared by Eco-engineering-Eco-logistics, 1997). In addition, many facets of nature can be used as the basis for an Ecotourism industry: mainland rain forests, island rain forests, coral reefs, marine turtle nesting, etc. It is therefore not surprising that many Caribbean countries (Belize, Dominica, Guyana and Trinidad & Tobago, to name a few) have opted to develop a strong Ecotourism component to their overall tourism product.

Green Tourists, in contrast, may not have as strong an interest in nature as Eco-tourists. However, they consider it important that the facilities which they use are designed and operated in such a way that adverse impacts on the environment are eliminated (or, at least, minimized). This is clearly a laudable approach, so why does it create a problem? Hotel operators in the Organisation of Eastern Caribbean States (OECS) can attest to the fact that enquiries received from European travel agents and tour operators now frequently include the question: «Is your hotel classified as environmentally friendly?». Implicit in this question is the assumption that there are accepted criteria for such classification; whereas in our region such criteria are not readily available. In the absence of ratings within the region, it appears that many potential tourists rely on environmental groups in their own countries to determine which facilities are «green», and which are not.

Green Classification

Criteria

Criteria for rating the «environment-friendliness» of any facility usually relate to:

* Operational Practices at the Facility,
* Services and Products used at the Facility, and
* Waste Disposal.

Operational practices cover a wide range of environmental concerns. External lighting of the facility and the nature and timing of sound emissions can affect neighbouring residents or wildlife in adjacent areas. The frequency of washing linen affects the water demand at the facility, as well as the volume of waste water that is generated. Similarly, the nature of detergents used will influence the type of impact which is experienced in receiving water bodies. In like manner, composting of part of the solid waste would reduce the load being placed on landfills.

In all cases, the diversity of the Caribbean region makes it very difficult to define a universally-applicable «best approach». For example, some facilities may reduce demand on the public electricity supply by the use of solar water heaters or on-site generation via windmills or solar cells.

This may not be a practical approach in other locations. Likewise, the use of treated waste water for irrigation of lawns and plants is very effective in dry islands like Barbados or the Bahamas. However, in places like Dominica or Trinidad & Tobago, irrigation during the rainy season has proved unmanageable.

In preparing this paper, enquiries were made to determine what criteria were used by international environmental groups in rating the «green» status of tourist facilities in our region. Unfortunately, no definitive answers were received. However, there was a clear suggestion that the criteria are applied uniformly across the region, without considering the diversity of the region.

Rating

Having decided on a set of criteria, the second question relates to the actual process of rating. Simply put, there are concerns about the information being used to rate facilities. These concerns relate to:

* the Accuracy of the Information, and
* the Currentness of the Information.

As with the criteria, we were unable to ascertain the sources of information being used to rate specific facilities. It is doubtful if this information comes from «Official Sources», because few (if any) of our governments collect and publish data on this type. We are also unaware of any International Environmental Groups which actually visit our region to collect such information. This leaves two sources: local environmental groups and surveys/questionnaires sent directly to owners/operators of tourist facilities. The first concern is that the information used in rating facilities should be accurate. Regardless of whether the source of the information is a local environmental group or a questionnaire/survey, the information must be validated. It would be foolhardy to assume that neither of these sources of information would bias the information to serve some ulterior purpose. In like manner, it is important that the information be kept up-to-date. Tourist facilities seldom remain in a fixed form over a long period. In the quest to satisfy their customers, frequent changes are made. Some of these changes would affect the «green» rating of the facility.

Transparency of the Process

Several owners/operators have complained that the present system of «green» ratings lacks transparency. Owners/operators of tourist facilities wish to know how the ratings are being done, and by whom. It is a fact that tourists (and by extension, travel agents and tour operators) consider these ratings (among other criteria) in deciding which facilities to use. The owners/operators feel that they should have access to the rating criteria (to make changes which would improve their rating), as well as the information used in rating (to ensure that it is accurate and current). The enquiries made in preparation of this paper suggest that such transparency is lacking.

Lack of Recourse

Because of the lack of transparency, owners/operators of tourist facilities feel that they have no meaningful recourse if they are disadvantaged by the present rating system. If they do not know how the ratings are being arrived at, they cannot correct errors. Even where they learn «through the grape vine» that they have been given an undeserved poor rating, they are unsure where their complaint should be directed.

Environmental Management Systems

Benefits of EMS

The implementation of Environmental Management Systems (EMS) represents one approach to addressing some of the problems indicated above. These tools permit the facility operator to devise an Environmental Policy which recognizes the uniqueness of his facility as well as his country. By their very nature, these systems also address local regulations and standards. Finally, the EMS relies on progressive improvement toward the goals, so that the operator is not faced with a «pass/fail» choice, but rather one of management by objectives.

Cost Implications

Anecdotal evidence suggests that the cost of implementing an EMS, per se, is not necessarily prohibitive. However, the cost of certification can be significant. In the circumstances, the following suggestions are made to bring the EMS within the reach of small and medium operators in the tourism sector:

(i) The OECS Region should invest in the preparation of a Handbook on EMS, specifically designed for the needs of the Tourism Industry. This is not intended to «re-invent the wheel», but rather should be tailored to exclude many details which are included in general texts but which are not directly relevant to the Tourism Industry.

(ii) The OECS Region should also provide broad-based training to operators in the Tourism Industry to ensure that the nature, objectives and procedures of EMSs are generally understood.

(iii) The OECS should support initiatives by regional organizations to become registered as EMS Certifiers. For example, the Trinidad & Tobago Bureau of Standards has indicated that they will shortly seek such registration with the International Standards Organization. Having such a registered organization within Caricom (in contrast to bringing certifiers in from the metropolitan countries) will certainly lower the cost of certification.

(iv) The OECS should explore whether economies can be gained by grouping facilities for the purpose of EMS certification. The concept of «grouping» is different from the «generic EMS» which has been discussed in some quarters, in that it would involve the selection of facilities which have features in common, and are similarly located.

Dialogue

In suggesting an approach to solving the problems highlighted above, several factors were considered:

* Customer-driven Green Tourism can be harnessed to the benefit of our Region. Thus, our thrust should be to improve, not to eliminate.
* International environmental groups tend to be very receptive to meaningful dialogue with local groups. Unfortunately, they have been less cooperative with «official» agencies.

The suggestion, therefore, is that the tourism industry in the Caribbean Region should engage the international environmental groups in a meaningful dialogue on the subject of «green» rating of individual facilities. This dialogue should be aimed at ensuring that ratings are based on criteria which are acceptable in the Caribbean and on data which is accurate and current. It should also seek to build the necessary transparency into the system. It is our opinion that an industry grouping, such as the Caribbean Tourism Organization, would be more likely to succeed in this endeavour than a governmental organization.

Tourism in the Polar Regions: Facts, Trends and Impacts

This section describes how polar tourism grew to become a mature and highly diversified industry in both Polar Regions; the characteristics of its current operations; and prominent factors that will affect its future. This information is essential for understanding tourism's present and future impacts on the Polar Regions.

Evaluating tourism impacts, both beneficial and otherwise, requires knowledge of total numbers as well as where, when, and how tourists cause impacts. For example, the many thousand cruise-ship passengers who passively view the Arctic from offshore, and occasionally disembark to visit land based souvenir shops, affect the region in ways that differ from the smaller numbers actively engaged in Ecotourism or wilderness recreations activities such as river rafting, mountaineering, and sport fishing. By accurately identifying the full array of tourist activities and their behavioural patterns, then placing that information within the context of their natural and human resource settings, we can begin to understand key relationships.

Nearly Two Centuries of Arctic Tourism

The Arctic has attracted tourists since the early 1800's. The earliest Arctic tourists were individual anglers, hunters, mountaineers, and adventurers attracted to abundant fisheries, exotic wildlife species, and remote regions. Many articles describing their recreational pursuits appeared in the growing genre of recreation, mountaineering, hunting, and fishing periodicals that emerged in the mid-1800's. During the same era, several pioneering travellers to the Arctic published journals that became popular guide books for future Arctic tourists.

Mass tourism in the Arctic has thrived since the mid-1800's when steamships and railroads aggressively expanded their transportation networks providing access to numerous destinations throughout the Arctic. Tourism entrepreneurs, such as Thomas Cook, formed partnerships with railroad and steamship companies and thereby pioneered the popular tourism industry. By the 1880's, the "Land of the Midnight Sun" in the Scandinavia Arctic, Alaska, and the popular excitement of the Klondike Gold Rushes firmly established the Arctic's mass tourism market.

During the past two centuries numerous advances in transport technologies have contributed to the steady growth of Arctic tourism. At the present time, advanced ship technologies together with improved marine charts and navigational aids have allowed cruise ship travel to increase exponentially. Diesel locomotives, four wheel drive and tracked vehicles further opened access to vast regions of the Arctic. And, most importantly, air transport in all of its forms, provides immediate travel to the Arctic. Collectively, these improved transport technologies not only added numbers of tourists, but also expanded the seasonal and geographical reach of Arctic tourism.

Antarctic Tourism

Antarctic tourism began in 1957-59 with four visits by Argentinean and Chilean naval transports, which accommodated tourists whose fares helped to pay costs of servicing the national expeditions. Antarctica received extensive international publicity from the explorations led by Richard Byrd, Vivian Fuchs and Edmund Hillary.

Entrepreneurial tour operators recognized the commercial value of feasible access and positive international publicity. In 1966 Lars Eric Lindblad began expedition cruising to the Antarctic and initiated the use of zodiacs to land passengers at diverse sites. As a result of the success of the Lindblad model, government affiliated voyages were quickly superseded by dedicated cruises in small 'expedition' ships carrying 50-120 passengers. For many years this type of travel dominated the trade. Increasing numbers of expedition ships are transporting larger numbers of passengers, and making more landings at several hundred sites. The first larger cruise ship to enter the field, Ocean Princess in 1990-93, had a capacity of 480 passengers, but carried only 250-400 on its annual Antarctic voyages. The most recent development has been the advent from 2000 of liners carrying between 800 and 3,700 passengers, including crew members.

Over the last decades, tourism activities have expanded tremendously with the number of ship-borne tourists increasing by 430 % in 14 years and land-based tourists by 757 % in 10 years (IAATO 2007). The tremendous increase of ship-borne tourism and its impacts on the Antarctic environment resulted in the members of the Antarctic Treaty adopting a resolution (May 2007) which recommends the Parties of the Treaty to:

1. Discourage or decline to authorize tour operators that use vessels carrying more than 500 passengers from making any landings in Antarctica; and
2. Encourage or require tour operators to:
    a. Coordinate with each other such that not more than one tourist vessel is at a landing site at any one time;
    b. Restrict the number of passengers on shore at any one time to 100 or fewer, unless otherwise specified in applicable ATCM Measures or Resolutions; and
    c. Maintain a minimum 1:20 guide-to-passenger ratio while ashore, unless otherwise specified in applicable ATCM Measures or Resolutions.

Commercial air transport of tourists to the Antarctic includes both small groups travelling to the continent and larger numbers viewing from over flights. Adventure Network International (ANI) has been providing flight services to Patriot Hills in the Heritage Range since 1985 and other charter air companies have provided tourist transport between South Africa and Dronning Maud Land, and between Punta Arenas, Chile and King George Island.

Polar Tourism Today – Diverse and Growing

Polar tourism is now a mature industry providing diverse experiences in both Polar Regions. The polar tourism industry is enticing an increasing clientele with expanding numbers of attractions, recreational activities, international destinations, and visitor accommodations. And now that regularly scheduled excursion travel is provided to both the Arctic and Antarctic, year-round polar tourism has become a reality. Polar Tourism's Diverse Markets

Polar tourism is not a single, monolithic industry, but rather a collection of diverse specialty markets that appeal to an equally diverse clientele. Each of these distinct markets is growing and expanding for an obvious reason – they appeal to tourists who are willing to pay for the unique experiences they offer. The five highly specialized market segments currently dominating the polar tourism economy are best defined in terms of their primary attractions and the ways in which those attractions are experienced. This approach to classifying tourist markets explicitly acknowledges tourist expectations, the service delivery methods used to realize those expectations, and the distinct impacts resulting from those activities. The five markets are:

1. The mass market, comprised of tourists primarily attracted to sightseeing within the pleasurable surroundings of comfortable transport and accommodations.
2. The sport fishing and hunting market, with participants who pursue unique fish and game species within a wilderness setting.
3. The Ecotourism market, consisting of tourists who seek to observe wildlife species in their natural habitats, and experience the beauty and solitude of natural areas. These tourists are also concerned with conserving the environment and improving the wellbeing of local people.
4. The adventure tourism market, providing a sense of personal achievement and exhilaration from meeting challenges and potential perils of outdoor sport activities.
5. The culture and heritage tourism market, a very distinct market comprised of tourists who either want to experience personal interaction with the lives and traditions of native people, learn more about a historical

topic that interests them, or personally experience historic places and artifacts.

Each market has distinct visitor experiences and economic dimensions, involving different tourists' motivations, expectations, on-site behaviour, and resource uses. Market segmentation provides a useful framework for understanding polar tourism in terms of the use of natural and cultural resources, economic activity, and visitor behaviour. But obviously, tourists themselves are not constrained by this classification: they participate freely in many types of activities.

The enormous geographic scope of the five markets deserves emphasis. All eight Arctic nations, and their seas and oceans host all five markets, while Antarctica hosts most of them with the exception of the sport fishing and hunting and the culture and heritage markets. Most of that geography consists of land masses that are true wilderness and oceans with the world's most severe maritime conditions. The challenge of managing tourism across those vast lands and seas is well known to the Arctic nations and to those concerned about Antarctic tourism.

Environmental, Economic, Social and Cultural Impacts of Polar Tourism

Environmental Impacts

There are serious concerns that tourism is promoting environmental degradation in the Polar Regions by putting extra pressures on land, wildlife, water and other basic necessities, and on transportation facilities (GEO 2002 and GEO 2006). According to the Arctic Council Working Group on the Conservation of Arctic Flora and Fauna (CAFF), the main environmental impacts of tourism in the Arctic are the following:

* The transport of tourists to the Arctic, in itself, increases the volume of ship and aeroplane traffic. In addition to the impacts on climate by long distance air and water traffic, increased ship traffic in these waters could lead to increased risks of groundings and other accidents, the results of which can include oil spills and other environmental consequences.

* Many visitors want to see areas of great beauty or richness, such as bird colonies, marine mammal haul-outs, and caribou aggregations. Because there are relatively few places where such sights are accessible and reliable, tourist traffic is often concentrated. Arctic vegetation is typically unable to withstand repeated trampling, and paths of bare ground have appeared in some heavily visited spots.
* Helicopters, used sometimes for recreational purposes, are noisy and produce a variety of sounds that are disturbing to seabirds. Helicopters cause panic flights and can lead to egg loss particularly in birds.
* In the forest-tundra areas of the Arctic, tourism, including sport hunting and fishing, attracts moderate though increasing numbers of visitors. This places additional pressure on the region's resources, sometimes leading to conflicts between local and visiting hunters. The forest-tundra in general has a low tolerance for trampling. Even the temporary presence of humans often leaves a lasting impact.
* Visits to Arctic seabird colonies by tourists are rapidly growing. Currently cruise ships visit or sail by colonies in the low and high Arctic of Canada, west Greenland, Iceland, Norwegian coast and Svalbard, eastern Russia, and the US (Alaska). Colonies chosen for visitation tend to be large and spectacular and usually are home to species such as murres, puffins, kittiwakes, and fulmars. During a colony visit, passengers typically board smaller boats from the larger ships, and cruise by colonies observing the seabirds and taking pictures. Occasionally passengers make landings at suitable colonies and view the seabirds from above or below the cliffs.
* Recreational activities, such as boating and fishing, cause local disturbance at bird colonies in several Arctic countries. In the Russian far-east, coastal and lowland species such as ducks, gulls, terns and Spectacled Guillemots are frequently disturbed by visitors.

* Garbage, waste, and pollution are significant problems for many tourism operations, especially as decomposition is slow and waste remains visible atop the permafrost in many Arctic areas.

In the Antarctic the most important impact of tourism concerns the disturbance of cetaceans. Certain studies have lent increasing strength to concerns that human activities may be influencing the fitness of these animals. Tourism activities in Antarctica present also a risk to the marine environment (pollution resulting from operations or maritime accident (e.g. grounding)) as well as to terrestrial ecosystems as over 80 % of the tourists land one or more times during their journey (introduction of alien species; disturbance of birds colonies; damage to the vegetative cover (e.g. lichen). In addition, high-risk unsupported (adventure) tourism can potentially impact on national research programmes in terms of search and rescue operations. The main positive impact of polar tourism, if well done, is its educational value. Arctic and Antarctic visitors are fascinated by the sheer beauty, wilderness and natural phenomena of the polar environment. This can be used to make them not only to ambassadors for the protection of the visited regions, but also supporters of conservation activities and organizations worldwide.

Economic Impacts

Growing public and private resource commitments to promote and further develop tourism demonstrate strong intentions to strengthen tourism's economic role in the Arctic. Given these circumstances, economic impacts, both positive and negative, include the following:

* Many Arctic people seeking economic security perceive tourism as a positive means for improving economic stability. From their perspective, reliance on predictably arriving tourists offers a more stable economic outlook than exhausting finite natural resources to meet the boom and bust needs of world markets.
* Arctic communities generally appreciate the economic benefits resulting specifically from the angling, hunting,

and nature tourism market because most tourist expenditures remain in the community. Tourists employ local guides, pilots, charter boat captains and crews, outfitters, and suppliers. They use local transport, stay in local accommodations, and eat in local establishments.

* Culture and heritage tourism provides critical support for language preservation, the practice of traditional ceremonies, and the perpetuation of ancient customs and art forms. The presence of appropriate and effective interpretation and education methodologies will dramatically impact effectiveness. Additionally, this form of tourism creates a market for art and other native manufactures and services.

* The cost of building, operating, and maintaining tourism infrastructure is a huge economic burden for Arctic communities and governments. Support facilities and services of all types are built and maintained to serve relatively large numbers of persons that exceed the resident population. Transport facilities, law enforcement, medical services, other emergency services, water and waste water utilities, and waste collection and disposal incur capital and operating costs, require advanced work force skills, spare parts, and need specialized supplies in order to sustain there functions. Tourism normally occurs for a few months of the year, but the infrastructure must be maintained under adverse conditions for the entire year.

* The economic and human costs of providing emergency services deserve special attention. Highly trained personnel, many of whom are volunteers, risk their lives in search and rescue operations. Expensive transport and medical equipment and supplies are required to evacuate victims and treat their injuries. Law enforcement resources must respond to large populations visiting their communities and need specialized equipment to patrol back country regions. Fire suppression service faces similar challenges.

* The cost of responding to environmental hazards is included in the budgets of all Arctic nations, but may not be sufficient. Oil spill containment and recovery, hazardous materials handling and storage, and hazardous waste disposal all represent substantial costs. Adequate funds and the availability of specialized equipment, trained personnel, and essential supplies may or may not be sufficient to respond to events.

* Finally, the question of who benefits economically from large-scale Arctic tourism is a very sensitive issue. Many of the transport, tour and hotel corporations conducting tourism in the Arctic are head quartered outside the region. Consequently, much of the money paid by polar tourists to those nonresident corporations escapes the Arctic people.

The continent of Antarctica derives absolutely no economic benefits from tourism, but can suffer environmental and heritage resource costs. Unlike most parts of the world, there are no indigenous people to benefit from tourism in Antarctica and thus tourism is not an alternative to local unsustainable economics activities. This blunt fact is a serious consideration for anyone motivated to propose tourism management practices on the southern continent. There is no continuous stream of money devoted to tourism management, environmental monitoring, emergency services, waste collection and disposal, the design and implementation of risk minimization or mitigation programmes, or any other "best practices" normally associated with reasonably managed tourism. Specifically:

* Aside from the fees collected by the Antarctic Historic Places Trust to maintain heroic era huts in the Ross Sea region, no revenues or fees of any sort are collected from either tour operators or the tourists themselves for the management of Antarctica's environmental resources. Some scientific stations and heritage sites generate revenues from the sale of souvenirs, but these are neither

dedicated to resource management nor sufficient to support tourism management programmes.

* As with all who travel to Antarctica, costs are incurred by tour operators for the preparation of environmental impact assessments required by the Protocol on Environmental Protection to the Antarctic Treaty. Scientific stations incur costs for the assistance they provide in emergency situations such as search and rescue or medical support. The true costs of emergency response include not only direct expenses for personnel and equipment, but the risk to additional lives and distraction from scientific missions.
* To the credit of many tourists who learn about Antarctica's economic dilemma, generous personal donations have been given in support of environmental research and heritage preservation projects in Antarctica and the sub-polar islands.

Social Impacts

There are serious concerns regarding the negative impacts of a growing tourism industry to the people in the Arctic world. Social norms, values and unique ways of life are all subjected to impacts from polar tourism. Tourism impacts affecting polar communities and their people are presented below.

* The most obvious social impacts result from the number of visitors that temporarily overwhelm the social norms of some Arctic communities during tourist season. Community institutions such as educational, religious, and civic organizations often experience altered roles and functions when the tourists are in town. Based on the attitude of the community, this may or may not be a major disruption, but large numbers of tourists relative to local populations always exerts a dominant presence.
* Social impacts of Arctic tourism can be mitigated by the terms and conditions of collaborative agreements between the tour operators and the local community. In some instances, tax revenues and special fees can offset

local costs. When tourist seasons are expanded there are greater economies of scale and efficiencies result from the extended use of infrastructure and longer duration of employment and income benefits.

Cultural Impacts

The Arctic environment is not merely a setting in which a rich diversity of Native People live, but rather it encompasses the essential resources upon which the lives and culture depend. Consequently, any events that endanger those resources place Native People at grave risk. By their own declarations the most severe threat facing Native People is climate change. The loss of Arctic sea ice with its attendant effects on wildiife habitat, numbers, and migratory behaviour; the transport routes needed to subsist; the duration of seasons; and the condition of fisheries are of critical importance to the cultural and economic wellbeing of Arctic people. According to a statement by Sheila Watt-Cloutier, former International Chair, Inuit Circumpolar Conference:

"What is at stake here is not just the extinction of animals but the extinction of Inuit as a hunting culture. Climate change in the Arctic is a human issue, a family issue, a community issue, and an issue of cultural survival."

The cultural impacts described below must be evaluated from that perspective.

* Large numbers of tourists can produce significant cultural resource impacts. They further stress increasingly scarce natural resources and that results in a variety of pressures on indigenous subsistence practices and value systems.
* Ironically, as traditional indigenous lifestyles succumb to change resulting from climate change, there will be fewer opportunities for tourists to support authentic cultural traditions. This will affect Arctic culture and economies.
* In addition to their numbers, the introduction of technologies and tourist service amenities can impact

Native People's desires to maintain traditional lifestyles.

* Intrusive, inappropriate visitor behaviour violates traditional customs. Tours that do not include educational practices can generate conflicts that damage both Native People's quality of life and the tourist experience. When that happens, both parties lose.
* In summary, the ways in which Arctic communities allow their natural and cultural resources to be used affects the character of those communities. As Arctic communities continue to achieve self determination, they will increasingly decide how their natural and cultural resources will be utilized and this will ultimately determine how those resources are managed. Arctic communities and Native People must determine how tourism will, or will not, occur and how natural and cultural resources should be used and safeguarded. They can be aided by good management practices that are relevant to their objectives. But the final decisions regarding natural and cultural resource uses must be made locally. Any other solution would be yet another example of intrusion from the "outside".

The Outlook for Polar Tourism: Reduced "Barriers to Entry"

Polar tourism expands because of a continuous reduction of what economists call "barriers to entry". The concept suggests that the extent to which these barriers are increased, reduced, altered, or eliminated directly controls the amount, geographic distribution, seasonal duration, and types of tourism likely to occur. Since its inception, the most difficult barriers confronting polar travel include difficulty of access, environmental conditions (both real and perceived), cost of travel, time to travel, and jurisdictional restraints. Both human-induced and natural events are making the Polar Regions increasingly accessible. Vastly improved geographic and hydrographic knowledge; advancements in transport and navigational technologies; more comfortable clothing; more durable recreational equipment;

significant reductions in the amount, extent and duration of sea ice; and a relatively more tolerable climate are all contributing to growing access to the Polar Regions. The cumulative impacts of these events are larger numbers of polar tourists spending more time in more locations.

Conclusion

Polar tourism was slow to start, but is now a popular and rapidly-growing industry that is expanding in terms of tourists, tour operators, diverse recreational pursuits, geographic scope, and seasons of use. Arctic economies have seen it evolve from an incidental activity to a vital sector upon which they increasingly rely. This has been particularly true for newly enfranchised indigenous people of the Arctic seeking self-sufficiency, and for gateway cities in the southern hemisphere eager to realize the economic benefits of Antarctic tourism.

Sustainable Tourism in the Polar Regions: Setting an Agenda

The conservation and sustainable management of polar environments and cultures including by means of good tourism practices will require both mutually accepted goals and a solid commitment to implement appropriate management techniques. Fortunately, the first of those tasks has been carefully deliberated by the international community. As previously stated, the United Nations Environment Programme and the United Nations World Tourism Organization engaged diverse stakeholders from around the world to establish 12 sustainability principles that are fully listed below. When summarized, those principles identify goals essential for achieving sustainable tourism. Again, those goals are:

* Conserving environmental quality.
* Preserving cultural and social values by means of participatory decision-making.
* Creating sustainable economies.
* Ensuring positive visitor behaviour, safety, and enjoyment.

Though relatively new, polar tourism is old enough to have established recognizable patterns of procedure, and mature enough-even in its newest venue Antarctica-to have accumulated extensive management experiences. Well documented knowledge of tourism management techniques, resource conservation programmes, industry practices, jurisdictional responses, economic strategies, and community opinions and expectations currently exist to provide the basis for sustainable polar tourism policies and practices.

Simultaneously, while tourism's presence is growing numerically and spatially, the polar environment itself is experiencing significant change. This section describes tourism management conditions, issues and techniques that are relevant to sustaining the environmental and cultural integrity of the Polar Regions. This information is further reinforced by examples of good polar management practices presented in the final section of this publication.

Management Conditions: Wilderness

Polar tourism most frequently occurs in immense wilderness regions, either de-facto or officially designated, and these vast areas are exceedingly difficult to manage. The Polar Regions contain the world's largest expanses of wilderness-places where human presence and development are virtually absent or not readily apparent. The continent of Antarctica is entirely a wilderness land mass. North America's and Eurasia's largest wilderness regions are located in the Arctic. Fully reliable sets of marine charts and hydrographic information for the Southern and Arctic oceans are not yet available.

These enormous wilderness areas and relatively unknown marine regions provide permanent habitat for highly adapted indigenous wildlife and seasonal habitat for immense populations of migratory wildlife. Arctic wilderness is the homeland of diverse Native Peoples who have practiced cultural traditions for millennia. The Antarctic contains important artifacts of the history of exploration and scientific discovery. Wilderness regions also possess highly esteemed scientific, inspirational and conservation values. For most of their existence these polar resources and values were protected by their remoteness and climatic conditions. Again, wilderness regions present unique management challenges. Comprehensive inventories of their natural and cultural resources are time-consuming and expensive to obtain. A competent knowledge of their dynamic ecological systems requires long-term investigations that are equally complicated and costly to accomplish. Establishing mutually acceptable methods to facilitate stakeholder participation in wilderness planning and management are difficult to implement, and frequently contentious.

Management Issues

Scarce Management Resources

The absence of development may be essential for sustaining the integrity of wilderness values, but it is also a huge obstacle in the performance of environmental and tourism management. The Arctic's scarce infrastructure in terms of transportation systems, number of trained personnel, and service facilities are severe constraints on managing the impacts of tourism. Operational functions essential for meeting the demands of large numbers of tourists, such as resource conservation, resource monitoring, scientific research, security patrolling, visitor safety, waste collection and disposal, and emergency response capabilities are all affected by the scarcity of infrastructure.

In the Antarctic the situation is even worse. Unlike the Arctic, there are no resources located on the continent specifically dedicated to supporting tourism's expanding presence and growing access. International policy strongly advocates environmental conservation of the entire continent, but the fact remains that because the Antarctic Treaty System cannot tax, there is no money to support on site management. Consequently, there are neither land nor marine Antarctic-based resources dedicated to the management of tourism activities. The Protocol on Environmental Protection to the Antarctic Treaty requires environmental impact assessments of tour operations. Although the inspection regime established under article 14 of the Madrid Protocol could also apply to tourism activities, there are no adequate international monitors to ensure compliance with assessment requirements or that proposed mitigation measures are implemented.

Both Arctic resource managers and Antarctic tour operators are keenly aware of these constraints and have adapted to them. Specialized wilderness management techniques affecting the number and distribution of tourists; educational programmes to promote appropriate behaviour; and self-reliant practices extending from waste collection to the provision of emergency services have been implemented. Valuable information regarding their effectiveness may be found in the wilderness recreation management studies published during the past 40 years.

Environmental Management Issues – Who did what?

Polar tourism must be conducted in a responsible manner and tourism management techniques are often suggested for conserving the polar environment. One of the supreme difficulties for accomplishing this objective is to accurately determine the environmental cause and effect and then manage tourism accordingly. In other words, when an environmental condition changes, the question becomes whether it was caused by a natural event, by tourism activity, or by some combination of both? The capacity to accurately monitor tourism, revise tourism management plans, alter visitor activities and behaviour, and implement appropriate environmental conservation measures depends on the answers to those questions. Realistically, the ability to assess and manage tourism impacts in the Polar Regions is vitally dependent on a competent understanding of those relationships.

Environmental cause and effect relationships affecting the Polar Regions also result from events occurring well beyond the high latitudes. Wildlife populations that seasonally migrate to the Polar Regions from other regions of the world are impacted by changing oceanographic conditions, environmental pollution, hunting and fishing pressures, and habitat transformations that are well beyond the jurisdictional boundaries of polar resource agencies. The cumulative impacts of these complex environmental changes are a colossal challenge to comprehend, much less competently manage. When polar tourism is mixed with this collection of dynamic, naturally occurring events, reliable understanding of those interdependency is further complicated.

Cultural Management Issues

Numerous cultural traditions pervade the Arctic, many of them derived from centuries of habitation by indigenous people. Others are the culmination of settlement patterns, resource uses, economic systems, and social customs evolved from empire building and the desires of sovereign nations. These very complex heritage and cultural traditions of Arctic societies are simultaneously tourist attractions and sensitive management issues. In Antarctica defining the 'allowable and acceptable' visitor uses of heritage sites and resources is a particularly difficult task. Internationally significant heritage resources associated with polar discovery, scientific inquiry, historical economic development, and human settlement are located throughout the southern polar region.

The abandonment of those sites, the absence of a permanent population to perform conservation, and severe weather has resulted in deterioration. Resource management issues at these sites include environmental remediation, heritage conservation, visitor safety, and the creation of interpretive services that simultaneously preserve the story of these places and enlist the respect of their visitors. These are daunting tasks given the absence of resources dedicated to these purposes.

The sub-polar islands in the southern hemisphere possess sovereignty status and the authority to implement heritage conservation programmes. Many resource conservation activities have taken place, but the scarcity of financial resources and the remoteness of the sites are ever-present impediments to this effort (UNEP-WCMC, 2006,a,b,c).

Managing Tourist Behaviour and Numbers

The history of tourism proves that increased access inevitably leads to increased numbers. This is a serious management concern. In fact, improved access causes various numbers to increase, e.g., number of sites visited, extended use of seasons, greater duration of stay, types of recreational activities pursued, additional support staff required, and more services needed. The results are an increased exposure of environmental resources to additional risks, the economic dependencies of local communities on tourism, threats to privacy, more cultural contacts, and growing demands on infrastructure.

An enduring criticism of tourism is tourist behaviour. Since its inception, tourists have been universally criticized for "inappropriate" behaviour and cultural insensitivities. When tourist behaviour results in resource damage, then condemnations and tough responses are well deserved. On other occasions, criticisms of visitor behaviour more accurately reflect opinion rather than proof of harm. In all instances, efforts are required to hold both the tourist and the tourism industry accountable.

From the tourist's viewpoint, the issue of numbers equates to perceptions of congestion, and this directly affects the quality of their tourism experience. The tourist's perception of congestion in the Polar Regions is an especially critical issue because these locations are strongly promoted as wilderness.

International Policy Issues

Polar climate and associated ecological changes are fueling international discussions concerning foreign policy. For tourism management, the resolution of those issues will be critical. Decisions regarding sovereign powers and jurisdictional boundaries determine the terms and conditions for allowable uses of Arctic resources. Alteration of wildlife, fishery and marine mammal treaty obligations, management practices and jurisdictional boundaries will directly impact tourism activities such as wildlife viewing, nature tours, angling, and hunting.

Arctic Governance Issues

The wilderness management dilemma faced by Arctic governments is to determine when, where, and how people should be allowed to use areas without destroying the natural character. In other words, what human activity should be permitted in an area universally defined as having no human presence? Governments throughout the world have responded to this challenge in a variety of ways. Management techniques range from strict restrictions of public access to participatory approaches that combine resource inventories, environmental assessments, and public involvement to define allowable uses. The most severe restrictions seek to achieve preservation by preventing human entry. The goal of the more collaborative approaches is to identify allowable uses based on science and citizen input and then test the effectiveness of those decisions by means of careful resource monitoring.

Enormous expanses of the Arctic are governed by the customs and traditional laws established and enforced by Native Communities. The Inuit in Canada, Greenland, and Eastern Russia, the Saami in Scandinavia, and diverse Native Peoples in both Russia and Alaska exercise combinations of traditions and sovereignty to determine the allowable recreational use of their land and water. These customs and the terms and conditions expressed in their management approaches offer valuable experiences that can be replicated in other parts of the Polar Regions.

Finally, it is acknowledged that politics and the competition for budgets are perpetual management issues affecting the governance of Arctic tourism. Officials responsible for wilderness recreation management realize that success in the political and budget arenas depends on providing quality tourism experiences to the public and economic benefits to local communities. They must demonstrate that the fees they collect from recreation activities and associated economic benefits to local communities justify their budgetary requests. Recreation managers have navigated this difficult course for a long time, and make considerable efforts to demonstrate that recreation participation is strong and growing.

Human activities in Antarctica are primarily regulated by the complex of multilateral agreements of the Antarctic Treaty System, in particular the Antarctic Treaty itself and its Madrid Protocol on Environmental Protection. The Antarctic Treaty was adopted on 1 December 1959. Its primary purpose is to ensure, in the interest of all mankind, that Antarctica shall continue forever to be used exclusively for peaceful purposes and shall not become the scene or object of international discord. The Treaty provides for freedom of scientific investigation and promotes international cooperation in scientific research. It also prohibits any nuclear explosions and the disposal of radioactive waste material in Antarctica. In order to further the protection of the Antarctic environment, a Protocol to the Antarctic Treaty on Environmental Protection was adopted in 1991.

The main purpose of the Protocol is to provide for the comprehensive protection of the Antarctic environment and dependent and associated ecosystems. The Protocol designates Antarctica as a natural reserve, devoted to peace and science; prohibits mineral resource activities other than scientific research; and sets principles and measures for the planning and conduct of all activities in the Antarctic Treaty area. Guidelines have been developed under this protocol to provide a framework for regulation of the potential negative impacts of tourism in the Antarctic. As tourist activities on the continent continue to grow the ATS is intensifying its focus on these issues.

Management Techniques

The UNEP and UNWTO have established 12 principles essential for accomplishing sustainable tourism. These principles represent guidelines for establishing and evaluating effective tourism management techniques. "The twelve aims for an agenda for sustainable tourism" are presented below and comprehensively discussed in the UNEP/UNWTO publication entitled Making Tourism More Sustainable A Guide for Policy Makers.

1. *Economic Viability:* To ensure the viability and competitiveness of tourism destinations and enterprises, so that they are able to continue to prosper and deliver benefits in the long term.
2. *Local Prosperity:* To maximize the contribution of tourism to the economic prosperity of the host destination, including the proportion of visitor spending that is retained locally.

3. *Employment Quality:* To strengthen the number and quality of local jobs created and supported by tourism, including the level of pay, conditions of service and availability to all without discrimination by gender, race, disability or in other ways.
4. *Social Equity:* To seek a widespread and fair distribution of economic and social benefits from tourism throughout the recipient community, including improving opportunities, income and services available to the poor.
5. *Visitor Fulfilment:* To provide a safe, satisfying and fulfilling experience for visitors, available to all without discrimination by gender, race, disability or in other ways.
6. *Local Control:* To engage and empower local communities in planning and decision making about the management and future development of tourism in their area, in consultation with other stakeholders.
7. *Community Wellbeing:* To maintain and strengthen the quality of life in local communities, including social structures and access to resources, amenities and life support systems, avoiding any form of social degradation or exploitation.
8. *Cultural Richness:* To respect and enhance the historic heritage, authentic culture, traditions and distinctiveness of host communities.
9. *Physical Integrity:* To maintain and enhance the quality of landscapes, both urban and rural, and avoid the physical and visual degradation of the environment.
10. *Biological Diversity:* To support the conservation of natural areas, habitats and wildlife, and minimize damage to them.
11. *Resource Efficiency:* To minimize the use of scarce and non-renewable resources in the development and operation of tourism facilities and services.
12. *Environmental Purity:* To minimize the pollution of air, water and land and the generation of waste by tourism enterprises and visitors.

As stated in the UNEP/UNWTO publication: "The order in which these twelve aims are listed does not imply any order of priority. Each one is equally important." While all of these principles cannot be applied in the Antarctic and some Arctic regions (because of the absence of indigenous population and the non existence of local economies), they provide a solid basis of management objectives and evaluative criteria for creating, implementing and evaluating sustainable polar tourism. Each principle also contains key words and phrases that identify factors that can be monitored to evaluate the effectiveness, equity and efficiency of those plans, strategies and techniques. Notably, the principles include factors that address both the quantity and quality aspects of the host region and the tourism experience. Given the diverse conditions found throughout the Polar Regions, the principles must be adapted to fit special circumstances.

The remainder of this section outlines tourism management techniques that have been effectively used in the Polar Regions. They are relevant to polar conditions and to the several distinct tourism markets operating in those regions.

Recreation Management in the Arctic Wilderness

As outlined in Section 3, the polar tourism market is now a highly diversified industry that attracts people to many wilderness recreation activities. Nature tourism, wildlife viewing, sport fishing, hunting, and wilderness adventures of all types are actively pursued throughout all regions of the Arctic. In response to these recreation demands, Arctic resource managers have established numerous, specialized techniques to safeguard both the environment and the tourist. These techniques have an extensive history of addressing the Arctic's environmental conservation issues and the opportunity exists to expand their use in the Arctic.

Wilderness recreation approaches used in the Arctic are normally an integral part of comprehensive wilderness resource plans. Responsible stewardship, defined as the conservation of its natural and cultural resources, requires the selection of objectives that define the appropriate and allowable uses of those resources and the establishment of management techniques that protect those resources from loss or damage. In the Arctic, as elsewhere, the primary wilderness management objective associated with tourism is to protect both polar resources and tourists from harm. This approach to wilderness management is employed by all Arctic nations.

Wilderness management plans and the recreation management techniques they endorse are the result of substantial stakeholder involvement. Government agencies responsible for resource management of protected areas seek advice from a variety of stakeholders. Participatory processes and competing interests vary among jurisdictions, but the issue of allowable tourism is always part of these lively discussions. Significantly, polar tourism is only one of many competing resource uses confronting Arctic wilderness managers as they attempt to reconcile economic development interests with the protection of wilderness values. A wealth of tourism management experience can be obtained from the public records that document those decision making processes.

The techniques described below are utilized by wilderness agencies to manage both the independent back country traveller and small groups pursuing recreation activities. The techniques are designed to optimize scarce management resources and, to a considerable extent, hold tourists personally responsible for their own safety. They also respond to the need to manage both general, short term use of wilderness resources and recreation activities requiring special expertise and the use of specific locations. They are especially applicable to three distinct polar tourism market groups: (1) the nature and Ecotourism market; (2) the sport fishing and hunting market; and (3) the adventure market.

Controlling and Monitoring Back country Use

Arctic wilderness managers implement land and water resource management plans that designate specific recreation entry points. These gateways to diverse wilderness experiences may be trail heads, information kiosks, interpretive centres, ranger stations, boat ramps, hunting zones, fishing sites, or kayak put-in sites. The primary purpose of these widely publicized locations is to intercept the tourist before they venture into the wilderness. When this "capture technique" is successful, managers can dispense vital information while simultaneously learning when, where, and how people are travelling through wilderness lands and waters.

This technique requires agencies to designate allowable recreation uses in specific locations and relies on tourists to let them know exactly how and when those resources are being used. Managers then monitor recreation activity locations to determine if current recreational use should be continued, modified or prohibited. Elements of this approach include:

* Before departure the tourists are advised to read all pertinent regulations, obtain maps, essential supplies and equipment, and relevant guide books.
* Given a scarcity of agency personnel or lack of funds for visitor centres, wilderness recreation information is often provided at entry kiosks, or by means of signage. Obviously, selecting the foreign languages to be used will directly impact the effectiveness of this information.
* Back country travellers are requested to identify their route and mode of travel. This is generally done by means of registrations at trailheads and boat launch sites. Identification of their intermediate camp sites and destinations is accomplished by back country permit registrations. Known hazards are identified and they are advised that their personal safety, including clothing and equipment, is their personal responsibility.
* In locations where search and rescue services are available, emergency instructions, such as communication frequencies and weather radio broadcasts, are provided with the assumption that the tourist has compatible communication equipment. Persons travelling by boat or kayak are required to possess proper vessel licenses and to have marine charts, tide tables, and adequate safety and navigational equipment on board. But there are rarely coast guard vessels to conduct inspections.

* Management objectives are enforced by periodic patrolling by authorized resource agency personnel. Patrolling is accomplished from strategically located fixed or seasonal bases. Patrols may be conducted by boat, aircraft and various modes of land travel. The availability and frequency of these enforcement resources is affected by financial and personnel resources, the ruggedness of the terrain, and weather conditions.
* Search and rescue and emergency response capabilities vary widely in the Arctic's wilderness areas. Their availability is generally dependent on agency resources, proximity to communities, terrain conditions, and the severity of the weather. For all remote Arctic settlements, the commitment by volunteers to perform these functions is vital.
* Resource monitoring is conducted by resource agency personnel or designated persons with special skills. The frequency and rigor of these monitoring and evaluation endeavors are dependent on the budgetary and personnel resources of the lead agency and support received from NGO's dedicated to support the agency's resource conservation mission. Arctic NGO's play a vital role in this regard. Their commitment of volunteer personnel, fund raising, public awareness, and political advocacy provide invaluable contributions to the conservation of Arctic resources. Therefore, it is well justified to ask polar tourists to become active supporters of such organizations.

These management techniques have been used by Arctic resource agencies in national parks for more than a century. National governance of Arctic wildlife refuges, forest reserves, and UNESCO World Heritage and Biosphere sites rounds out a list of prominent environmental settings offering important sustainability experiences. Site management practices, participatory decision making processes, partnerships with stakeholders, and commitment to international resource conservation agreements are all embodied in the roles and responsibilities of these resource agencies.

Licensed Guides and Special Use Permits

One of the most successful management techniques for conserving Arctic resources and directly influencing lawful visitor behaviour is guide licensing. Wildlife managers realized long ago that an effective way to insure regulatory compliance was to require anglers and hunters to employ licensed guides. Guide licensing programmes have been established by wildlife management agencies in all Arctic nations. The programmes instruct specialized knowledge of environmental conditions, resource laws and regulations, survival skills, and emergency response skills. Guide licenses are issued based on demonstrated competency of that knowledge and skills. In most jurisdictions refresher courses are required to sustain both educational knowledge and practical skills.

Guide licensing in the Arctic has expanded well beyond angling and hunting. The pursuit of Arctic recreation activities such as mountaineering, rafting, kayaking, and wildlife photography frequently require licensed guides with the special skills required to safely conduct those activities. Licensing requirements vary considerably among Arctic jurisdictions and responsible resource agencies, but fundamental requirements required by all include: proven knowledge of specific locations, technical skills, safe and efficient recreation delivery systems, waste removal, emergency response systems, and detailed reporting of activities and observations. This skill and knowledge takes time to acquire, thus Arctic jurisdictions established a process that evolves from apprenticeship to master status.

States exercising jurisdiction in the Arctic hold guides directly responsible for both resource protection and visitor safety. Critical management issues concerning liability for resource damage and human harm are explicitly addressed by a combination of license requirements that include adequate insurance coverage, bonding, and indemnification. Based on the huge risks they are legally required to accept, guides very diligently monitor the behaviour of their clients. Guides accept the professional and financial risks of their profession for the privilege of pursuing a unique way of life.

They generally spend a considerable amount of time teaching their clients appropriate behaviour, and respond quickly to instances when clients willfully disregard this information. Guide licensing regulations not only have beneficial affects on tourist behaviour, but on tourist numbers also. Legal prescriptions effectively limit tourist access by requiring they be accompanied by a licensed guide. Numbers are controlled by means of guide to visitor ratios, length of season, and sometimes duration of stay at a particular location. All of these methods strictly control the maximum number of people that may be on site. These requirements may be further specified in special use permits used to govern recreation activities. By example, the terms and conditions of river rafting, mountaineering, and wildlife viewing expeditions can be defined by special use permits.

Arctic guide licensing and the issuance of special use permits have proven to be effective polar tourism management techniques. They are an integral part of resource conservation programmes, such as wildlife management; they directly affect appropriate visitor behaviour and numbers; and the reports filed by guides provide vital resource monitoring information that would otherwise be unavailable. This approach to sustainable tourism has also established mutually beneficial partnerships between local communities and resource agencies. Native People and local residents who depend on polar resources for their cultural and economic wellbeing often serve as guides or possess special use permits to conduct recreation activities.

They are the strongest advocates of sustainable management of polar resources, and as guides, they provide a direct method for accomplishing wise stewardship. The application of a guide licensing programme to Antarctica deserves serious consideration. To date, Antarctic tourism has been conducted by knowledgeable persons who often have distinguished records of scientific service in Antarctica, but no formal training in the skills and techniques of guiding. As the number of Antarctic tourists increase there will be a corresponding need to supply more qualified guides. Proficiency in variety of skills including subject expertise, knowledge of the landing sites, emergency response and communication skills, and tourist management should constitute the basic requirements of the Antarctic guide.

These skills would help protect Antarctic resources; enhance the safety of the tourism experience; and advance the development of universal operational and communication protocols needed to respond to emergencies. For ship-based tourism, in particular, an education programme in polar tourism for guides should be considered. Cruise companies interested in high quality educational skills of their guides may support such an initiative and could request a certificate for their guides. Cooperation with environmental organizations in this field could lead to increasing benefits for conservation through advanced education.

The Special Case of Adventure Tourism the Arctic

Significant management challenges confront those responsible for accommodating the adventure tourism market. Principally, it is nearly impossible for Arctic recreation resource managers and licensed guides to competently know if the skill levels, health and psychological preparation of the participant are sufficient to meet the rigors of their sports.

Inspection of equipment should be conducted, but managers, guides and operators rarely have that opportunity, and usually do not have spare parts and repair facilities to correct deficiencies. Maps, marine charts, tide tables can be supplied and it is hoped that adventurers will responsibly seek these essential aids to navigation. Emergency communication instructions in the form of emergency radio frequencies, protocols, directional beacons, and Standard Operating Procedures for search and rescue (if available) can also be provided. Again, it is essential for the adventurer to avail themselves of these in order to safely pursue their activities.

The Antarctic

For several decades Antarctica has attracted increasing numbers of adventure tourists. These activities range from relatively traditional outdoor sports to extreme events. More traditional pursuits have included mountaineering expeditions and numerous cross country skiing challenges. The more extreme sports include sky diving at the South Pole and scuba diving. A comprehensive discussion of this market and its management implications are found in Lamers, Stel, Amelung 2007.

Cultural Resource Management

The Arctic

A fundamental Arctic tourism management goal is to achieve balance between the public, commercial display of cultural features and the preservation of cultural integrity. Each culture has its own tolerance level for visitation and sharing its resources. Individual Arctic societies define acceptable visitor behaviour in terms of the types, magnitude, geographic location, and seasons of resource use. Consequently, cultural tourism management in the Arctic is subject to a set of 'host conditions' in which cultural preservation, economic necessity, and scarce natural resources are continuously debated. The conservation of ancestral homelands, scarce resources, and vulnerability to irreversible change are all significant tourism management issues facing Arctic indigenous societies.

From approximately the mid-1970s to the present, Native People have implemented a variety of policies, programmes, and techniques designed to uniquely reflect their approach to cultural tourism. In many instances these approaches are an affirmation of self-rule. When Alaskan Native Corporations and Villages were established they were empowered and capitalized to create economic development programmes. Several organizations pursued very conventional tourism development, such as hotels and similar commercial attractions, others instituted heritage tour programmes that represented their cultures. In the Canadian Arctic, the Inuit attained governance of Nunavut, a territory spanning one fifth of Canada's entire land mass. Nunavut has pursued various forms of tourism development during the past 25 years in response to this opportunity.

Attainment of Homeland Rule by the Inuit of Greenland in 1979 resulted in the initiation of a very aggressive tourism development programme that includes ambitious commercial activity in Nuuk and diverse venues in rural areas. The Saami throughout Norway, Sweden and Finland are especially active in designing, funding, and operating numerous types of tourism venues that reflect the diversity of their cultures. And the most recent entrant to the Arctic cultural tourism market is Russia's Association of Indigenous People of the North (RAIPON), established in 1990 to accomplish many goals, one of which is tourism development.

As with other forms of tourism management, there is a substantial history of cultural tourism experience in the Arctic. The lessons learned, both good and bad, provide valuable guidance for those seeking to either establish or modify cultural tourism programmes. But the foremost lesson is that Native People and their governments must be vitally involved in decisions regarding how their culture and resources are shared with others.

The Antarctic

Antarctic heritage sites are popular attractions because of their historical significance and because of family and cultural ties to the pioneering settlers who once worked there. Management responses to these demands for visitation have ranged from prohibited entry to cordial invitations. For example, despite the popularity of Sir Ernest Shackleton's exploits, tourist access is denied to Stromness, South Georgia because of environmental protection concerns, while visitor access to Grytviken, where 'the Boss' is traditionally toasted at his graveside, is encouraged. Antarctic heritage sites in the Ross Sea are permitted with strict, but hospitable controls, and the refurbished 1940s research station at Port Lockroy, in the Antarctic Peninsula Region, actively promotes tourism to share its colorful heritage and to commercially support its postal concession.

Managing the Mass Market

The Arctic

The Arctic's tourism management opportunities and constraints are obviously well known to its people, governments, conservation organizations, and the tour companies that operate there. In response to a strong desire to influence the growth and development of polar tourism, a meeting of affected stakeholders was facilitated in 1995 by the World Wildlife Fund Arctic International Programme (WWF Arctic, 1996). The result of that collaborative effort was the publication in 1996 of Linking Tourism and Conservation in the Arctic which contains ten principles for Arctic tourism and associated codes of conduct for both tour operators and tourists.

The participatory process and its product, as described by WWF Arctic, involved: "Representatives from local communities, governments, different sectors of the tourism industry, conservation organizations and scientific institutions used their experience to create these guidelines for arctic tourism. The principles were also adopted into Codes of Conduct for tourism business and tourists which contain more specific information on what to consider when doing business or travelling in the Arctic."

The Arctic's consensus-based Principles and Codes of Conduct offer a responsible approach to polar tourism management. The ten principles contain an appropriate collection of resource conservation goals, the essential starting point for resource management. Environmental conservation, cultural integrity, economic benefits, visitor safety, and respect for polar resources are comprehensively included in the Principles for Arctic Tourism. The principles are to be realized by two ten point Codes of Conduct for Tour Operators and Tourists in the Arctic, respectively. The direct relationships between the conservation goals and tourism practices by both operators and tourists are clearly described and represent the strength of this approach. The Principles and Codes are implemented by means of a comprehensive advocacy programme. Stakeholders collectively promote the Principles and Codes through information dissemination, consumer education, and personnel training. To date, they have been diligent in their efforts. The Principles and Codes are described in further detail in the Good Practices section of this publication.

The Antarctic

The first tourism-specific regulations were adopted by the Antarctic Treaty as early as 1966 with the emergence of commercial tourism activities. These regulations were setting rules for visits by tourist groups to Antarctic stations maintained by the Parties. In 1975 a Statement of Accepted Practices was adopted. This was modified and expanded several times and resulted in the Tourism Guidelines adopted in 1994 by the Parties to the Antarctic Treaty. Aside from establishing guidelines for tourist expeditions, the Parties to the Antarctic Treaty also require tourist expeditions to submit reports on their visits.

On August 2005 the UN Secretary General reported on the UN General Assembly on the "question of the Antarctica". The report recognizes that "Antarctic tourism activities are increasing, as is their diversity (camping, climbing, kayaking and scuba-diving), presenting new management challenges". As a first step towards a more rigorous control of tourism activities, the Antarctic Treaty Consultative Meetings (ATCMs) adopted two resolutions to enhance information exchange and consultation and to further the development and implementation of site-specific guidelines.

However, according to the Secretary General report, "no consensus has yet been reached on critical issues, such as land-based and high-risk (adventure) tourism, leaving tourism to be regulated to a large extent by the industry itself". The annual Antarctic Treaty Consultative Meetings (ATCMs) have been discussing tourism and tourism regulation in details since 2001. The Antarctic Treaty parties have adopted guidelines for visitors to the Antarctic. These guidelines are intended to ensure that wildlife and vegetation are not disturbed, protected areas and research programmes are respected, and activities are conducted with a high regard for safety. Guidelines for operators request that they provide advance notification of their activities, confirm visits to scientific stations, ensure that their passengers are properly supervised and report on their expeditions.

The requirements of the Madrid Protocol and other components of the Antarctic Treaty System are implemented by each Treaty party in its own laws, according to its legal system. Visitors to the Antarctic should ensure that they are familiar with the legal requirements that apply to them-for example, the applicable laws may be those of the country where the expedition is being planned, or the country from which the expedition departs. The most important legal requirements relate to prior environmental assessment of the proposed activities, prohibition on taking or harming flora and fauna, waste disposal, contingency planning and the need for permits if visits to protected areas are contemplated.

Complimentary to the regulatory framework created by the Antarctic Treaty System, one on-site management technique currently available for conserving the resources of the entire continent is self regulation of tourist operations and behaviour. The International Association of Antarctic Tour Operators was founded by seven private tour operators in 1991 and, as of 2007, had grown to include 80 members from 14 countries. The majority of tourist ships to Antarctica are members of the Association and some yacht operators are joining them. The members of IAATO endeavored to comply with Recommendation XVIII-I: Guidance for Visitors to the Antarctic by creating visitor guidelines that addressed the environmental protection of landing sites, the safety of the guests, and the establishment of operational protocols to provide emergency assistance. Both guests and all tour operator personnel receive these instructions.

As the UN Secretary-General's Report to the GA in 2005 on the Question of Antarctica states, "since the Twenty-fifth Antarctic Treaty Consultative Meeting, the IAATO has continued to focus its activities on increasing cooperation and field coordination among its members; promoting effective environmental impact assessments; preventing the introduction of alien organisms; promoting self-sufficiency and proper conduct among visitors; developing emergency response and contingency plans; and promoting specific guidelines for sites where the growing bulk of tourism occurs".

The self-regulated approach to tourism management in Antarctica, developed in accordance with the existing regulatory framework, currently depends on the following premises: (1) the tourist industry instructs their clients about appropriate behaviour and does not alienate them; (2) voluntary coordination among cruise and tour directors is the only means of managing site visits; and (3) responses to emergency situations are completely dependent on voluntary efforts and the skills of those who, fortuitously, are willing to respond. To date this approach has been effective, but the inherent environmental conditions of Antarctica, its remoteness, and, most importantly, the growing number of tourists will test the sustainability of this approach. As passenger numbers increase, there is a need for increased vigilance at some of the sites. Towards this end, the indicators proposed by UNWTO for the assessment of the sustainability of tourism in Antarctica provide a good base for a monitoring programme.

Conclusion

Key elements of an agenda for sustainable tourism development in Polar Regions have been developed through the efforts of a combination of governments, intergovernmental bodies, NGOs, business initiatives. They are:

* The 12 principles for sustainable tourism development that have been endorsed by UNEP/UNWTO. While all of these principles cannot be applied in the Antarctic and some Arctic regions (because of the absence of indigenous population and the non existence of local economies), they provide a solid basis of management objectives and evaluative criteria for creating, implementing and evaluating sustainable polar tourism.
* In response to unique circumstances, Arctic governments, Arctic natural resource agencies, NGOs, the tour industry operating in both hemispheres, and Native People have created innovative management techniques that are now applied in both Polar Regions. Some of the most important of these techniques include the Antarctic Treaty tourism Guidelines, and the WWF 10 Arctic Principles.

* Recognizing the need to simultaneously protect many resources from adverse impacts, existing tourism management techniques employ a comprehensive approach to influence appropriate tourist behaviour and resource conservation practices.
* An immense amount of information pertaining to the laws, participatory decision-making process, native customs, and numerous techniques employed to manage polar tourism and polar resources has been produced.
* A multitude of good tourism management practices exist throughout both the Arctic and Antarctic that should be evaluated for either expansion to new regions or modified for current tourist activity zones.
* Improved knowledge of the many natural events affecting the environmental conditions of the Polar Regions is growing rapidly. This knowledge is an essential ingredient in the design of tourism management policies and programmes, which must also be adjusted and as necessary reinforced in the face of growing tourist numbers.

What is now needed to advance sustainable polar tourism policies and programmes is the assembly of existing information and open access to that information. Since virtually all polar tourism management documents are in the public record and the Arctic is supremely well connected in this digital age, this is a very feasible agenda that can produce immediate positive results.

Remote Arctic communities seeking to manage tourism in a timely manner need immediate access to this type of information. Stakeholders concerned about Antarctic tourism should have access to the full spectrum of available resource conservation and tourism management techniques. The collection and dissemination of appropriate tourism management and resource conservation laws, customs, treaties, codes of conduct, techniques, and customs will provide significant benefits to both Polar Regions. This free flow of information will allow the benefits derived from tourism in Antarctica by a limited number of persons or commercial entities to be weighed against the global values at risk. Antarctica offers unique opportunities for scientific monitoring of, and research on processes of global and regional importance and was declared a natural reserve devoted to science and peace. A regime for its protection was also developed in the interest of mankind as a whole. As stated in the SG report, "the tourism industry has increased tremendously over the last decade. Efforts should be continued to ensure that commercial activities will not impact on the successes of the Antarctic Treaty system, in particular in securing Antarctica as a natural reserve, devoted to peace and science".

Defining 'Nature Tourism'

Nature in Tourism

In its broadest sense, nature in tourism involves experiencing natural places, typically through outdoor activities that are sustainable in terms of their impact on the environment. These can range from active to passive and include everything from bush walking and adventure tourism experiences to sightseeing, scenic driving, beach experiences and wildlife viewing. In many instances a visitor may combine several of these in the one trip. For keen outdoor enthusiasts, and there are many, the great majority of adventure activities directly depend on nature and natural environments for their successful conduct. Fundamentally, the role of nature can vary from 'crucial to the visitor experience' to 'enhances the visitor experience'- particularly in relation to such variables as active or passive measures of the activity involved.

For passive and active visitors alike, nature is also playing an increasingly important role in giving something back to people (relaxing, enriching the spirit, getting back to basics). By doing so, it is able to enhance their broader experience of a destination. And for mainstream domestic visitors, these benefits tap more accurately into nature's deeper meaning-see resource paper No 3, The deeper significance and role of 'nature' in tourism. Nature-based experiences are intimately linked to all other aspects of the visitor's total experience of a destination, such as food, culture, relaxation, health, escape, family needs, accommodation, transport, etc. All serve to complement each other and together form the basis of a visitor's overall satisfaction with their holiday.

Ecotourism

Eco tourists, with their strong focus on learning about the natural environment, minimising negative impacts and contributing to its care, lie at one specialist end of the nature in tourism spectrum, albeit an important one. They are in effect ambassadors (or early adopters) for a set of personal values towards which it now appears many other market segments, potentially comprising much larger visitor numbers, are moving. Conserved and protected areas (including Marine and National Parks), the Earth's biodiversity, and respect for local culture and those who have been traditional guardians of our natural environments, can be central to their interests. Eco tourists are also characterised by knowing what they want and being strongly self-active in accessing it. They will often plan and book their experiences and travel needs themselves, leaving tourism operators with more time and the broader opportunity to pursue tourists with more mainstream nature-based interests, and those seeking adventure activity.

Soft and Hard Adventure Tourism

Soft and hard adventure tourism activities also comprise a subset of activities strongly associated with the natural environment and nature-based tourism. Related market segments include 'adventure sports' such as mountain biking. Anecdotal evidence from Australian tourism operators suggests that demand for both soft and hard adventure tourism is growing. Research suggests that spending by nature-based tourists (particularly those with an interest in adventure activities and visiting significant nature destinations including national parks) is often substantially above average, per visitor and per night.

It is important to recognise that international source markets can culturally differ over which activities they will describe as 'soft' and which as 'hard' (e.g. snorkelling, surfing, ballooning and orienteering may be viewed as soft by one market and hard by another). Similarly, differences in outlook can arise between younger and older visitors from the same source market. For many major international markets (e.g. Asian and American), soft activities rather than hard are more frequently preferred by those interested in adventure-based experiences in natural areas. Soft adventure activities commonly require a moderate level of physical involvement by participants and are less physically challenging than hard activities. They can include– hiking/bush walking, mountain biking/bicycling, camping, horseback riding, orienteering, walking tours, wildlife spotting, whale watching, river and lake canoeing and fishing. The numbers undertaking such activities can be substantial – e.g. the NSW Fisheries estimates that recreational fishing is enjoyed by over 1 million New South Wales residents each year, as well as around 300,000 visiting anglers.

There is evidence from leading natural destinations that bush walking activity rates are also significantly increasing, particularly when support facilities are good, with highest participation rates in the 'under 2 hours' and '2 hours to a full day' categories. Wildlife viewing also achieves high levels of participation. Hard adventure activities commonly involve a higher level of physical or rugged involvement or a potentially greater personal challenge for participants. The risk factor can also increase. Hard adventure activities with a nature basis or need include– caving, scuba diving, trekking, white water rafting, kayaking, rock and mountain climbing, cross-country skiing, safaris, surfing, windsurfing, ballooning and ocean sailing. By contrast, bungy jumping does not depend on a nature setting. At the more challenging end of the hard adventure scale, support equipment can be involved or be absolutely necessary-e.g. climbing gear, oxygen tanks, ocean-going kayaks.

Special Interest Tourism

Nature-based tourism and its various subsets can also encompass some particularly challenging, but potentially high spending, special interest market segments. These often comprise socially and environmentally aware, highly educated and potentially demanding visitors who travel both to learn and to achieve personal and social goals.

Most of these visitors are serviced and targeted by specialist tourism operators and suppliers who often provide highly expert guides as part of the service. Examples include the 'not for profit' travel sector in the United States whose interests can range widely, encompassing anything from wildlife expeditions to scientific and cultural tours.

The major non-profit institutions of North America, such as natural history museums, zoos, universities and botanical societies, commonly promote their own worldwide travel programs to membership, alumni and donor bases that can run into the millions. Accessing and converting their small groups travel market can be difficult. It takes time, effort and a great commitment to high quality standards and delivery. An equally dedicated nature-based special interest visitor segment exists with bird-watching. Enthusiasts will travel long distances (and often at short notice) to sometimes remote and hard-to-access destinations, in order to sight new and rare species. In addition, readily identifiable communication channels (such as the ornithologists' special interest newsletters) can exist for accessing such market segments.

Wildlife Tourism

Wildlife tourism involves travel to observe wildlife in natural environments and preferably their native habitat. It is a further subset of nature tourism and one in which significantly high levels of domestic and international interest exist. Wildlife tourism involves wild and non domesticated animals and can encompass free-ranging and captive circumstances. Given the unique character and special appeal of most of Australia's wildlife, this suggests it may represent a tourism opportunity area for some destinations. The Blue Mountains, Barrington Tops, North and South Coast areas and Outback New South Wales possess great potential in this regard given their species diversity and relative convenience as destinations from major source markets and ports of entry. Wildlife tourism encompasses the chance to encounter fauna (and flora) in terrestrial, aquatic/ marine and aerial settings and to gain some further understanding of a wide variety of species (including viewing kangaroos, koalas, whales, dolphins, seals, fish and birds). Undertaking this activity in a manner that is environmentally responsible is important to ensure less disturbance to wildlife and habitats.

In terms of major visitor trends, 'appreciative tourism' involving observation, photography and interaction with wild animals is large scale, prominent and growing. Consumptive tourism involving such activities as hunting and (non-catch and release) fishing is also large scale, but declining. Ideally, wildlife tourism should include some element of education and an increased appreciation of nature and conservation issues.

Potential new models for wildlife tourism in Australia are being developed. These involve wildlife sanctuaries with feral free habitats attempting to use tourism and other enterprise based revenue sources as a means to help protect endangered native species and develop recovery plans for the species.

Activities directly related to wildlife viewing, such as scuba diving and whale watching, are experiencing rapid worldwide growth in popularity and it is clear that the concept of wildlife viewing itself is gaining global currency with visitors. It has been estimated to generate $30 billion worldwide in revenues each year. Alaska has experienced strong tourism growth in recent years, particularly in wildlife tourism, with more than 46% of its visitors engaging in this activity.

Nationally in the USA, wildlife viewing is the third highest purpose for trips each year (671 million) after sightseeing (1037 million) and family gatherings (778 million).

It is expected that wildlife activities will increase 61% nationally over the next 52 years to Year 2050 (Outdoor Recreation in American Life: A National Assessment of Demand and Supply Trends, 1999 – quoted in Nature: The leading edge for regional Australia). 43% of Canadians are involved in outdoor recreation each year and 18.6% have a wildlife component to their trip. 74.5% watch wildlife on the media and this is a major influence on driving wildlife tourism. The worldwide value of whale watching is estimated at over $2 billion. In Australia it has been estimated to generate $100 million with almost one million people watching each year. In New South Wales alone, more than 200,000 people annually pay for whale watching tours– double the number of 10 years ago.

Wildlife tourism should also seek to maximise the benefits to local communities, while avoiding problems such as disturbance to wildlife and pollution. Types and magnitudes of environmental impacts associated with wildlife tourism vary with the type of tourist activity pursued – some impacts are obvious and easily identifiable while others are indirect and difficult to quantify. The impacts on particular animals should not be considered in isolation from the broader environmental settings and wider animal population. The conservation benefits of wildlife tourism can include – its financial contribution; practical (in kind) contribution; socioeconomic incentive for conservation; and education.

Sustainable Tourism

Sustainable tourism is envisaged by the World Tourism Organisation (WTO) as "leading to management of all resources in such a way that economic, social and aesthetic needs can be fulfilled while maintaining cultural integrity, essential ecological processes, biological diversity and life support systems".

Sustainable tourism might also be defined as "tourism which is economically viable but does not destroy the resources on which the future of tourism will depend, notably the physical environment and the social fabric of the host community". Furthermore, "A clear distinction should be made between the concepts of Ecotourism and sustainable tourism: the term Ecotourism itself refers to a segment within the tourism sector, while the sustainability principles should apply to all types of tourism activities, operations, establishments and projects, including conventional and alternative forms".

The goal of 'ecologically sustainable development' is to improve the total quality of life, both now and in the future, in a way that maintains the ecological processes on which life depends. Supplementary definitions with significant relevance to nature in tourism.

Geotourism

Geotourism is concerned with sustaining or enhancing a destination's geographic character – the entire combination of natural and human attributes that make one place distinct from another. Geotourism encompasses both cultural and environmental concerns regarding travel, as well as the local impact tourism has upon communities and their individual economies and lifestyles. Aesthetics, heritage and the wellbeing of residents are included as some of its concerns. Geotourism has also been summarised as restorative and reconstructive forms of tourism that enhance a destination's natural and cultural distinctiveness, as well as provide a high-quality visitor experience. Geotourism is obviously closely related to sustainable tourism, even though it has its own refined concerns and focus.

Ecologically Sustainable Development

"Using, conserving and enhancing the community's resources so that ecological processes, on which life depends, are maintained and the total quality of life, now and in the future, can be increased."

Conservation

"The management of human use of the biosphere so that it may yield the greatest sustainable benefit to present generations while maintaining its potential to meet the needs and aspirations of future generations." (National Conservation Strategy for Australia.) "The protection, presentation, maintenance, management, sustainable use and restoration of the natural environment (and its ecosystems)."

The issue of management is vital in relation to tourism. The environmental impacts of tourism as a service industry must be recognised and never dismissed, but they also need to be placed in perspective. Ecological sustainability will never be achieved through a focus on environment and biodiversity alone. Social and economic values and needs must become integral concerns of nature conservation management. Likewise the tourism industry must address the concerns of natural area managers and recognise them as important partners in delivering sustainable experiences to visitors. Managed protected areas and other conservation sites now provide accessible means by which all visitors can experience at first hand nature in its wider diversity (and come to appreciate its values). Effectively planned and managed, this can foster conservation benefits – the basic challenge is to deliver good management, planning, education and resourcing. Interpretation (directed at visitors)

1. "A special process of stimulating and encouraging an appreciation of the natural and cultural heritage of a region, as well as a means of communicating nature conservation ideals and practices."
2. "A means of communicating ideas and feelings which helps people enrich their understanding and appreciation of their world, and their role within it." The first definition sees interpretation from a visitor's perspective as a means of value-adding to their experience because of the added interest it creates when more is known about an attraction or experience. The second definition places the responsibility back with the visitor to arrive at their own understanding based on their collective experiences.
3. "An educational activity which aims to reveal meanings and relationships through the use of original objects, first hand experience and illustrative media, rather than simply by communicating factual information."

Principles for Successful Interpretation

Successful interpretation typically reflects a number of key principles: People learn better when they are actively involved in the learning process. People learn better when they are using as many senses as appropriate. It is generally recognised that people retain approximately 10% of what they hear, 30% of what they read, 50% of what they see and 90% of what they do. Insights that people discover for themselves are the most memorable as they stimulate a sense of excitement and growth. Learning requires activity on the part of the learner. Being aware of the usefulness of the knowledge being acquired makes the learning process more effective. Enhancing the quality of interpretation at visitor centres, attractions, on tours, along trails/drives and 'in the field' or on site, is a major opportunity area for 'nature in tourism' in New South Wales.

As far as possible, interpretation needs to capture a visitor's imagination, intellect or emotions (even momentarily) and in so doing grab their interest. Differences such as age, and cultural background are also obvious considerations. When pursuing excellence in interpretation, there are as many paths of possibility open to visitor managers as there are creative ideas in the world. To fail to explore these is to risk having an audience label the interpretive approach adopted as too dull, tired, serious, patronising, over-complicated, overwhelming, superficial, cautious, etc. Great creative ideas resulting in exciting interpretation outcomes are often achieved more successfully if more innovative creative development processes (e.g. those developed by Edward De Bono) are applied, and the creative net cast more widely.

Building wider creative alliances by involving other people with different 'skill sets' (e.g. who are known for their innovative & 'wildcard' thinking capacities as well as essential sense of humour & fun) can often prove of value-particularly if they are properly rewarded for the business significance of their personal contribution to the results. A capacity for simple but effective delivery coupled with good commonsense and empathy also helps. Summarising its benefits, interpretation is an effective way of adding value to the experience, employing more locals, creating a cultural connection for visitors, building understanding and differentiating an operator's product in the market.

Tourism Feels the Heat of Global Warming

The promoters of 'adventure-' or 'Ecotourism' have popularized slogans such as: "Go visit the last paradises... before they'll be destroyed by tourist hordes." In a similar fashion, the British daily The Observer recently suggested that world travellers need to hurry up if they want to see the '10 wonders of a vanishing world'. According to the related article, the most wondrous natural tourist attractions we can no longer take for granted due to global warming include:

Africa's highest mountain-the spectacular Kilimanjaro in Tanzania will never look the same as snows are disappearing at an alarming rate.

The Caribbean coral reefs – particularly the Meso-American reef, the world's second biggest, stretching from the coast of southern Mexico down past Belize and into Honduras, is threatened by a threefold environmental disaster: Warmer water disrupts coral growth; acidic water affects coral's abilities to secrete new skeletons; and increasingly intense hurricanes break it up. As a result thousands of marine species are on the brink of extinction. The Maldives in the Indian Ocean-many tropical islands forming the Indian Ocean archipelago are likely to become submerged in the next two decades as a result of rising sea levels and increasing numbers of heavy storms.

Traditional ski resorts in the Alps such as Kitzbuhel in Austria for example will disappear from the tourist map within 20 years because of the lack of snow. Furthermore, the future of many unique animal species that have attracted wildlife tourism is in jeopardy as habitats, breeding grounds and migration routes are changing. If global warming gets worse, entire populations of polar bears in the Arctic region, Wildebeests in East Africa, Mountain Gorillas in Uganda and Rwanda or Monarch Butterflies in Mexico may be destroyed.

Tourism World Wakes up to the Climate Crisis

Climate is an essential resource for tourism, and especially for beach, nature and winter sport tourism, and the phenomenon of global warming already gravely affects the industry and an increasing number of destinations. In 2003, the Madrid-based UN World Tourism Organization (UNWTO) convened the 1st International Conference on Climate Change and Tourism in Djerba, Tunisia, to help the travel and tourism industry to respond to these issues. The UNWTO, that only a few years ago became a special UN agency, is traditionally driven by a strong Business Council that aggressively advances the interests of the world's most powerful tourism-related corporations. That the UNWTO declared climate change a priority issue shows the growing awareness among industry leaders and policy-makers that the impacts of global warming pose a serious threat to tourism-one of the world's largest and fastest growing industries, generating over 10.4 percent of world GDP, according to the World Travel and Tourism Council (WTTC). Notably, the Djerba conference recognized that the relationship between climate change and tourism is twofold: Not only is tourism affected by a changing climate, at the same time it contributes to climate change by the consumption of fossil fuels and resulting greenhouse gas emissions. It was concluded that there was an "urgent need for the tourism industry, national governments and international organizations to develop and implement strategies to face the changing climate conditions and to take preventive actions for future effects, as well as to mitigate tourism's environmental impacts contributing to climate change.". Also the burgeoning international Ecotourism industry feels challenged. At the recent Global Ecotourism Conference 2007 (GEC07) that was jointly organized by The Ecotourism Society (TIES), Ecotourism Norway and the UNEP in Oslo, Norway, it was agreed that "Climate change has increasingly become a major threat affecting the very resources on which Ecotourism depends – natural areas and local and Indigenous communities around the world....Stronger leadership and strategies are needed in order to substantially decrease Ecotourism's carbon footprint generated from multiple sources including facility operations and transport-related greenhouse gas emissions."

This article will offer some explanations as to why travel and tourism leaders are now feverishly working at the climate change front. Firstly, the economic costs of climate change for the industry will rise inexorably if it takes a business-as-usual attitude. Secondly, tourism relies more than other industries on a good image, but its reputation as a beneficial and environmentally acceptable activity has rapidly faded during recent debates on the causes of global warming.

Aviation, Cruise Ship Industry Major Climate Change Culprits

The aviation industry in particular is now facing enormous

pressure since the Intergovernmental Panel on Climate Change (IPCC) and environmental campaign groups have singled out the responsibility of air travel in accounting for a considerable portion of global greenhouse gas emissions. Globally, the world's 16,000 commercial jet planes generate more than 600 million tones of CO2 per year, almost as much as from all human activities in Africa each year, according to Friends of the Earth. The huge increase in aircraft pollution is largely due to the rapid growth of tourism and related air traffic. A WWF briefing paper on 'Tourism & Climate Change' (2001) states that the actual tonnage of CO2 emitted will increase by over 75 percent by 2015; concomitantly, from almost 700 million international travellers in 2000, numbers are expected to jump over one billion by 2010 and 1.6 billion by 2020. "As a consequence, the role of air travel within the tourism industry is likely to expand, cause considerable environmental damage, and to have knock-on effects on the tourism industry itself," concludes WWF. Given the recent negative publicity, tourists in Western countries are changing their behaviour and tend to fly less. There are now even voices in Europe that go so far to suggest that flying away on holiday is immoral and should be stopped altogether. "Warming stops global roaming", wrote the Australian newspaper Daily Telegraph recently. A survey in Australia done by a holiday website found nearly 20 percent of respondents considered giving up air travel as it causes irreparable harm to the environment, while only 16 percent said they do not care about climate change and it would not affect their travel choices at all.

Similarly, a study prepared for Greenpeace in the UK showed a clear shift in consumers' perception: 61 percent of the respondents were of the opinion that "We should limit our air travel voluntarily", 33 percent agreed that "Air travel is now too cheap", 52 percent agreed that "There should be a tax on fuel for air travel", and 61 percent of the respondents supported the idea that "There should be a pollution warning on air tickets".

Apart from aviation, the worldwide booming cruise ship industry has also come under fire. Cruise ships that can carry up to 5,000 tourists are not only notorious for creating tremendous amounts of waste and sewage but also belong to the biggest contributors to greenhouse gas emissions within the travel and tourism industry. The US-Bluewater Network that campaigns against the pollution of the world's oceans by ships has found that in one port visit, a single cruise ship can generate the emissions of more than 12,400 cars. The ship smokestacks release toxic emissions that lead to acid rain, global climate change, and damaging health effects to communities situated near ports. Despite the fact that ocean cruise liners are more energy efficient than other forms of commercial transportation, marine engines operate on extremely dirty fuels, known as 'bunker oil'. To compound the problem, engines on these ocean-going ships are currently not required to meet the same strict air pollution controls as cars and trucks are required to do.

Global travel and tourism could only grow by leaps and bounds because the transport networks that enable the movement of people and goods around the world are heavily subsidized. Tourists can enjoy to travel the world at incredibly low prices. As the New Economic Foundation study 'Up in Smoke?' explains "...much international trade lives in a bubble. International aviation and marine fuels are immune from any kind of taxation that would indicate and internalize the real environmental cost of freight and shipping. Greenhouse gas emissions from international freight are also exempt from the emissions targets set for rich countries to meet under the Kyoto Protocol of the UN Climate Change Convention."

Growing consumer awareness on these issues and a burgeoning citizens movement calling for fuel taxes and stricter regulation of the transport industry can severely curb future tourism growth targets and, thus, cut deep into the profits of plane-makers, airlines, travel agencies, cruise ship-operators and other tourism-related businesses. No wonder then that companies are now scrambling to talk about hard-earned environmental advances and new initiatives to protect the environment.

At the Paris Air Show in June, for example, Airbus' top salesman John Leah, told a press conference that Airbus is "saving the planet, one A380 at a time". The company's promotional brochures featured a silhouette of the new two-deck super-jumbo-dubbed the "gentle green giant"-set against images of dolphins, rain forests and fishing boats on a misty pond. Boeing representatives were also keen to display ecological bona fides and claimed the industry has reduced fuel consumption by 70 percent since the jet age began, reported Dow Jones Newswires. While the global travel and tourism lobby has adopted the rhetoric of corporate social and environmental responsibility, reality checks on the ground show that tourism's environmental performance has remained very poor. Neither the UN-initiated International Year of Ecotourism 2002 or multilateral environment agreements such as the Tourism Guidelines under the Convention of Biological Diversity (CBD), have achieved anything to stop tourism from pervading pristine coastal areas, islands, forests and mountainous areas.

On the contrary, more fragile ecosystems and biodiversity are destroyed, local communities displaced and traditional livelihoods destroyed-all for the establishment of huge exclusive resorts, golf courses and marinas. These massive tourism complexes are also notorious for high per capita consumption of energy and water. But however damaging and wasteful these projects may be, with the right PR efforts, they can still pass as 'Ecotourism' developments and even raise their profile thanks to eco-accreditation schemes, or environmental Best Practices awards. As long as no proper legally binding frameworks are in place to check and redress excessive and damaging tourism activities, 'green-washing' continues and climate change culprits are likely to get away scot-free. Ecotourism promoters' intention to help minimize tourism's carbon footprint is laudable. The GEC07 Oslo Statement, for example, outlines an action plan that aims at "encouraging adapted travel patterns (e.g. increase length of stay per trip); promoting more energy-efficient, alternative or non-motorized transport options; utilizing reduced and zero-emission operation technologies; and increasing participation in reliable high-quality carbon offsetting schemes."

But many of the new initiatives that promote 'zero-carbon' or 'carbon-neutral' tourism businesses need critical examination because they may just be marketing gimmicks. For instance, The Guardian (UK) announced in January that Per Aquum, the brand behind some of the world's most luxurious resorts, was the owner of the first 'zero-carbon' five-star beach resort designed by architects in London. The developers of the resort, due to open in 2008, claim the project will have no negative environmental impact and will be totally self-sufficient, using only energy from the sun and wind and producing little waste or carbon emissions. "The only drawback, environmentally speaking, is its location-thousands of fuel-guzzling miles away in Nungwi, Zanzibar," cautioned The Guardian.

Six Senses Resorts and Spas, a Bangkok-based luxury hotel chain with properties in Thailand, Vietnam and the Maldives is now specialized in 'carbon-cutting getaways' for millionaires who do not want their "vacation dampened by global warming guilt". Apart from introducing energy-saving innovations at the luxurious island resorts, all visitors are required to pay a tax for their flight, which goes into a carbon offset fund. The project owners say the fund will be spent on renewable energy projects for villages in Sri Lanka and India, thus, offsetting among the poor the carbon emissions caused by jets transporting the rich to their holiday destination. Yet, can Six Senses really be called an environmentally friendly company considering that it consumes exorbitant amounts of water to run their spa facilities, for example?

Bibliography

Bryson, McDowell: Concierge: *Key to Hospitality: A Training Manual,* New York, Wiley, 1992.

Clark, Mona: *Interpersonal Skills for Hospitality Managers,* London, Chapman Hill, 1995.

Conroy, B. : *Quality in Education and Training for Tourism,* London, Tourism Society, 1997.

Cukier, J. : *Tourism Employment in Bali: Trends and Implications,* London: Thompson, 1996.

Davidoff, Donald M.: *Customer Service in the Hospitality and Tourism Industry,* Englewood Cliffs, Prentice Hall, 1994.

Donald, M.: *Customer Service in the Hospitality and Tourism Industry,* Englewood Cliffs, Prentice Hall, 1994.

Douglas C: *Practical Tourism Forecasting,* Oxford, Butterworth Heinemann, 1996.

Elio, C.: *The Hospitality Law Desk Reference,* Miami, Southern Beverage Journal, 1994.

Foster, Douglas: *Travel and Tourism Management,* London, Macmillan Educational, 1985.

Ghimire, Krishna: *The Native Tourist*: Mass Tourism within Developing Regions, London, Earthscan, 2001.

Graham M S: *Language of Tourism,* The, Wallingford, CAB International, 1996.

Ireland, Lewis: *Quality Management for Projects and Programs,* Upper Darby, PMI, 1991.

Kotler, Philip: *Marketing for Hospitality and Tourism*: New Jersey, Prentice-Hall, 1998.

Larkham, P J: *Building a New Heritage: Tourism, Culture & Identity in the New Europe,* London, Routledge,1994.

Lewis, Robert C.: *Cases in Hospitality Marketing and Management*, New York, John Wiley, 1997.

Lock, Dennis: *Project Management*, New York, Wiley, 1996.

Marcussen, Carl H. : *Internet Distribution of European Travel and Tourism Services*, Research Centre of Bornholm, Denmark, 1999.

Morrell, J. : *Employment in Tourism*, London: British Tourist Authority, 1985.

Nancy N.: *Choosing a Career in Hotels, Motels, and Resorts*, New York, Rosen Pub. Group, 1997.

Pearce, Douglas: *Tourism Today: A Geographical Analysis*, Harlow, Longman, 1995.

Peters, M: *International Tourism*, London, Hutchinson, 1969.

Richards, G. : *Tourism in Central and Eastern Europe: Educating for Quality*, Tilberg, Tilberg University Press, 1996.

Rocco, M.: *An Introduction to Hospitality Today*, Orlando, Educational Institute, 1998.

Rogers, H Anthea and Slinn, Judy A: *Tourism: Management of Facilities*, London, Pitman: M & E, 1993.

Rosemary, E.: *Managing Employee Relations in the Hotel and Catering Industry*, London, Cassell, 1995.

Rosenzweig, J. E.: *Organisation and Management*, New York, McGraw Hill International, 1963.

Rue, Nancy N.: *Choosing a Career in Hotels, Motels, and Resorts*, New York, Rosen Pub. Group, 1997.

Schwaninger, M: *Trends in Leisure and Tourism for 2000 - 2010*, Prentice Hall, 1989.

Slinn, Judy A: *Tourism: Management of Facilities*, London, Pitman: M & E, 1993.

Swarbrooke, J.: *Marketing Tourism, Hospitality and Leisure in Europe*, London, International Thomson Business Press, 1996.

Thomas, F.: *Introduction to Management in the Hospitality Industry*, New York, Wiley, 1995.

Timothy R.: *Cases in Hospitality Management: A Critical Incident Approach*, New York, Wiley, 1995.

Index

N

O

P

R

S

T